# RELIGIOUS EXPERIENCE
# AND TRUTH

*Other books edited by Sidney Hook*

**Determinism and Freedom in the
Age of Modern Science**

**Psychoanalysis, Scientific Method, and Philosophy**

**Dimensions of Mind**

# RELIGIOUS EXPERIENCE AND TRUTH

## A SYMPOSIUM

Edited by Sidney Hook

*New York University Press*

© 1961 by New York University
Library of Congress Catalog Card Number: 61-15886
Manufactured in the United States of America
By arrangement with Washington Square Press, Inc.
ISBN: 0-8147-3393-X (paperback)
      0-8147-0202-3 (hardbound)

*The contents of this volume comprise the proceedings of the fourth annual New York University Institute of Philosophy, held at Washington Square, New York, October 21–22, 1960.*

# CONTENTS

## Part I—Continued

## Part II. The Nature of Religious Faith

# Part III. Meaning and Truth in Theology

# PREFACE

One of the most impressive features of the intellectual scene in midcentury America is the revival of interest in theology among philosophers and the concern of theologians with modern trends in philosophical analysis.

On the part of philosophers, the revival of interest in theology has been fed by various sources—some friendly to, and some critical of, theological traditions. Existentialism as a philosophy, whether in its religious Kierkegaardian form, or in its irreligious Sartrian expressions, raises issues which are similar to those over which profound religious thinkers from Augustine to Pascal have pondered and agonized. The continuing crisis of modern civilization, which after two world wars lies in the shadows of sudden death by nuclear holocaust or the living death of a totalitarian take-over, has turned the thought of multitudes to religious salvation in the hope of finding an assurance and comfort that earthly history cannot give. Since man's reason cannot be denied, this has led, among some philosophers, to a renewed quest for a concept of metaphysical intelligibility which will vindicate belief in God, freedom, and immortality in the face of modern skepticism.

On the other hand, both naturalist and rationalist philosophers, who have observed the revival of supernaturalism in popular religious thought, and see the secular and humanist gains of the last few centuries threatened in consequence, have returned with vigor to the critique of the old theology and the new. They base their critique, not merely on the progress of modern theoretical science which all sophisticated forms of religion now profess to accept, but on theories of meaning and confirmation that call into question the very significance of some central doctrines of theological belief.

The revival of interest in philosophy among theologians has to a considerable extent been a result of developments in contemporary philosophy itself. Pragmatism, operationalism, and logical positivism were all committed to a thesis which made the meaning of empirical terms depend upon their verifiability. Common sense and the sciences were taken as the paradigms of intelligible discourse. A statement describing a state of affairs was considered meaningful only if one could indicate the condition or set of conditions under which it could in principle be verified by some observation. Except for a few theologians who were willing to enter the lists with assertions purporting to rival or supplement the statements of science, this criterion barred theologians from the kingdom of cognitive sense. Not merely was their chance to make good in describing the furniture of heaven and hell denied to them, but their very right to be heard was also denied. Theologians glared at philosophers over a semantic gulf which they denounced as arbitrary but were powerless to overcome.

It was Wittgenstein who, in a sense, released the theologians from the ban which his earlier work had helped to pronounce on them. Instead of asking, as a condition of meaningfulness of a word or statement, whether it was verifiable, Wittgenstein suggested that the meaning of an expression is to be found in its *use*. Once we are able to describe the standard occasions of the use of an expression and the rules of departure from these occasions in all their complication we can be said to truly understand its meaning. There need be no implicit reference to verifiability by observation at all.

Of one thing theologians were certain. They had been using words all their lives and distinguishing between their proper and improper uses in theological contexts. They need now have no fear of linguistic analysis. On the contrary, it was a method which could be employed both to clarify theological usage and to preserve its autonomy against "rude" requests from scientists and naturalists to talk sense as defined by the parochial criteria of the scientific and commonsensical mode of discourse. There is not a single language-game that can be laid down in advance as binding upon all who would speak, whether in storytelling, describing, commanding, or praying. Each mode of discourse has its own language, its own rules of sense, to be discovered by analysis, not settled by decree.

A perusal of theological periodicals and recent theological volumes will show to what extent the new doctrine of meaning was experienced as a liberating force. Its indisputable effect was to make the theologians no longer shy of confronting philosophers, and to revive a common interest in common problems concerning meaning and truth. The question of truth once more becomes of paramount importance.

This explains the selection of the theme of the Fourth Annual Meeting of the New York University Institute of Philosophy. A few words are necessary to describe certain features of the proceedings as published which differ from the actual proceedings. The first and third sessions appear here in reverse order because it turned out that the theme of the meaning and justification of religious symbols raised large questions which, it is believed, readers will find more illuminating if they precede consideration of more specific issues. Professor Paul Tillich's paper, "The Religious Symbol," published as the Appendix, was distributed at his request to all participants prior to the Institute meeting. His paper, "The Meaning and Justification of Religious Symbols," which opens the volume, is a restatement of his position in the light of the criticisms made of his views at the Institute sessions.

The contributions of the individual participants appear under the specific themes to which they are directed. Contributions which contain comments on all three of the main themes appear naturally in the discussion of the third theme.

The New York University Institute of Philosophy wishes to express its appreciation to the Rockefeller Foundation for a grant which made possible these intellectually exciting sessions. Instead of passing one another by, philosophers and theologians met in keen yet amicable discussion of problems which border both disciplines. The confrontation was one of the frankest in modern times. It is hoped that it will also prove fruitful.

*Sidney Hook*

# RELIGIOUS EXPERIENCE AND TRUTH

# PART I

## The Meaning and Justification
## of Religious Symbols

# 1

## THE MEANING AND JUSTIFICATION OF RELIGIOUS SYMBOLS

*by Paul Tillich, Harvard University*

Religious symbols need no justification if their meaning is understood. For their meaning is that they are the language of religion and the only way in which religion can express itself directly. Indirectly and reflectively religion can also express itself in theological, philosophical, and artistic terms. But its direct self-expression is the symbol and the united group of symbols which we call myths.

### *I.*

In order to understand religious symbols we must first understand the nature of symbols generally. And this is a difficult task, because the term symbol is being applied to things which should not be called symbols at all, e.g., signs, symptoms, metaphors, etc. But since the linguistic development can hardly be reversed, one can save the genuine meaning of "symbol" only by adding an adjective whenever "symbol" is meant. Symbols which deserve the name shall be called "representative symbols," following a suggestion by John Randall, in contrast to the symbols which are only signs, such as mathematical and logical symbols—which one could call "discursive symbols." The realms in which representative symbols appear are language and history, the arts and religion. They show common characteristics which must be presupposed if one speaks of symbols in each of these groups. The common characteristics in all realms of representative symbols are the following:

## Religious Experience and Truth

First and most fundamental is the character of all symbols to point beyond themselves. Symbols use "symbolic material": the ordinary meaning of a word, the empirical reality of a historical figure, the traits of a human face (in a painting), a human catastrophe (in a drama), a human power or virtue (in a description of the divine). But this symbolic material is not meant in its proper and ordinary meaning. When it is used as symbolic material, it points to something which cannot be grasped directly but must be expressed indirectly, namely through the symbolic material. This "something" can be the connotations of a word which transcend the empirical reality of this person, or it can be a dimension of reality which is not open to an ordinary encounter with reality as the artistic forms, or it can be ultimate reality, expressed in symbols whose material is taken from finite reality.

The second characteristic of all representative symbols is to participate in the reality of that which they represent. The concept of representation itself implies this relation. The representative of a person or an institution participates in the honor of those whom he is asked to represent; but it is not *he* who is honored, it is that which or he whom he represents. In this sense we can state generally that the symbol participates in the reality of what it symbolizes. It radiates the power of being and meaning of that for which it stands.

This leads to the third characteristic of the representative symbol: it cannot be created at will. It is not a matter of expediency and convention, as signs are. Therefore, one can metaphorically say that a symbol is born and may die. Even if individual creativity is the medium through which it comes into existence (the individual artist, the individual prophet), it is the unconscious-conscious reaction of a group through which it becomes a symbol. No representative symbol is created and maintained without acceptance by a group. If the group ceases to accept it, it may, like the ancient gods, become a metaphor or maintain its poetic-symbolic value, but, as a religious symbol, it becomes lost.

The fourth characteristic of a representative symbol is its power of opening up dimensions of reality, in correlation to dimensions of the human spirit, which otherwise are covered by the predominance of other dimensions of spirit and reality. The historical symbols show historical potentialities which are covered by the everyday historical events and activities. Artistic symbols—in fact, all artistic creations—open up the human spirit for the dimension of aesthetic experience and they open up reality to the dimension of its intrinsic meaning. Religious symbols mediate ultimate reality through things, persons, events which because of their mediating functions receive the quality of "holy." In the experience of holy places, times, books, words, images, and acts, symbols of the holy reveal something of the "Holy-Itself" and produce the experience of holiness in persons and groups. No philosophical concept can do the same thing, and theological concepts are merely conceptualizations of original religious symbols.

One may add a fifth characteristic of representative symbols: their integrating and disintegrating power. This function of symbols refers both to individuals and groups. The history of religion gives an endless number of examples for the elevating, quieting, and stabilizing power of religious symbols. In the larger, and sometimes even narrower, sense of the word, one can speak of the "healing" power of religious symbols. All this is equally true of the three other groups of representative symbols. But in contrast to their integrating function, symbols can also have a disintegrating effect: causing restlessness, producing depression, anxiety, fanaticism, etc. This depends partly on the character of that to which they point, partly on the reaction of those who are grasped by them. Symbols have the same creative or destructive effect on social groups. Symbols are the main power of integrating them: a king, an event, a document in the political realm of representative symbolism, an epic work, architectural symbols, a holy figure, a holy book, a holy rite in religion. But here also are disintegrating possibilities as in some political symbols such as the Führer and the swastika, or in religious symbols such as the Moloch type of gods, human sacrifices, doctrinal symbols producing a split consciousness, etc. This characteristic of symbols shows their tremendous power of creation and destruction. By no means are they harmless semantic expressions.

## II.

In the preceding general analysis of the nature of symbols, we frequently have mentioned religious symbols. They must now be considered in their particular character. In the language of religion a problem is intensified which appears in every kind of expression, the problem of the "referent." To what does a religious symbol refer, one asks? How can it be reached? And if it can be reached by symbols only, how can we know that something is reached at all? Such questions are certainly justified. One can sum them up by asking: Is there a nonsymbolic statement about the referent of religious symbols? If this question could not be answered affirmatively the necessity of symbolic language for religion could not be proved and the whole argument would lead into a vicious circle. The question then is: what is the referent of religious symbolism and how can it be known except by symbols—known namely in the one and only respect that it is the referent for religious symbols.

There are two ways which lead to the same result, a phenomenological and an ontological one. Excluded by the very nature of the subject matter is the inductive way. For it can lead only to a finite part of the universe of finite objects through observation and conclusion. But the intention of every religious symbol is to point to that which transcends finitude. Nothing finite, no part of the universe of finite relations can be the referent of religious symbols, and, therefore, no inductive method can reach it.

The phenomenological approach describes the holy as a quality of some encounters with reality. The holy is a "quality in encounter," not an object among objects, and not an emotional response without a basis in the whole of objects. The experience of the holy transcends the subject-object structure of experience. The subject is drawn into the holy, embodied in a finite object which, in this encounter, becomes sacred. An analysis of this experience shows that wherever the holy appears it is a matter of ultimate concern both in attracting and in repelling, and of unconditional power, both in giving and in demanding. The phenomenological analysis of the experience of the holy has been carried through in an excellent way by Rudolf Otto and others. It shows what is meant, if religious symbols are used. But it cannot go beyond the description. Phenomenology cannot raise the question of validity of the phenomena it makes visible.

The other way of reaching the referent of religious symbolism is the ontological one. It analyzes the kind of being man is, in interdependence with his world. It analyzes the finitude of the finite in different directions, it points to the anxiety which is connected with the awareness of one's finitude, and it raises the question of being-itself, the *prius* of everything that is. This approach tries to find the referent of religious symbolism not in a particular experience, that of the holy and of the ultimate concern implied in the holy, but it tries to find it in the character of being as such, in everything that is. The ontological method, as indicated here, does not argue for the existence of a being, about which religion makes symbolic statements, but it gives an analysis of the encountered world with respect to its finitude and finds through this analysis its self-transcending quality, its pointing beyond its finitude. That to which this analysis leads is the referent in all religious symbols. One can give it metaphoric names, like "being-itself" or "power of being" or "ultimate reality" or "ultimate concern" (in the sense of that about which one is ultimately concerned). Such names are not names of a being but of a quality of being. If religious symbols express this quality in divine names, classical theology has always asserted that the referent of these names transcends their nonsymbolic meaning infinitely.

The two ways of finding the referent of symbolic language, the phenomenological and the ontological, corroborate each other. That which is the implication of the phenomenological description is also the focal point of the ontological analysis and the referent of the religious symbols.

*III.*

There is an almost endless amount of religious symbolism in the history of religion. This is not so by chance. It follows from the fact that in a particular encounter with reality everything can become a bearer of the holy. Nothing is prevented from becoming a sacred thing. Only historical contingencies prevent it. But they have not prevented exemplars of almost every class of things from actually becoming sacred things. This produces the impression that the history of religion is a mere chaos of incoherent imaginations. But this is not the case; there are many keys for the understanding of the dynamics of this large realm of human experience. There are also keys for an understanding of the immense amount of religious symbols. Without considering their historical dynamics I want to distinguish certain basic kinds of religious symbols in order to overcome semantic as well as material confusions.

The first distinction needed is that between primary and secondary religious symbolism. The primary symbols point directly to the referent of all religious symbolism. In order to do so they establish a "highest" being, attribute characteristics to him the symbolic material of which is taken from human or cosmic experiences and extended *via eminentiae* to that which to the religious intention transcends all such characteristics. This refers to qualities like personality, power, love, justice, etc. It has been asked whether qualities like being, becoming, essence, existence, can be attributed nonsymbolically to God. It seems to me that such an assertion makes out of that which transcends all beings a being of higher order. The rejection of this attempt agrees with the contention of classical theology that God is "beyond" the split between essence and existence, as well as beyond being (in a static sense) and becoming. This "beyond" is an expression of a symbolic use of these terms.

A second level of primary religious symbolism is the way in

which religion speaks of divine actions like creation, providence, miracles, incarnation, consummation, etc. It is especially important to emphasize the symbolic character of these symbols, because they often are understood literally, with the consequence that they fall into insoluble conflicts with the scientific interpretation of reality. In all these symbols the religious imagination subjects that which is ultimate reality to the categories of time, space, substance, and causality. This is unavoidable and without danger as long as the symbolic character is being recognized. But if this is not done, the whole relation between God and the world becomes a nest of absurdities, as, e.g., God's "predestining" or his "almighty" actions.

The third level of primary symbols lives in the realm of divine manifestations in finite reality, divine incarnations in holy things or objects. In the dynamics of the history of religion this level must be considered as the "oldest" one. For the basic religious experience is that of the presence of the holy in concrete things, persons, or actions here and now. The "sacramental presence" of the holy is the lasting basis of all religious experience, and the radical transcendence into which the divine was elevated is a later development, the result of the fight of the higher religions against the demonic distortions of the sacramental religions.

These three basic levels of primary religious symbolism are permeated by a host of secondary religious symbols. Secondary are supporting symbols like water, light, oil, or poetic symbols in which a primary religious symbol is artistically resymbolized, or metaphoric expressions as they appear in parables or are used in poetry. They should not be raised to the rank of primary symbols. In the Psalmist's phrase "The Lord is my shepherd," the word "Lord" is a genuine and primary religious symbol, the word "shepherd" is a poetic metaphor. It must be added that the distinctions made here are neither exclusive nor static. The levels are mixed with each other and, often symbols of one level originate on another level, e.g., secondary religious symbols had once an independent standing as primary religious symbols and vice versa. But the distinction itself is valid.

## Religious Experience and Truth

*IV.*

If one asks about criteria of religious symbols we must state generally that the measure of their validity is their adequacy to the religious experience they express. This is the basic criterion of all symbols. One can call it their "authenticity." Nonauthentic are religious symbols which have lost their experiential basis, but which are still used for reasons of tradition or because of their aesthetic value. The criterion of authenticity is valid but not sufficient. It does not answer the question of the amount of truth a symbol possesses. The term "truth" in this context means the degree to which it reaches the referent of all religious symbols. The question itself can be answered in two ways, a negative and a positive one. The negative quality which determines the truth of a religious symbol is its self-negation and transparency to the referent for which it stands. The positive quality which determines the truth of a religious symbol is the value of the symbolic material used in it. Both statements need interpretation.

It is the danger and an almost unavoidable pitfall of all religious symbols that they bring about a confusion between themselves and that to which they point. In religious language this is called idolatry. The term does not express (or should not express) the arrogant and indirectly idolatrous judgment of one religion over all the others, but it expresses an implicit tendency of all religions to elevate themselves to ultimacy in power and meaning. On the other side, all religions live from the system of symbols by which they have been created and which they continue recreating. They live as long as a whole of symbols is the expression of their particular character. With the end of the power of its symbols a religious group comes to its own end. When, however, the symbols are in power their idolatrous misuse is almost unavoidable. The symbol of the "Cross of the Christ," which is the center of all Christian symbolism, is perhaps the most radical criticism of all idolatrous self-elevation. But even it has become again and again

10

the tool of idolatry within the Christian churches. This consideration is the answer to the question of the truth of religious symbols
from the negative point of view. The measure of their truth is the
measure of their self-negation with respect to what they point to,
the Holy-Itself, the ultimate power of being and meaning.

The other criterion is the quality of their symbolic material.
There is a difference whether they use trees and rocks and stones
and animals or personalities and groups as symbolic material. Only
in the last case do the symbols comprise the whole of reality; for
only in man are all dimensions of the encountered world united.
It is therefore decisive for the rank and value of a symbol that its
symbolic material is taken from the human person. Therefore, the
great religions are concentrated on a personal development in which
ultimate concern appears and transcends the personal limits, though
remaining in a person. The positive criterion for the truth of a
symbol (e.g., creation) is the degree in which it includes the valua-
tion in an ultimate perspective of the individual persons.

The negative and positive criteria of the truth of a religious
symbol show that their truth has nothing to do with the validity
of factual statements concerning the symbolic material. However
problematic the symbolic material in its literal meaning may be,
its symbolic character and its validity as a symbol are not determined by it.

It seems to me that an understanding of the language of religion
in the line developed in this paper is the precondition for an adequate interpretation of religion and for a creative interpenetration
of the theological and the philosophical task.

# 2

## TILLICH'S CONCEPTION OF
## A RELIGIOUS SYMBOL

*by William P. Alston, University of Michigan*

As Professor Tillich himself has said, "The center of my
theological doctrine of knowledge is the concept of symbol. . . ." [1]
And it must be apparent on the most cursory reading of his works
that in Tillich's enormously influential reinterpretation of Christian
theology, and more generally of the nature and function of religion,
the concept of a religious symbol is made to bear a great part of
the weight. The examination of this concept is, therefore, of the
very first importance for an evaluation of Tillich's whole enterprise.
In this essay I shall proceed as follows: First, I shall set out a
concept of religious symbols, which I think reflects fairly accurately
the actual use of symbols in religion, and which I take to be a
refinement of the traditional conception. Second, I shall explore
Tillich's deviations from this conception, and indicate the points
at which they seem to me to be disastrous.

A religious symbol is some concrete object or aspect of a concrete object which is taken to represent the ultimate object of
worship or some aspect thereof.[2] Thus a shepherd is taken to
represent the providential care God takes for His creatures; a
mountain or hill, or more abstractly, height, is taken to represent
God's majesty, His perfection, or His immutability. (The plurisignification of symbols is one of their most marked features.) It is
important not to confuse, as I fear Tillich sometimes does, the
symbol in this fundamental sense with symbolic language, which
is symbolic in a derivative sense. An utterance can be said to be
symbolic when it does its job through using terms which denote
symbols. Thus we might speak of God as our shepherd, or say

that "We are the people of His pasture and the sheep of His hand," or "Thus saith the high and lofty One that inhabiteth eternity, whose name is Holy. I dwell in the high and holy place." Here these words, including the words 'shepherd,' 'high' etc. are not symbols in their own right; but the utterance has the significance it possesses through the fact that 'shepherd' denotes what is a symbol, and thus the utterance can be called symbolic in a derivative sense. It can be interpreted as an injunction to take a shepherd as a symbol of God, or, perhaps, as an expression of the conviction that a shepherd can appropriately be taken as a symbol of God.

Now, what is meant by saying that a shepherd is taken to represent divine providence? It may roughly be defined as follows: seeing or thinking of a shepherd, or a picture of a shepherd, tends to call up a complex of feelings, attitudes, and thoughts which are appropriate to divine providence (deep thankfulness, a feeling of an unshakable underlying security, attitude of complete submission, etc.); and in addition any person who construes a shepherd in this way would be both able and willing to specify God's providential care for His creatures as that which is being symbolized. Both conditions seem to me to be necessary. Without the first, one might know that the shepherd had this symbolic significance for others, but it would not actually be functioning as a symbol for oneself. Without the second we would be hard pressed to give any sense to saying that the object was taken to represent anything other than itself; it would simply be an effective stimulus for certain emotional states. Concepts without feelings are empty; feelings without concepts are blind.

I am not, indeed, asserting that every time a person responds to *x* as a religious symbol, he tells himself what it is this object symbolizes. But I am saying that he would be capable of specifying the symbolizandum on demand. And note that this in turn implies that it is possible to say this in nonsymbolic language. Confronted with the question, "What does a king symbolize in this religious community?" one could hardly answer by pointing to the sun, even if in the community both a king and the sun do function

13

as symbols of the same aspect of the divine nature. And if this will not do, neither will a supposed specification in symbolic language, which ultimately amounts to no more than pointing out certain objects to be used as symbols. We certainly do not succeed in locating that which is symbolized, if all we do is enumerate more objects which symbolize something-or-other. What is required is an effective identification of the symbolizandum—one which will make it possible to decide whether you and I (or myself at two moments, for that matter) are taking the concrete object to symbolize the same thing. What this means in practice is that religious symbols function against the background of a complex system of beliefs about supernatural beings, a system which furnishes the material for the requisite identifications of symbolizanda. As to the character which such beliefs or the utterances which express them must have, that is a question for another essay. Here I will only affirm my conviction that, in order to furnish descriptions from which effective identifications can be made, the component assertions in such a system must at some point yield implications concerning experienceable states of affairs, though that does not mean that it will be possible in practice to put them to an empirical test.

This is not to say that a symbolic statement is translatable into a nonsymbolic one, and still less is it to say that responding to a symbol is the same as reflecting on a theological doctrine. The symbol and the symbolic utterance contribute something to the religious life which could never be extracted from theologizing. The symbol presents in a vivid and striking way a concrete analogue of a characteristic attributed to God, and in so doing condenses the significance of that characteristic into a single point so as to make it intuitively assimilable, and so as to actively engage such typically religious feelings as awe, wonder, and adoration. The analogy can be of various sorts and degrees. Sometimes it concerns features of the symbol itself (the care of the shepherd for his sheep, the height of the mountain); sometimes the way the symbol affects us (the sense of awe or sublimity we get from gazing at the mountain). But in all cases, the whole range of our experience of the object, the diverse associations it has acquired, contribute to a wealth of felt significance which makes the symbol a concrete focus for religious responses.

Nor am I suggesting that we first develop theologies and then cast about for appropriate symbols to enliven them. I am saying nothing about the order of development. I suspect that the two grow up together. It may even be that responding to certain objects with awe, wonder, a sense of significance, etc., sometimes precedes *any* theological formulation; and that theological formulations then result from the attempt to say what goes on in such encounters. It may be that first the members of a community reacted in this way to, e.g., bulls, and then later developed the notion of a supernatural person manifested in bulls as a way of giving a sort of explanation of their reactions. Moreover, irrespective of origins, I would suppose that a theology derives part of its meaning and most of its vitality from the fact that its adherents do have encounters of this sort with objects which present analogies with characteristics attributed to the deity in the theology. I only wish to maintain that even so the theology does not solely consist in registering such experiences of sacredness, but goes beyond such a registration in specifiable ways; and that unless and until the encounter with sacred objects is meshed into a theology involving such an assertive overplus, we cannot speak of the objects as religious *symbols*.

Now, Tillich deviates from the traditional conception for a number of reasons. I would suppose that the most important are these: (1) He does not see any reason to believe in the existence of God conceived as an immaterial, personal being Who literally enters into various relations with human beings. And yet he does not want to abandon Christianity. (2) The religious attitude, as he conceives it, is directed to a reality more ultimate, more unconditional than anything which is *a* being among others. (*Systematic Theology,* hereafter referred to as *ST*) [3] Given these convictions we can understand why Tillich proposes to take what were symbolizanda in the traditional scheme and make them into symbols too. Thus the personal creator of the universe and all His attributes and activities are lumped together with the sun, kings, mountains, and bulls under the heading of symbols.

In tossing them all into the same bag, Tillich fails to make certain distinctions which are vital to his project.

A. He fails to note the following contrast: whereas the objective existence of natural objects is taken for granted when they are treated as symbols, we can, in Tillich's program, treat a supernatural God and His doings, e.g., the Incarnation, as symbols without making any assumption of objective existence. Once this contrast is brought out into the open, we see that, when Tillich argues that since the personal God of theism is a symbol the question of His *existence* is of no religious importance (in *Dynamics of Faith,* hereafter referred to as *DF*),[4] he cannot claim to be deriving the principle of the argument from the way symbols are *generally* treated in religion. Again, this means that we cannot literally encounter the supernatural "symbol" as another existent, but must "encounter" it as conceived, imagined, or pictured. And this would seem to carry with it important differences between the *modi operandi* of the two classes of symbols, differences which Tillich has not considered.

B. The failure to draw the right sort of distinctions between symbols and symbolic language leads Tillich into various confusions. For example, Tillich says (in an article in *The Christian Scholar,* hereafter referred to as *CS*), ". . . it is obvious that symbols cannot be replaced by other symbols." [5] But it is *quite* obvious that the mere substitution of one word for another in our talk about God, e.g., arbitrarily replacing 'holy' with the hitherto unused phoneme sequence, 'kona,' would be entirely possible in a way that an interchange of symbols would not be possible, e.g., replacing Jesus Christ with Hitler, or replacing a personal supernatural creator with the dialectical movement of history. These latter replacements could occur only as the result of very fundamental cultural changes.

C. Tillich sometimes talks as if unattained goals like financial success or the attainment of scientific knowledge can be religious symbols in just the same sense as presently existing objects like the state or a person (e.g., *DF, 3*). But obviously there are important differences in the ways we can relate ourselves to "symbols" of these different sorts. In the ensuing discussion I shall occasionally make reference to some other difficulties into which Tillich is led by his failure to make these distinctions. But since I believe that these difficulties could be eliminated by a more careful working-out of the position, I do not wish to dwell on them further.

Let us return to the main thread of the discussion. If what was the ultimate referent of religious symbols in the traditional scheme has now become another symbol, is anything left for symbols to symbolize? Now clearly Tillich wants to find such a referent. He does not want to view religion as nothing but an organization of human activity and experience. And so, in line with the basic conviction regarding the thrust of the religious attitude noted above, he thinks of religious symbols as symbolizing not *a* being of any sort, but being-itself. In an article reprinted in *Religious Symbolism* (hereafter referred to as *RS*), he writes, "the religious symbol has special character in that it points to the ultimate level of being, to ultimate reality, to being itself, to meaning itself. That which is the ground of being is the object to which the religious symbol points." [6] One crucial consequence of this is that symbolic language becomes autonomous. In the traditional scheme symbolic language is at least partly dependent on doctrines expressed in nonsymbolic terms. A necessary, though not sufficient, condition for the appropriateness of using a shepherd as a symbol of God is the truth of the doctrine that God providentially cares for His creatures, or does something else for which the activities of a shepherd furnish an analogue. (This condition is not sufficient because it is also necessary that the symbol effectively perform the evocative job for which it is employed.) But in Tillich's scheme this will not be the case. As the ground of all being, being-itself is beyond all differentiations that mark off one sort of being from another. Hence it is not susceptible of any characterization.

> The statement that God is being-itself is a nonsymbolic statement. . . . However, after this has been said, nothing else can be said about God as God which is not symbolic.

17

> As we already have seen, God as being-itself is the ground of the ontological structure of being without being subject to this structure himself. . . . Therefore, if anything beyond this bare assertion is said about God, it no longer is a direct and proper statement, no longer a concept. It is indirect, and it points to something beyond itself. In a word, it is symbolic (*ST*, 264–65).

Since we can say nothing nonsymbolically about being-itself, a given symbol cannot be judged in terms of the reality or unreality of that aspect of being-itself which it is being used to symbolize. We are unable to specify any such aspect. Symbolic utterance becomes the primary, and indeed the only, type of religious utterance. And that means that the affirmations of religious faith are not subject to criticism in terms of the canons applied by science and common sense to statements of fact.

To achieve an objective reference for religion without relinquishing immunity from criticism in terms of evidence is a notable accomplishment. But we still have to ask: What does it mean to say that a religious symbol "points to" being-itself? Remember that in the traditional scheme to say that x is a symbol of y means, roughly, that x tends to evoke feelings, attitudes, and behavior appropriate to y, and that the person for whom x is a symbol of y could, on demand, identify y as the symbolizandum. If we try to apply this analysis here we will run into trouble on both counts. Taking the second first, it would seem that one could *specify* being-itself as what certain symbols point to only if he went through something like the ontological discussion Tillich goes through in introducing the concept. But that would mean that religious symbols function as such only for metaphysicians, indeed, only for metaphysicians of a certain stripe—a conclusion which would surely be as abhorrent to Tillich as to anyone else. As for the first component of the analysis, when I asked, "What sort of feelings, attitudes, etc. would be appropriately directed to being-itself?" I do not know how to answer—and justifiably so. If being-itself does not admit of any characterization as this rather than that, there is no ground for considering one sort of attitude or feeling more

18

appropriate to it than another. This latter point will emerge again in the discussion of ultimate concern.

We might try to get a clue from Tillich's oft-repeated assertion that religious symbols, like other symbols, participate "in the reality and power of that to which they point." (*CS,* 189) But I fear this is not of much help. For one thing it will not provide any differentia of religious symbols. On Tillich's principles, everything constantly participates in being-itself, as a necessary condition of its being anything (*ST,* 263). Of course it may be that religious symbols participate in being-itself in some special sense of 'participate.' But, to my knowledge, no such sense has been provided.

Perhaps our lack of success in finding a meaning for 'points to being-itself' is due to our failure to connect this notion with another of Tillich's fundamental notions—ultimate concern. As I understand Tillich, he maintains that religious symbols function as such only in the context of ultimate concern (*RS,* 111; *DF,* 10). Ultimate concern as presented by Tillich involves the following elements:

(1) An unconditional surrender to something (x), the willingness to recognize x to hold absolute authority over one's life.

(2) An expectation that one will somehow receive a supreme fulfillment through one's encounter and commerce with x.

(3) Finding in x a center of meaningfulness. That is, everything in one's life and one's world gets significance insofar as it is related in some way to x.

(4) Experiencing x as holy (in Otto's sense of the term 'holy,' in which this experience involves a unique blend of awe, fascination, and a sense of mystery).

Now Tillich speaks of religious symbols *expressing* ultimate concern (*DF,* 41, *ST,* 238), and this may be true of symbolic utterances, but nonverbal symbols themselves have, on Tillich's own account, the somewhat different role of objects or foci of ultimate concern—that to which the various attitudes and feelings which make it up are directed. (This is one of the points at which a failure to distinguish between symbols and symbolic language gets Tillich into trouble.) Thus ultimate concern might be directed to one's nation, one's class, the scientific enterprise, one or more supernatural beings supposed to exist, a great leader, etc. And whenever this happens the entity in question can be said to be functioning as a religious symbol. (If we try to put various examples Tillich gives of religious symbols into this position, we will be struck by the impossibility of making goals, like financial success, fit. One could hardly surrender to a goal, and still less could one expect to receive a supreme fulfillment from a goal. The attainment of such a goal might be a fulfillment one would expect from some person or group.)

But however illuminating this may be as a characterization of religious and near-religious modes of experience, what light does it throw on the claim that religious symbols point to being-itself? The claim is that *really* ultimate concern is directed only to being-itself.

> The question now arises: What is the content of our ultimate concern? . . . *Our ultimate concern is that which determines our being or non-being.* . . . Man is ultimately concerned about his being and meaning. . . . Man is unconditionally concerned about that which conditions his being beyond all the conditions in him and around him. Man is ultimately concerned about that which determines his ultimate destiny beyond all preliminary necessities and accidents (*ST,* 17).

This argument represents an extraordinary conflux of two serious ambiguities. First, "man is ultimately concerned about his being and meaning" in the sense of 'concern' in which it means something like 'being worried about' or 'being anxious about.' ("I am concerned about his state of health.") But this is a quite different sense from that which Tillich has given to the phrase 'ultimate concern.' Surely Tillich is not suggesting that we are worried about the fate or condition of being-itself! Second, as Tillich explained 'ultimate concern,' the ultimacy is psychological; it consists in the supremacy of that concern in the psychic structure of the individual. It is in a quite different way that being-itself is thought by Tillich to be ultimate. It is ontologically ultimate by virtue of the fact that it is the ultimate ground of all being. Once this distinction is made, we can see that there is no reason to suppose that (psychologically) ultimate concern must be concern directed to what is (ontologically) ultimate.. But the verbal identity may make the transition seem obvious. This drift is clearly exemplified in another passage. "The unconditional concern which is faith is the concern about the unconditional. The infinite passion, as faith has been described, is the passion for the infinite. Or, to use our first term, the ultimate concern is concern about what is experienced as ultimate" (DF, 9).

But apart from doubts about the soundness of the argument, it is not at all clear what one could mean by saying that one is ultimately concerned, in Tillich's sense, with being-itself. I can understand what it would be to surrender oneself to a person or a movement, to expect fulfillment from a person, or find a center of meaningfulness in him. But as Tillich explains 'being-itself,' it makes no sense at all to speak of surrendering oneself to being-itself, or expecting anything from it, etc. This becomes even clearer if we remember that in Systematic Theology Tillich said that "Ultimate concern is the abstract translation of the great commandment: . . . 'You shall love the Lord your God with all your heart, and with all your soul, and with all your mind, and with all your strength" (ST, 14). But what would it mean to love being-itself so intensely, or even less intensely?

Tillich has an answer to these questions, which is at the same time an answer to the questions: "What has happened to the religious symbols on which ultimate concern was said to be focused?" and "Just how does the fact that ultimate concern is directed to being-itself help us to understand how religious symbols point to being-itself?" It would be a mistake to think of a religious symbol and being-itself as alternative candidates for the position of an object of ultimate concern. They are both involved in different ways. In Chapter IX of Systematic Theology, I ("The Meaning of God"), Tillich points to a "tension" in ultimate concern. On

21

the one hand it is driven, by its ultimacy, to transcend every special being and to direct itself to being itself; on the other hand, "it is impossible to be concerned about something which cannot be encountered concretely, be it in the realm of reality or in the realm of imagination" (*ST,* 234). Again, "The ultimate can become actual only through the concrete, through that which is preliminary and transitory" (*ST,* 242). Thus ultimate concern is directed to being-itself "in and through" one or another symbol. The symbol is serving as a manifestation of the Ultimate for the person who is focusing his concern on it. He is focusing his concern on it because he is experiencing it as ultimate, or as a "medium" or "vehicle" through which he can be "grasped" by the power of being-itself (e.g., *ST,* 16). Thus a religious symbol can be said to point to being-itself in the sense that it plays the role we have just specified in this three-termed interrelationship.

But this does not really help. We have simply moved from 'point to' to a set of new metaphors which we are equally unable to pin down—'manifestation,' 'medium,' 'vehicle,' 'grasp.' Given Tillich's explanation of 'being itself,' it would seem that in any sense in which we could speak of anything being a manifestation or a vehicle of being-itself everything would equally be so. Remember that "everything finite participates in being-itself and in its infinity. Otherwise it would not have the power of being" (*ST,* 263). And the only sense I can give to 'manifesting being-itself' or 'serving as a vehicle of being-itself' is a sense in which these phrases are alternative metaphors for saying approximately what is said by the use of the phrase 'participating in being-itself.' And if that is so, these terms do not serve to mark off those situations in which an object is functioning as a religious symbol. For they apply to every conceivable situation.

The unsoundness of Tillich's conceptual foundations is reflected in the difficulties into which he falls at several points in the development of his ideas. I shall examine two such points. One of the most serious difficulties concerns his attempts to evaluate religious symbols. Although Tillich has barred himself from using the traditional canons of criticism, still he wants to be able to say that some symbols are more adequate than others, and, as a Christian theologian, he wants to be able to say that the Christian symbols are the most adequate. Of course, in one sense a religious symbol is adequate if it effectively expresses (or evokes) ultimate concern (*ST,* 266; *DF,* 96). This might be called subjective adequacy. But since Tillich is concerned to insist that religion points beyond the sphere of human experience to the ultimate ground of being, he also tries to make discriminations, within the group of symbols which are subjectively effective, in terms of the effectiveness with which this pointing is done (*DF,* 96–97). The key concept here is that of idolatry. A symbol is idolatrous to the extent that it fails at this job of pointing. A consideration of the vicissitudes which attend Tillich's attempts to formulate a criterion of idolatry will further reveal the basic strains in the concept of a religious symbol.[7]

Tillich often says that a symbol becomes idolatrous when it is put in the place of the Ultimate. "In true faith the ultimate concern is a concern about the truly ultimate; while in idolatrous faith preliminary, finite realities are elevated to the rank of ultimacy" (*DF,* 12). Symbols "always have the tendency (in the human mind, of course) to replace that to which they are supposed to point, and to become ultimate in themselves. And in the moment in which they do this, they become idols" (*CS,* 193). But what is this place which is occupied by the Ultimate when everything is going as it should and which is usurped by the symbol when we degenerate into idolatry? As we have seen, the answer is that the Ultimate is being pointed to by a finite object which is the focus of ultimate concern. Thus for a symbol to be put in the place of the Ultimate would be for it to be pointed to by another symbol in just the way in which a symbol points to being-itself. Is this conceivable? It is, of course, possible for one symbol to symbolize another symbol, as the cross hanging in a church symbolizes the crucifixion, or perhaps, the atonement, which is itself a symbol, at least according to Tillich. But in the first place, this is clearly not the sort of thing Tillich wants to brand with the label 'idolatry.' And in the second place, although one symbol can point

23

to another, it seems extremely doubtful that this is anything like the sense of "point to" in which Tillich wants to say that symbols point to being-itself, however that latter sense is finally explicated. We have already seen that the ordinary sense of symbolize, in which one finite reality is said to symbolize another, is not the one which Tillich needs.

But perhaps Tillich's point is better put by saying that a symbol becomes idolatrous when it loses its pointing function altogether and simply is treated as an object in its own right.

"Innumerable things, all things in a way, have the power of becoming holy in a mediate sense. They can point to something beyond themselves. But, if their holiness comes to be considered inherent, it becomes demonic. . . . Holiness provokes idolatry" (*ST,* 240). Again, this can happen. We might still find value in sacred music, or religious poetry, or icons even after we had ceased to regard them as pointing beyond themselves to an ultimate object of worship. But in that case there would be no basis for calling them religious symbols any longer, and hence they would not be subject to that particular perversion of the religious called "idolatry." In Tillich's account, being a religious symbol is linked by definition to pointing to being-itself.

What is undercutting these attempts is the fact that, as Tillich depicts the situation, all the constituents must be in their proper places if there is to be a religious symbol at all. This rules out the kinds of variation on which Tillich tries to base the distinction between genuine and idolatrous symbols.

Tillich does make use of other criteria. For example, he sometimes suggests that one can recognize an idolatrous symbol by the fact that the promises it makes are not fulfilled, that in the long run it disintegrates rather than integrates the personality, etc. (e.g., *DF,* 11). These are promising suggestions. But they achieve this promise at the cost of bypassing the supposed connection between religious symbols and being-itself. They are not stated in terms of that connection.

The second difficulty I want to mention is this. As his own principles demand, Tillich explicitly disavows any intent to interpret a religious symbol by specifying the aspect of the Ultimate to which it points. "Every symbol opens up a level of reality for which nonsymbolic speaking is inadequate" (*CS*, 191). And yet when Tillich actually goes about explaining various theological terms, it looks very much as if he is trying to translate them into ontological terms.

> If we call God the "living God" . . . we assert that he is the eternal process in which separation is posited and is overcome by reunion (*ST*, 268).

> Will and intellect in their application to God . . . are symbols for dynamics in all its ramifications and for form as the meaningful structure of being itself (*ST*, 274).

> It is more adequate to define divine omnipotence as the power of being which resists nonbeing in all its expressions and which is manifest in the creative process in all its forms (*ST*, 303).

I do not know how to read this other than as an attempt to translate symbolic language into nonsymbolic language. (If they were intended to be simply the replacement of one symbol by another symbol, they would be grotesque failures. No one would suppose that "dynamics in all its ramifications" is a better religious symbol, i.e., performs a symbolic function better or more clearly than "will.") The fact that Tillich is unable to carry out his own principles when he comes to try to explain particular religious symbols is very instructive. It demonstrates the strain involved in the notion of an indescribable symbolizandum.

In spite of these difficulties, which I do think are fatal to Tillich's enterprise as a whole, I believe that he has made some important contributions to our understanding of religious symbols, as well as other aspects of religion. The account of ultimate concern seems to me to constitute an admirable phenomenology of the religious attitude. I would suggest that Tillich's talk about being-itself (in this connection) could be profitably taken as a part of that phenomenology. Thus a phenomenologically apt way of describing the experience of a sacred object would be to say that through it one is grasped by the power of being-itself, that the object is a channel through which one participates in the Ultimate, etc. All this would then be simply a description of the experienced impact of religious symbols. But the fatal difficulties in which Tillich becomes entrapped in his attempt to use these concepts in an account of the extra-experiential reference of religious symbols demonstrates vividly that he cannot claim such reference while refusing to make claims which are responsible to objective criteria. If we are not satisfied with a purely naturalistic account of religious symbols, there is no short cut around the traditional scheme, which makes their justification rest, at least in part, on the truth of those nonsymbolic assertions which specify their symbolizanda.

## NOTES

1. "Reply to Interpretation and Criticism," in *The Theology of Paul Tillich*, ed. Charles W. Kegley & Robert W. Bretall (New York: The Macmillan Company, 1956), p. 333.

2. Cf., "A symbol is a representation of something moral or spiritual by the images or properties of a natural thing." *Webster's Collegiate Dictionary*.

3. Paul Tillich, *Systematic Theology* (London: Nisbet and Company, 1953), I, 17, 24.

4. Paul Tillich, *Dynamics of Faith* (New York: Harper and Brothers, 1957), p. 47.

5. "Religious Symbols and Our Knowledge of God," *The Christian Scholar*, XXXVIII, 191.

6. "Theology and Symbolism," in *Religious Symbolism*, ed. F. Ernest Johnson (New York: Harper and Brothers, 1955), pp. 109–10.

7. For a fuller treatment see my article, "Tillich on Idolatry," *Journal of Religion* (1958), XXXVIII, 4.

# 3

# THE OUTSIDER
*by Virgil C. Aldrich,* Kenyon College

Once there was a small family with a great expectation. They saw in things the portent of the coming of a wonderful person to be with them a while. They would talk earnestly and urgently about it. In such converse, their language grew to accommodate the event, by giving it an articulate place to occur in. Then the person came to the place thus prepared for him. They wondered at the personality they saw expressed in his bodily presence, and lost their souls to him. After he left them, one of them, who was a painter, expressed what they had seen in a picture, beneath which they appended the story of what had happened. The words and the picture fused for them into a single composition in which they could see the personality, portents of which they had previously seen in things. These, in an inarticulate or minimal way, had shown to them what was later manifested in the person, the story, and the picture. In the end, they took to chanting and praying parts of the story before a cross, thus elaborating it in congregational enactment. The story thereby became more and more articulate, presenting or expressing more and more of what they had seen. This seemed to purify their hearts and with this went a clearer and clearer seeing of the personality. It disturbed them when some other people were mystified by their form of expression which had become their language and their form of life, their way of looking at things. Before those people could understand, they had to become communicant-members of the congregation and speak its language, since the seeing was with the congregational eye. This was the problem. It was those people who had earlier brought the person to a tragic end.

## Religious Experience and Truth

The family, which was now a congregation, lived on the ground floor of a three-story house. One of them, Saul Brillig by name, would occasionally go up to the second floor which was a sort of hall of mirrors and cameras. Certain individuals lived there; that is, they did not comprise a congregation. Their form of life involved making representations of objects. There were the objects on the one side, and the pictures—mirror images, photographs, sometimes models and maps—on the other side. The ultimate concern of these people was to make accurate representations of objects, and thus the whole function of the picture was to point at, describe, stand for something else. Given a representation, the procedure was to check it by looking for something outside it which it pointed at. The very language of these individuals reflected this. Indeed, this language controlled their way of looking at things. It consisted mainly of verbal signs that pointed at objects. Outside the linguistic medium were these objects which the terms of the language indicated. Understanding and using language this way was these individuals' form of life. Observation of objects was therefore decisive, and this was their mode of perception of things, which categorically required that things be seen as objects, and objects themselves as the ultimate concern. In short, the place prepared for the encounter with things in this outlook and its mode of representation was objective, vis-à-vis the observer as the subject of the experience but who, in this view, was also an object, of another kind from sticks and stones.

Saul Brillig, in his converse with these people on the second floor, came to understand all this so well that he began to look at the picture and the story on the ground floor that way. That is, he occasionally ceased to see it with the congregational eye. Then, of course, he began the quest for the object outside the picture which he thought the picture pointed at. He could not find it in the dim religious light on the ground floor. Nor, looking that way, could he find it on the ground outside. He remembered the person, of course, or the event that had occasioned the picture. Was not that the object? But the individuals upstairs, and the other people outside, also knew of that event, and claimed that the portrayal was a misrepresentation. Observation of the original as object, and of the present relevant evidence, presented another truer picture, not nearly as expressive of what the congregation saw in their picture story.

Brillig was worried. He was still a member of the congregation, but he was becoming objective, an outsider. He looked for objects outside pictures, the objects they pointed to. And he could not find an object that the sacred picture story stood for, as a true description or representation. He went up again to the second floor to search more closely there for the corresponding object, asking for help from the experts at that language game. They did help him, but not by finding the object. They told him that, on the third floor, some people lived who made a profession of asking such mixed-up questions as were stinging Brillig like hornets. So up he went another floor.

There he found a collection of individuals even lonelier than the crowd on the second floor. Brillig himself was becoming lonely, so felt some of the tension going out of him in their presence. They told him that he must be more sensitive to differences in the ways in which languages and things signify. Things and linguistic terms signify as symbols and as signs. His picture story on the ground floor is a symbol; whereas, on the second floor, the concern is with signs. But, said Brillig, don't symbols point at something outside them? Of course they do, he was told; but unlike signs, which merely point, the symbols also participate in what they mean. You mustn't trample on a flag because it participates in the country it points to; thus does it symbolize its object. Then, after all, he said, a symbol has an object which transcends it or is outside it, and which it points to? Yes, they answered, but be careful from here on about what you mean by object; and, moreover, watch that whole subject-object distinction, together with the symbol-object distinction. The object that a symbol represents could be another symbol of a higher order. There can thus be quite a hierarchy of symbols comprising different sorts of objects. But the highest symbol in the hierarchy, said Brillig—is there something outside it that it points to? They looked at one another, then upward at the ceiling, and said, yes, but it's not another object. It transcends all objects. But since we refer to it by the word "it," and other substantives such as Absolute, it *must* be something or other, way up there beyond all comprehension, outside the whole hierarchy of symbols.

So Brillig climbed up onto the flat roof of the three-story building, in search of the something or other that he still thought was outside his beloved picture story down on the ground floor. The tragically wonderful person, he had learned, was himself a symbol, near the middle of the hierarchy of symbols. Supreme Being was at the top, symbolized by the person at the middle, and Being itself, as a diffuse sort of conceptual object, symbolized something outside it. So, from the rooftop, Brillig looked around and up at the outside. He felt pretty homeless, sat down, and went into a cross-legged trance. He began to think of the outside as itself a diffuse sort of symbolic object at the top of a hierarchy, symbolizing something transcending it which in his heart he called the All-Encompassing. He realized sadly that that too was a symbol pointing to something outside it. He became lonelier and very much needed a personal encounter. Then something happened. Gazing this way at the bright outside, which he was taking for a symbol standing for a nameless ultimate beyond, he saw it break into fragments. The emptiness in the broken object became replete, resplendent, and luminous with a light-of-light, which consumed and etherealized the pieces, annihilating their objectivity. With this transfiguration of what had been an object, he felt his own lonely subjectivity dissolved away; the experience confirmed for him the doctrine of the people on the third floor, that the subjective emerges only in opposition to the objective. Sublimate the one and you sublimate the other. They are thus *aufgehoben* in something higher. In the experience which transcended this distinction, Saul Brillig felt not so lonely. The presence of something personal had been realized. He had seen it in the broken symbol. The unbroken symbol, he thought, is an idol; and, like an idol, it must be broken to make room for the wondrous reality that it points at. So he resolved to be an iconoclast.

Yet, in his thinking about all this, there up on the roof outside,

Saul continued to picture the essence of the revelation, even during the revelation, as still outside even the broken symbol. But now it was pictured as very close to him or in him, an absolute essence which he grasped with a certainty too intimate for knowledge or understanding, since knowledge and understanding require an object. He thought that it was this ineffable absolute that objectifies itself in the symbol and partly reveals itself within the symbol's limitations when the symbol is broken. Indeed, it is this absolute as subjective certainty which itself makes the nihilistic demand that the symbol be broken, because the symbol after all is a kind of object even after being broken and sublimated. The transfiguration of the symbol helps, but, alas, it does not quite reveal what the ultimate concern it expresses is about. This, as such, remains unexpressed or unobjectified, in any symbolic formulation of it, broken or not. Thus, it seemed to Saul that what he was seeking is after all outside any symbol whatsoever, howsoever broken. . . .

One of the communicants of the congregation on the ground floor missed Saul and went upstairs to bring him home in time for the communion. He found Saul in the twilight sitting cross-legged, head bowed, his eyes fixed on the figure of his intersecting legs. This is a good place to study astronomy, the communicant said. What are you looking *down* at? I am looking neither up nor down at anything, Saul answered, I'm looking *for* something—the meaning of our picture story, what it points to, what transcends it. Then you'd better come down and see again what's *in* the picture, his friend said.

Saul was again lonely, and he remembered that it helps to break symbols. So he started downstairs to break some. He gave the people on the third floor a knowing look in passing, saying, symbols must be broken. They nodded in grave affirmation. On the second floor he got a glimpse of a black-and-white photograph of two little children walking away from under trees into the light. This brought him momentarily to a halt. So this is a *sign,* not a symbol, he thought to himself. I wonder what it would be like to break a sign? His companion nudged him and they went on down home into the dim religious light below.

There Saul braced himself to look again, but this time with an

31

iconoclastic eye, at the beloved symbol. He was resolved to see new being in it, to see the merging of essence and existence, and to see the absolute, since this is what is outside the picture story, its meaning, not revealed by the symbol until it is broken, and even then only partly. He wasn't going to see in it the life and death and the spirit of just the wonderful person and of the congregation that had, with one accord, become the mystical body of the event. That symbol, he thought resolutely, must be broken, to make room for being and the absolute which transcend it, a glimmer of which may be got in the properly broken symbol. This would be the occasion for a personal encounter with the ultimate, not with the person. Saul Brillig inferred that the wholeness of such a view of the whole truth would integrate his whole person into a whole man. It would make him whole, protecting him from the disintegration of idolizing the unbroken symbol, in which capacity it was not a god but a demon with the power to break the believer. Either you break the symbol, or get broken by it. He had discovered, he thought, a new and a good way to be objective, without being taken in by objects.

Looking thus at the picture story, Saul waited for the revelation of the new being in it as of a white light. He found himself *thinking* of the new being, and of Being *simpliciter* beyond that, and of the absolute beyond being and nonbeing, instead of seeing anything in the symbol. He *saw* less in the symbol than he had seen before, though there it was broken wide open under the impact of his concepts. He sensed that he must not let the ontological concepts replace and interpret the symbol. The symbol must be allowed to function in its own mythic way. For a moment he lapsed into the earlier way of looking and again was consumed with the kind of understanding that is tragic love. He was perplexed to find that, when this happened, he did not seem at all to be worshipping an idol and a demon, though he did see the sacred picture as the person, with all heaven and earth and hell concentrated in his wonderful personality. There was the symbol, radiantly expressive and unbroken by concepts, all in a dynamic field of faith.

Saul got down on his knees with the congregation for a moment, then left in quiet desperation, leaving the devotees behind. He *had* to discover what the symbol pointed to outside itself. The notion of space endlessly leading beyond anything given still haunted him. He went outside into the moonlight and saw there, on the ground, the loneliest looking man he had ever come across. The man was carelessly dressed and seated on a stone. He had a stick with which he sketched a figure on the ground. Brillig saw it first as a duck, then, when he approached closer, as a rabbit. Without looking up, the man on the stone asked Saul: Do you think that this contour scratched on the ground *is* a rabbit? Of course not, Saul said, but I can see it as one, or as a duck. What if you idolized it or thought it *was* a rabbit, not a picture of one, asked the man who looked like an idiot, would you then say you see it *as* a rabbit, *could* you then see it that way?

Brillig took some time over this question. The idiot stopped talking and wove a figure in the insubstantial, moonlit air with his stick. It was rather like a cross. For a moment Brillig saw it as the substantial cross the wonderful person had hung and died on. The image of this pervaded and animated the region of the drawing. He could see it in the the wake of the weaving stick. The figure was broken and transfigured by the animating image. For the first time, the strange man looked up with a teasing smile. Beware of the moonlight, he said; you are seeing things.

Saul went on imagining silently. The wonderment grew upon him. He was imagining things, yes, but he was also in a sense seeing an aspect of the aerial drawing that any member of the congregation could have seen, with the congregational eye. But what intrigued Saul most was having had, there, down on the ground, the sort of ethereal experience he had had on the roof up in the sky. Even seeing the duck-rabbit picture as a rabbit was in some respects like that, though with differences he now wanted to explore. It too involved the breaking and trans-figuration of an observable something by the animating presence of an image.

The key thing that impressed Brillig in all this was that, though he *was* imagining or seeing things, he was *not* being deceived or

33

taken in by anything. He was not mistaking certain objects for others. He had not thought that the drawing was a rabbit or the cross, though he had seen the two drawings, the one as a rabbit and the other as the cross. If he *had* made this mistake in thinking, he would not and could not have seen what he had seen. Seeing *that* something is something is quite different from seeing it as something which it is not observed to be. "Observe," thought Saul in his new trance, *there* is a useful word for the sort of seeing that presents you with things as objects and their own qualities. He had "observed" the drawing and its contours, which had a likeness to another object he had observed. This had been the occasion for another sort of seeing which was not objective in that sense at all; in fact, it revealed an aspect which animated the thing, in which capacity the thing was not experienced as an observable object. Saul decided that he would call this sort of awareness "pre-hending," not observing. It is still a mode of perception, but not of things as objects with qualities; rather, of things as presences with aspects that animate them. So Brillig began to conceive a thing *simpliciter* as something that, in one special mode of perception called observation, can be seen as an object with qualities; and in another special mode of perception called prehension, as a presence with aspects. *This* is neither an objective nor a subjective way of experiencing the thing. That distinction does not make sense in this case. And things lend themselves as nicely to this mode of being and being perceived as to the observational.

Out of this meditation Brillig came with the realization that he had been thinking too much in terms of broken *symbols*. Why not, instead, say that a symbol is a broken *sign*? The drawing on the ground was a sign, insofar as it was observed to have a certain shape (quality) like that of a duck or a rabbit, and thereby pointed to or referred to or described one of those objects. In that capacity it makes one think of something beyond it—outside it. This is its use as a sign. And words of an object-descriptive language function that way, as on the second floor. Even a flag can mean a country in this manner, as a sign, to unpatriotic people who do not form a congregation. In fact, the cross picture drawn in the air frequently has that sort of object reference, pointing to the cross proper. But even these can be, and commonly are, broken by the animating image or presence of the original, when they are seen as the original. Saul remembered the photograph of the little children walking hand-in-hand into the light. Then they are expressive symbols instead of pointing signs. Inasmuch as anything means by pointing, it is a sign; it may be broken by the animating presence of aspects, and it then is a symbol.

But here Saul, standing stock-still in the moonlight beside the idiot, remembered the things that are symbols in a more special sense: a crucifix, bread and wine, a statue, even a flag or a man. These can be made into idols, and one who does this is an idolator. Brillig's iconoclasm had been directed at such iconic symbols; he had wanted to break these as he would break wooden and stone images. These were certainly different from the duck-rabbit sketch, already innocently broken by the presence of an animating image, there on the good earth. Brillig did not feel that, in seeing the picture as a rabbit, he was idolizing anything; though he was noticing something not confirmable in the observational view of any object. He felt no obligation to break the picture, because a symbol of that kind is not an idol and is not generally idolized. The picture did participate in what it meant, and not merely point to it; and so it was a symbol on that count by his own standard. But still it was not an idol. It had more to do with the symbolism that becomes conspicuous in art, not in religion. What, then, is an idol? Why must it be broken, and how does one do it?

Brillig was gravid with these questions. He remembered first that, in the presence of the flag, you quite properly stand still and straight, and with your hat off your head on your breast. But if, afterward, you see someone touch the flag by accident, and expect to see him drop dead as a consequence, you are idolatrous and the flag in relation to you is an idol. It then needs to be broken, or it will eventually break you. He remembered the story that idolized the ark of the covenant. But in the case of the ritual of the respectful stance in the presence of the flag, idolatry was not necessarily involved; because there the flag was an iconic *symbol,* not an

35

idol. If it had been an idol, it could be broken this way in favor of, or into, an iconic symbol which itself needs no breaking.

But when shall a symbol be said to be iconic? Brillig wondered. How does it differ from a presentational symbol animated by the image of something? In the case of the flag, even more obviously in the case of a religious symbol such as, say, the cross, and the person on it, the notion of some *object* outside the symbol, the *image* of which animates the symbol itself, seems not to apply. The flag does not *picture* something as the duck-rabbit sketch did; nor does the cross. So the visual emphasis of seeing something as something must be dropped without dropping the notion of something animating something with its presence for the prehensive sort of experience. Nor strictly do the *flag* and *cross* themselves seem to participate in what gets expressed with their help. Thinking they do is what tempts one on to idolatry. What then is the vehicle, the carrier, of the expressed presence where iconic symbols are involved? For certainly the presence of something is realized somehow in something in such situations.

Saul heard the liturgical chant of the congregation kneeling before the cross on the ground floor and thought of a man by the flag with his hat off, and the answer came to him like oxygen to a climber on a high mountain.

It is the *participants* in the ritual act who, with the iconic symbol as the occasion, become animated with the presence of the power and the glory. It is *they* who, in a personal encounter, participate in what the iconic symbol symbolizes; the icon itself does not do this. Realizing this deliteralizes or breaks the *idol* into an iconic *symbol* which, as such, needs no breaking. In the whole sacramental enactment by the congregation, the iconic symbol takes its place as one of the expressive terms, and the communicants experience the liturgical form of their own performance as animated with the presence. Of course, they do not *observe* this. They prehend it, and in the prehension are made whole. Thus did Saul get a confirmation of something he had thought before: that the ritual act *constitutes* the spiritual community. By partaking of the bread and wine, in remembrance of the person, and hearing the intoned words, the kneeling congregation experiences itself *as* the transubstantiated body of the animating presence. They realize in the sacred rite and in their own persons the spirit of the person, much as those who were there when he was crucified saw it in his crucified body and trembled. And this is not mistaking the bread and the wine and the crucifix for things they are not. It is using them as iconic symbols or terms in that language. Nothing is being idolized in the practice, although sometimes mistaken theory about it assumes it is. So nothing needs to be broken except the bread.

But the tragic person himself, how does one interpret him and justify the interpretation? Is he too an iconic symbol, not to be idolized? The idiot on the stone looked up, as if in answer to Saul's unspoken question, saying, when you see a smile transfigure a face, are you *observing* the shape of a mouth and making inferences? Saul had himself said no to a question like this before; in such a case one sees a presence that transfigures the medium of the manifestation, annihilating its status as an object of observation. The nitwit was looking down again, so Brillig went on thinking. The family, he thought, had originally encountered the person that way, not as one observes a body in motion and infers the cause. In that personal encounter, were they confronted by a *symbol* of any sort? Was it not rather an experience that confirmed the sort of experiences they had previously in the presence of the portents as signs of the event-to-come? And was it not that experience which was subsequently revived and remembered with the help of the iconic symbols? It now seemed to Saul that the experience of the person was the datum for the whole form of expression which had become the congregation's form of life.

But, still, Saul continued to wonder about *what* they had experienced and he after them—the interpretation of what the life and death of the person expressed. Granting that something had been shown somehow in a nonobservational way, the question remained: What? The iconic symbols, the whole liturgy, the sacred rite, were occasions that realized and revealed a presence. But this language of realization is not enough. *What* presence, the presence of what?

# Religious Experience and Truth

For a moment Saul inclined towards breaking some more symbols with ontological concepts, but he found he no longer had the heart. Instead he noticed his thinking about the question become articulate in the language of the high argument about God. In this idiom, he now sensed that God is not a symbol, nor *simply* presupposed. Rather, He is the presupposition of all the symbols, as was the person. Thus are the symbols and the argument grounded, while they interpret the ground with an ever-deepening penetration, not questioning its existence. So he realized that the language of the high argument has its taproot down in the non-observational way of looking at things. Things lend themselves to this mode of perception of them, in which they are given as portents of Will. The formulation, the articulation of this experience of things shows God as its ultimate concern, its ultimate presupposition, its final category of explanation.

Saul was turning to join the congregation when the idiot said enigmatically, but there are other languages and forms of life. Yes, yes, said Saul, other myths, science, psychology, ontology, and all that. He paused to smile at the man whom he now strangely felt of as a companion, as if he had learned something from him. Saul said to him, I think I've heard of you and know who you are. The idiot on the stone smiled back. Yes, he said, you are Brillig and I am Schuldig Nitwitstein; are you going back in to break some more symbols? Saul said that he was going to break bread with the congregation, and to tell them afterward that more must be made of transfiguration as the meaning of crucifixion.

# 4

## SOME PROBLEMS FOR A
## PHILOSOPHY OF RELIGION

*by J. M. Bochenski, O. P., University of Fribourg, Switzerland*

> ". . . and besides, what would be the
> use of processions," thought she, "if
> people had all to lie down on their
> faces, so that they couldn't see it?" So
> she stood where she was, and waited.
> Alice's Adventures in Wonderland

In the following I have tried to state in a sketchy way some problems which occurred to me during the discussions at the symposium. Most of them are concerned with what may be called the epistemic aspect of religion. This, of course, does not deny that there are other aspects and consequently other types of problems in religion, which is a highly complex phenomenon. Moreover, most of the problems mentioned here are such that they may be treated by means of logical and semantic analysis, which again does not mean that all problems of religion are of this type. I think personally that a fully developed philosophy of religion would have to use phenomenological *and* analytical methods, while relying at the same time on the results of psychology. However, it seems to me that such problems as can be treated by the analytical method are, on the whole, the most fundamental and interesting.

Some of the questions I have stated here I think I can answer; a few of them are not problems at all to me, for I believe that their solution is obvious. But the purport of this paper is not so much to state my own views, as to formulate *problems,* for the recent developments in analysis allow us to state many new problems in our field and reformulate some of the old ones.

# Religious Experience and Truth

I only hope that the word "philosophy" in the title will be noticed. This is *not* a theological paper, i.e., it is written under complete abstraction from any religious belief. Religion is considered here as a datum accessible by empirical and rational means, and only insofar as it is accessible by them.

*1. Can religious discourse be submitted to analysis by means of formal logic and semantics?* I think personally that it can. But some Protestant theologians present at the symposium seemed to deny this; consequently, the necessity arises for justifying the above view. This should be done, I believe, by showing that religious men are *men,* i.e., that they must use human language when they talk. The fact that they talk about things divine does not change the fact that they talk *human* language.

*2. Is there a direct experience of God?* There can be no doubt that some men and women, namely, the mystics, have claimed to have had such experiences. And nowadays not only those saints but also many Protestant theologians, who do not pretend to be saints, claim that sort of experience for themselves and perhaps for many among their faithful also. I would suggest, therefore, that a thorough psychological and semantic study of some religious communities should be performed so that we might know to what extent the claim is true. I think personally that the claim is false and that persons who have had a direct experience of God are quite rare.

*3. Is there a specific religious experience?* That there is a complex phenomenon called "religious experience" can hardly be doubted. But this could be a complex of experiences which, taken in isolation, are all moral or esthetic experiences of different sorts. R. Ingarden has shown, in a penetrating study,[1] that a work of literature is composed of many levels. Each carries some peculiar aesthetic values and the value of the work as a whole consists in the interplay of those many-leveled values. Perhaps something similar also happens in religion. Then it would be necessary to say that there is no *specific* religious experience, no peculiar quality or value we could call by that name. I am now strongly inclined to think that this is the case.

4. *What is the syntactical status of the term "God"?* Some Protestant theologians seem to believe that it must be a name, i.e., a noun. But for someone who has not had any direct experience of God, the only way to give a meaning to the term "God" is by description. This is, I think, the position assumed by Professor Ziff and I fully agree with him here. But the explicit statement of that view seems to me to be necessary if we are to avoid some considerable semantic difficulties.

5. *Does religious discourse necessarily contain some indicative sentences?* Again, some of the speakers at the symposium seemed to hold that this is not the case, that religious discourse is composed exclusively of nonindicative phrases. To me this is an impossible position, at least in regard to the religious discourse of the great religions, especially of Christianity. It seems to me that both Professor Niebuhr and Father Weigel did show very well that a believer always believes *something,* namely, a proposition. Yet, the correct way to show this would be, I think, not by using abstract considerations, but by analyzing concrete religious discourse, e.g., the professions of faith in their context. I am afraid I do not know of any such analysis.

6. *Does the believer, who uses indicative sentences in his religious discourse, intend them to have a meaning similar to the meaning of sentences in profane discourse?* This seems to be denied by Professor Tillich. To him the utterances used in religious discourse have no meaning at all; they are not signs of the ordinary type, but, as he puts it, symbols, i.e., they do not symbolize anything in the way in which most utterances do in other types of discourse. This is, I must insist, a *factual* problem. It can be resolved only by seeing what people really do intend when they use indicative sentences in religious discourse. A study of this sort seems to be very necessary, in spite of the fact that everyone acquainted with authentic religion knows pretty well that the answer to our question is affirmative: the believer *does* intend to have the

said meaning. Of course, one can try to operate a "demythologiza-tion." But this, I submit, if successful, would lead to a complete change of attitude for the believer. I think, consequently, that Professor Tillich's analysis is not an analysis at all, but a proposal to influence believers in such a way that they would become non-believers. In linguistic translation it is a proposal to use the term "faith" in a way other than most believers use it.

7. *Can indicative sentences in religious discourse have a meaning?* This is a completely different problem from (6); there, a question of fact is stated; here, we deal with a semantic problem. It might very well be that the believer *intends* to give meaning to his utterances but that this is semantically impossible. The present problem should be treated, I think, in the usual way, namely, by asking about the conditions of significance and of truth. As far as the first class is concerned, the problem may be restricted to that of the predicates which are applied to God—because once the meaning of the term "God" is secured, a correct definition of other religious terms may be easily given.

8. *Is the theory of analogy an adequate solution of (7) and if so, under what conditions?* I think that anybody who is not ignorant of the efforts made to resolve problem (7) will agree that up to now only *one* serious theory has been offered in that field, namely St. Thomas Aquinas' doctrine of analogy. But this doctrine needs, I think, a far more precise restatement. I myself have tried to interpret analogy (of proportionality) as isomorphy,[2] i.e., to understand it in this way: (1) out of the meaning of words used in profane discourse we apply only relations to God; (2) from these relations we transfer to Him only their formal properties. This theory (which needs a considerable mathematico-logical apparatus to be stated and justified—for example, it uses relations with eight terms) is open to some objections, which were formulated for the author by Professor H. Hermes. Is there any other possible interpretation of analogy? How can the interpretation proposed be readjusted? Can it meet the major difficulties? All those problems should be, I think, seriously studied by means of modern logical and semantic tools.

9. *What is the logical structure of faith?* I mean, of course, not

the *act* of faith, but its object, *what* is believed. In order to illustrate what I mean, I shall sketch a view I developed recently in this respect. I think that faith is intended to be *a system* of propositions. The verbal expression of that system contains at least the following three elements: (1) *the objective faith,* a class of object-linguistic sentences about God, salvation, etc.; (2) *the heuristic rule,* a metalinguistic rule which allows the believer to determine what sentences belong to the objective faith; (3) *the basic dogma,* a meta-linguistic sentence stating that all elements of the objective faith are true. I do not pretend that all those elements are always explicitly formulated, but I think that they are always more or less consciously admitted by the believer. Also, I would not like to dogmatize in that field; other analyses may be proposed. But I found that the above is useful for the statement of the problems connected with the truth-conditions and I shall therefore use it in the following.

*10. Are the indicative sentences contained in religious discourse thought by the believer to be verifiable and falsifiable?* This is equivalent to the question of whether the believer admits that there are truth-conditions for such sentences. I think personally that to state this question is to answer it in the affirmative—for there can be no meaning to a sentence which has no truth-conditions attached. Faith presents, however, a peculiar problem here: it seems that it always includes a sort of certainty that the sentences in question cannot be false. I think that the solution of this problem lies in a distinction between the awareness of the conditions under which a sentence *would* be false (this is always present, I think) and the admission of the possibility that some such conditions might be *realized* (this, it seems to me, is excluded by faith).

*11. What are the truth-conditions of the objective faith?* This partial problem of the truth-conditions in religious discourse appears to be astonishingly easy, if not trivial, for they can be stated in purely syntactical terms. Suppose the heuristic rule states that, for all sentences *P*, if *P* is found in the context *T*, then *P* belongs to the objective faith. Then the problem of verification is a syntactical one.

*12. What are the truth-conditions of the proposition on which the heuristic rule is based?* The rule as such can, of course, have no truth-conditions; but there is always a corresponding sentence which expresses a proposition. We can and must ask for its truth-conditions. I must confess that I do not know the answer to that special problem. It is not quite clear to me what the connection between the heuristic rule and the basic dogma may be—though some such connection is certainly present.

*13. What are the truth-conditions of the basic dogma?* This appears to be the central and most difficult problem. It seems to me that two aspects of the situation are often confounded: the psychological and the logical. Psychologically, the act of faith is an act of free choice, the believer has neither immediate evidence nor deductive proof that the basic dogma is true; the logical counterpart of this situation is the lack of strict demonstrability of the dogma. But, if the act of faith has to be anything other than pure fancy, it must be a reasonable act; there must be a degree of rationality in performing the said act. But the degree of rationality is subject to logical study. My personal opinion is the following: I think that the believer formulates the basic dogma first of all not as a dogma, but as a hypothesis, in a way very similar to that of a scientist. Then, by the act of faith proper, he changes that hypothesis into a dogma, which is recognized now as absolutely true. How such a leap comes to be performed is, I think, the business of psychology to explain, and that sort of psychology will, of course, be also of interest to the philosopher of religion. But his main interest will be directed toward the rational process preceding the act.

*14. What is the difference between the religious and the scientific hypothesis?* That there is a difference seems obvious to me. Moreover, I think that the difference does not consist solely in the leap described above. I think that there is already a considerable difference on the level of hypothesis, because I cannot understand otherwise the justification of the leap which occurs in faith and does not (or at least should not) occur in science. My personal solution is this: while a scientific theory has as its basis only a restricted subclass of empirical sentences, the religious hypothesis serves as an explanation of the totality of the subject's experience. And I think that that totality includes also all his moral and esthetic experience.

*15. Is it necessary to assume a determinate epistemology in order to acknowledge the possibility of the logical justification of the basic dogma?* My personal answer is yes. I believe, in particular, that a strictly positivistic epistemology—in particular, one which denies that moral and esthetic experiences can be expressed by indicative sentences—forces its partisans to say that there is no possible logical justification of the basic dogma, that this is, consequently, a sort of fancy. The minimum required is the recognition of the indicative character of moral and esthetic sentences. There may be also other requirements. I think that a great deal of clarification could be obtained by a thorough analysis of those epistemological requirements.

*16. Why is faith so difficult to falsify?* That it is so, nobody will doubt. But why? One reason is perhaps supplied by the answer I suggested to problem 9, namely, by the theorem that faith is a system. It is a well-known fact that the discovery of some contradictions in the system does not lead to the immediate rejection of a well-established theory in science. The situation must be similar here. Moreover, it seems to me that because the inductive basis of the religious dogma is so much broader than that of any scientific theory this phenomenon should be understandable. Yet, I feel that much research should be done here.

*17. What is the logical structure of the loss of faith?* It is an empirical fact that some believers *do* abandon their faith at a certain moment. Why? Logically there may be two explanations: (1) the number of elements of the objective faith which have been shown to contradict other sentences, recognized as true, may be felt intolerably great; (2) new experiences in the moral and aesthetic realm may suggest that the religious hypothesis assumed is inadequate. I personally believe that the second way is the most common.

*18. Does faith change in time?* That it does in some way seems to be universally recognized (there is, e.g., a Catholic theory of the evolution of dogma). Some penetrating studies have been made of it in the 19th and 20th century. But I feel personally that very little has been done to clarify the change from the point of view of modern semantics. I think that the theory of the axiomatic system combined with something like the above (9) analysis of faith forms a rather powerful apparatus which would allow interesting results. But once more, this problem of philosophy of religion seems to be largely a *tabula rasa in qua nihil est scriptum* in modern terms.

*19. How do errors arise in religion?* Curiously enough I have never found a theory of theological error. Of course, there is a sort of general recognition of the fact that there may be errors; this is implied (at least in those theologies which have been somewhat thought out) by the distinction between faith and theology. But it seems to me that a believer can err in many ways without being a theologian. There may be, e.g., a logically wrong application of the heuristic rule; there may be a misinterpretation of the meaning of words used in some element of the objective faith. One very important error of this sort is an unwarranted acceptance of some sentence as belonging to the objective faith. I think that a full philosophy of religion should include also a well-developed logical and psychological theory of religious error.

*20. How is religion related to other fields of experience?* I said above (13) that the religious hypothesis which precedes the acceptance of the basic dogma is based on the totality of the experience of the subject. But this does not entail that the objective faith is coextensive with the class of all sentences held to be true by him. On the contrary, they seem always to form only a proper part of the latter. But there will certainly be a tendency to form a sort of universal system, embracing all the said sentences, and consequently some sort of logical relations between the two sets will be present. What those relations are is another problem for philosophy of religion.

These are a few examples of many problems which seem to be offered to a philosophy of religion by the actual situation in logic and semantics. I have the feeling that a philosophy of religion,

46

elaborated on these lines, would be something very, perhaps radically, different from much of the things which are now being expounded under the same title.

## NOTES

1. R. Ingarden, *Das Litterarische Kunstwerk,* 1926.
2. J. M. Bochenski, "Ueber Analogie," in *Logisch-philosophische Studien,* Paderborn, Schöningh, 1958. This is a corrected translation of a paper "On Analogy" published previously in *The Thomist*; the original English paper contains a misprint which makes one of the main proofs unintelligible.

# 5

## SYMBOLISM
### by Brand Blanshard, Yale University

Symbolism is a favorite subject in recent philosophy. White-head wrote a book about it; Urban wrote a much bigger book about it; Cassirer wrote a vast three-volume work about it; semanticists discuss it endlessly; theologians look to it for essential light on theological thought. I am puzzled by all this. I get little light from the study of symbols, and do not understand why others find it so instructive.

Why is it that people expect illumination from such study? Presumably because they think there is some important relation between the symbol and what it symbolizes which, once we have grasped it, will illuminate the nature of our knowledge, the nature of the object, or both. Now there is, to be sure, one fixed though rather remote relation between symbol and symbolized, a utilitarian relation; the symbol is a means or vehicle that helps us fix our thought on something beyond it. We cannot think clearly of an abstraction such as justice or rectangularity until we get hold of the word that symbolizes it; if we try to think of a complex concept such as communism, we find ourselves doing it with the help of some visual aid, such as the image of a bear or a hammer and sickle; and the inferences of mathematics would be impossible without the aid of symbols. Symbols are a means of fixing and sustaining attention. But the symbol is not the thought, nor is it the object of thought, and these are the things of importance. The symbol itself does not in general throw any light on either.

The reason is that apart from this aid to the attention there is no general relation between the symbol and the symbolized; symbols have the wildest variety of relation and lack of relation to what they stand for. Sometimes they resemble their objects, as when a poster of Mr. Kennedy looks like him. Sometimes there is no resemblance whatever, as when a crescent stands for Islam. Sometimes the symbol is associated with some conspicuous character of the object, as when the image of Gibraltar stands for the Prudential Insurance Co., or a flying horse for Mobil gasoline. Sometimes the symbol is drawn from some incident connected with the object, as when the cross symbolizes Christianity, or an empty tomb, immortality. The same symbol may stand in different minds for totally different things, as when the stars and stripes symbolize national glory for the American and a hated imperialism for the Cuban. Finally, different symbols may stand for the same thing, as when 'rouge,' 'rot,' and 'red' all stand for the same color.

The relations of symbols to what they symbolize are thus inexhaustibly heterogeneous, and are formed on no principle whatever. Where this is true, a study of these relations is not very profitable. The hope of finding some single law governing our use of symbols seems to me idle, nor would such a law be very significant if we were to find it. If symbols generally resembled their objects, one might throw some light on the object by scrutinizing the symbol, but since no such resemblance in general exists, one can secure such light only if one knows already that the object is like the symbol, and then study of the symbol is needless.

It is clear from his thoughtful and suggestive paper that Professor Tillich would not agree with all this. He plainly thinks that the study of religious symbols is important and enlightening. Why? He does not state the reasons formally, but in reading his paper I seem to find three of them clearly at work.

One appears at the outset of his paper "The Religious Symbol" (see Appendix, p. 299) in the distinction between a symbol and a sign. "The sign is interchangeable at will. It does not arise from necessity, for it has no inner power. The symbol, however, does possess a necessary character. It cannot be exchanged." The word 'red,' for example, would no doubt be a sign, since it could perfectly well be replaced by 'rot' or 'rouge.' On the other hand, the flag would be a symbol, since it cannot be replaced by any other

49

flag and thus "possesse[s] a necessary character." Now what does this necessity consist in? There is, of course, no logical necessity about it; it is quite conceivable that the nation could have adopted some other flag. So far as one can see, the necessity is only one of established association; through long experience, a set of feelings and ideas have come to cluster about the flag, and these are evoked when the flag is displayed. Professor Tillich describes this as a possession of the part of the symbol of "innate power." Why innate? Is it suggested that if some other flag had been adopted, it would not have possessed the same power to evoke feeling as this one? That can hardly be intended. Indeed, it is not easy to discover any meaning that can be called 'innate' to this flag, or any 'necessary character' in the meaning it does convey. It happens, in fact, to carry a rich volume of associated ideas and feelings, and, therefore, its presence in a parade or a battle may be rousing and exciting. And no doubt a psychologist could learn something of how Americans feel about their country by observing how they respond to the flag. But surely this is not the sort of light the philosopher is seeking. He had gathered that there is some sort of relation between the symbol (the flag) and the symbolized (the country), by study of which he could gain a new insight of some kind going beyond these psychological associations. It remains a puzzle to me what this insight is. I do not see that on this point the symbol is more revealing than the sign. Both are related in the most contingent way to their objects. The fact that symbols have collected emotions about them and are, therefore, more potent in practice does not make them more illuminating about those objects. The distinction between symbol and sign is not that one possesses something 'innate' or 'necessary' which the other does not; it is at most a matter of degree, and that difference of degree is of psychological, not philosophical, importance. It is a difference in the comparative volume of associations.

A second reason why Professor Tillich attaches such importance to the study of symbolism is the very broad meaning which he gives at times to 'symbol.' At the beginning of his paper a symbol is something used to carry a reference to something else. But in the discussion of the "cultural-morphological" theories, it has a far wider sense. A symbol now seems to be anything whatever that is expressive of a state of mind. "In the style of works of art, concepts, legal forms, and the like, the soul of the culture from which they derive finds expression. By means of this conception of style all objects or forms of cultural life become symbols." Though Professor Tillich does not identify himself with these theories, he includes such expression among the functions of the symbol. There can then be no doubt that symbols are important.

But the term is now so vast in its scope that it is almost beyond profitable discussion. Freudian lapses of memory and slips of the tongue will be symbols, not because they carry a reference to something else, but because they express something in the agent's mind. The symbol is here a symptom. 'Ouch' and 'cheers' are presumably symbols, though they refer to nothing. A symphony is a symbol, even though its composer may insist that in a cognitive sense it means nothing. The Parthenon is a symbol; so is a Bostonian's accent, a dream, a sonnet, or a football game. Indeed, it is hard to think of any human activity that is not a symbol, for they are all expressive of their agent's minds. But this is clearly not the sense of 'symbol' that we started with. The artist or the football player is not using his work to refer to something else; if he were asked what his acts symbolized he would be at a loss to know what was meant. They are expressions, embodiments, outlets, or displays of his inner feelings or interests. Such expressions are, of course, very important as diagnostic of the individual or cultural soul. But if for that reason they are to be called symbols, then the study of symbols will be virtually coextensive with the study of civilization.

If symbolism has come to be thought so important a study, the reason thus lies in part in the ambiguity of the term. There is no clear understanding as to what the word 'symbol' signifies. Nothing in its ordinary sense would make one suppose its study to be of great importance. But this sense has been gradually stretched to include a vast hinterland of vaguely analogous meaning. The critic who keeps to the original and definite meaning and complains

51

of its use to cover every form of human expression is then suspected of shallow verbalism.

A third reason for Professor Tillich's stress of symbols is his belief that they serve as our only available bridge between finite and infinite. God is for him "the unconditioned transcendent," who "surpasses every possible conception of a being, including even the conception of a Supreme Being." Infinity exceeds the grasp of finite thought. Hence religious thinking is symbolic in a double sense. It is symbolic in the familiar sense in which the symbol carries the thought beyond itself, but it is symbolic also in the sense that the thought carried by the symbol is itself symbolic only; it never reaches the object, never apprehends it as it really is. Religious thought here differs from ordinary thought. When the chess player reads the notation "P to K4" he knows precisely what square on the board is referred to; when the student sees his college pennant, he can bring to mind easily enough the sort of things it stands for. The case is very different when the religious man refers to the absolute. The cross may serve as a symbol which carries his thought of the incarnation, but what is the character of this thought itself? Unlike the thought of the college or the square on the chessboard, it is a reference to what is beyond all thought, what is wholly incomprehensible. In such thinking it is not only the image of the cross that is symbolic, it is also the concept carried by that image. No matter how ambitious the concept may be, it falls short, indeed infinitely short, of its object.

What are we to say of this account of religious symbolism? It has, I think, an important element of truth. Professor Tillich is surely right in holding that the ultimate nature of things is beyond the reach of our present powers; we can only say, with Goethe, that existence divided by human reason leaves a remainder. Whether this means that God is a 'wholly other' or differs from man in degree only has been much disputed; I hold the latter view. But the notion of the completely other has been powerfully advocated. The most effective statement of it was made, not by Kierkegaard, but by his great English contemporary, Dean Henry Mansel, who was as much superior to Kierkegaard in scholarship and intellect as in style. Anyone who claims to have caught the absolute in butterfly nets of his reason will come away from Mansel's *Limits of Religious Thought* with his pretensions thoroughly chastened.

But granting this, what is the upshot of Professor Tillich's insistence on 'the unconditioned transcendent'? He is confronted, I think, with a dilemma. If God is really thus transcendent—transcendent of all the prescriptions of human reason in metaphysics and ethics—then any attempt by reason to construe his nature or his will must end in complete misconstruction. Kierkegaard concedes this and rubs his hands over it. God, he holds, is "the most absurd of beings," and the readiness in man to accept a "teleological suspension of the ethical," even to the point of murder, is the ultimate proof of faith. If God is 'wholly other,' the attempt of rational men to live reasonable lives is as little likely to represent his will as the life of some wayward beatnik or some dervish from Berchtesgaden. This conception of God as a being who is discontinuous absolutely with human reason and moral standards has made strange headway of late in some of our theological schools. It is best to speak plainly about it. If this is what Christianity means, there are thousands of us, brought up to believe in "a faith that inquires," who want no part of it. Such "reactionary irrationalism," as D. C. Macintosh rightly called it, not only builds a wall between religion and the rational mind, but exposes religious leanings to the suspicion of immorality. Once the compass of reason has been thrown overboard, how is one to tell whether the wind of inspiration in one's sails is of divine or satanic origin?

Now it is plain that Professor Tillich is not in this sense an irrationalist. If the call came to him which Kierkegaard thought divine in the case of Abraham, he would surely refuse to obey it, on the ground that anything so irrational could not possibly be divine. Here all rationalists would be with him. But in taking this line, is he not to all intents and purposes a rationalist himself? If a mandate purporting to be revealed requires what reason disallows, he will reject its claim to revelation rather than act in an irrational way. This is to measure revelation by reason, not reason by revelation. What is the difference, after all, between one who takes reason as the guide of life and one who, accepting revelation as the guide, imposes the test of reason on the candidates to revelation? The two are Tweedledum and Tweedledee.

Speaking as a rationalist who is interested in religion, I am tempted to lay claim to Professor Tillich as one of us. Where does he differ from us? Not in holding that infinity is beyond our powers, for on that we agree. Not in holding, like some of his colleagues, that it is sinful pride of intellect to ask that dogmas should make sense, for he tries hard to make them intelligible. The difference is rather in his insistence that what religious thought symbolizes is an 'unconditioned transcendent,' between which and the thought of which there stretches an impassable gulf.

Now the gulf is not wholly impassable. To say that our judgments of truth and good must be reversed in the ultimate reckoning is to make every judgment absurd, including this one. It is well to recall McTaggart's reminder that no one ever tried to break logic but that logic broke *him*. An absolute that goes beyond reason in the sense of being wholly alien to it is a notion without meaning. Revelation comes through reason if it comes at all. Between ultimate truth and the fragmentary truth that we know, there is a difference undoubtedly, but there is no discontinuity. And if I venture to claim that Professor Tillich is on our side, it is because he so often speaks and acts as if this were so. Holding to an 'unconditioned transcendent,' he finds this transcendent at work in him immanently, appointing its own characterization, rejecting false descriptions and illicit 'divine imperatives.' He is a rationalist *malgré lui*.

# 6

## RELIGIOUS SYMBOLS
## AND/OR RELIGIOUS BELIEFS
*by Raphael Demos, Harvard University*

Religion includes many things: love, worship, ritual, and right conduct. But it does not exclude belief; on the contrary, belief is the essence of religion. Surely, if love be its heart, then belief is its spinal column. Religion cannot stand *up* without belief. For this reason I am much disturbed by Professor Tillich's procedure of interpreting Christian doctrine symbolically ("all knowledge of God has a symbolic character"; objects that possess a holy character are not empirical . . . but symbolic"; "religion is greatly indebted to modern research by recognizing the problematic character of the empirical element and by emphasizing the importance of the symbolic element"). Doubtless, we do have to interpret some of the elements of the Christian doctrine symbolically—for instance the six days of creation in Genesis—but once we have begun on this task where do we stop? Professor Tillich tells us that the doctrine of God as being-as-such must be taken literally (empirically?) and everything else symbolically; but by what criteria does he decide that *this* doctrine is literally true and the others not?

The problem may be conveyed by the following metaphor: once you start going down the steps of the staircase, why stop here rather than farther down, why, indeed, not go all the way to the foot of the stairs? And if you do, what has become of the necessary element of belief in the Christian religion? What prevents one from saying that the *whole* of Christianity is no more than an agreeable story? Thus, the story of Jonah and the whale surely must be taken symbolically (to say the least); so with at least some of the miracles, but what does one do with Jesus? We are told that his resurrection has only symbolic significance; then, what about his birth, his life, his death? Did Jesus really exist—I mean Jesus, the Christ? And if we deny that Jesus is a historical ('empirical') figure what is left of orthodox (non-Unitarian) Christianity?

The danger of the symbolic interpretation is the de-historization of Christianity, the denial of the Incarnation. Yet one of the cardinal claims of Christian theology is that Christianity is unique among the great religions in ascribing to history an ultimate significance. Such a claim becomes a worthless check when we find ourselves unable to cash it at the bank of actual history.

In the second volume of his *Systematic Theology* (pp. 97–118), to which Professor Tillich suggests that we should look in order to get a better understanding of his views on symbolic meaning, the reader notes the following. Professor Tillich says that the 'Christian event' is a combination of two parts: (a) Jesus is (b) the Christ. The first must be dealt with by the methods of historical inquiry, the second is known by faith, the 'believing receptive' side of man. This separation of functions is valid. It stands to reason that no historical inquiry could possibly certify that Jesus is the Christ; at best, it could certify the existence of a certain man called Jesus. But in fact, as Professor Tillich says, historical research can provide only probability. The two parts form one integral whole in the Christian doctrine; if there is no Jesus, he cannot be the Christ. "The paradox of the Christian message is that in *one* personal life the essential manhood has appeared under the conditions of existence without being conquered by it." Good; but if one leg of the body of the Christian doctrine is crippled ('more or less probable') can the other leg sustain this body alone? Of this more below.

The content of *faith* is symbolic—not literally or 'empirically' true. When a believer asserts that Jesus is the Son of God, Professor Tillich asks him "What do you mean by the term 'Son of God' "? This is only fair. Professor Tillich's own answer is that the phrase is a symbol of the essential unity of God with man; it does not denote a "family relation." He speaks disparagingly of the literal-ism which imagines "a transcendent being who, once upon a time, was sent down from his heavenly place and transmuted into a man. In this way, a true and powerful symbol becomes an absurd story. . . ." Absurd perhaps, but does Professor Tillich's con-struction leave any substantive content to the Christian doctrine? Not only is there no virgin birth, no resurrection (no crucifixion?), but the conception of the Holy Trinity—of three natures in one person—is abandoned. Professor Tillich dislikes absurdities but he welcomes paradoxes; I find it hard to draw the line between paradoxes (dialectical contradictions) and absurdities.

Surely we must welcome Professor Tillich's aim to make Christian doctrine credible to the modern mind. But a balance must be struck between the claims of rationality on the one hand, and the mystery of Christian doctrine on the other. This balance was, more or less, achieved by the Cappadocian theologians and the Nicene Creed, in which Christian doctrine was stated in terms borrowed from classic Greek thought; the formulation is rational (although difficult and complex) and is presented as meaningful. I fear that Professor Tillich has jettisoned too much precious cargo in his effort to save the ship from the winds of modern thought. I repeat my earlier question: once you start retreating, why not abandon the whole battlefield? Why talk of Jesus at all? The latter question brings me once more to the problem of the historicity of Jesus.

Of the complex sentence 'Jesus is the Christ,' we have discussed the second part and now we will take up the first. At first sight it seems that Professor Tillich agrees that the first part (the existence of Jesus) is essential to the truth of the whole statement. Thus he writes, "If the factual element in the Christian event were denied, the foundation of Christianity would be denied." But how, I ask, can the foundations be firm, if the ground underneath is shaky, if the existence of Jesus be no more than probable, proba-ble more or *less,* with a probability which might diminish to zero?

Professor Tillich faces up to this problem. The Christian doctrine, he says, "guarantees a personal life in which the New

57

Being has conquered the old being. But it does not guarantee his name to be Jesus of Nazareth. Historical doubt concerning the existence and the life of someone with this name cannot be over-ruled. He might have had another name . . . . Whatever his name, the New Being was and is actual in this man." Another man with another name: where did he live and when? And why assume that he was born in some time past; why should he not belong to the future? Indeed, given the probabilities of history, how can Professor Tillich be sure that such a person with whatever name did exist? And if he cannot be thus sure, what becomes of the certainty about the Christ? To labor the obvious, if we cannot know for sure that Jesus (or somebody like him) existed in the past, we cannot be sure that Jesus (or somebody like him) was the Christ. One is surprised, therefore, to find Professor Tillich writing, "Historical research can neither give nor take away the foundation of the Christian faith." But he soon calms our surprise by going on to write, "Faith can guarantee only its own foundation; namely, the appearance of that reality which has created the faith." The last phrase is vague; I can only interpret it to mean that history is no part of the foundation; to change the figure, the plant of Christian doctrine is not rooted in the earth but grows in water.

To sum up, in Professor Tillich's presentation (*a*) the historical element of Christian doctrine is so downgraded as to become worthless, and (*b*) the content of faith is so thin as to be—like the Emperor's new clothes—nonexistent. Christians are faced with an ineluctable Either/Or: either we believe in the full sense of believing that something is the case, or we are not believers. Perhaps the trouble with Professor Tillich is that he has all the answers; I miss that anguish of doubt which, he tells us, is part of faith.

# 7

# THE ATHEISM OF PAUL TILLICH

*by Sidney Hook, New York University*

Paul Tillich is one of the heroic figures of religious thought. He carries to completion the process of religious freedom begun with the Protestant Reformation, the upshot of which is the recognition of atheism as a religion among others, with truth claims that seem better warranted, on Tillich's own showing, than its rivals'. That this is accomplished by the use of the traditional language of religious piety will be puzzling only to those who have old-fashioned notions about the ethics of words and who have failed to realize that the validity of religious assertion does not depend upon actual historical or natural fact but upon the therapeutic function it plays in healing fractures in the spirits of believers. This liberation is accomplished in Tillich's case by a refurbishing of the myths of German idealism, including the romantic and magical idealism of the German *Natur-philosophen*. Certain things, like water, bread, and wine, certain words, like the names for God, certain colors, like gold, have an intrinsic sacramental significance which makes them essentially adequate as carriers of the transcendent, the holy, the divine. This adds an aura of poetic obscurity to the iconoclastic tendency of his work. But it muffles the sound of falling idols in an almost impenetrable fog, and sharpens the vision of the idol-worshipers to the high moral ideals which shine through the watery metaphysical mists.

The God whom many millions of men have worshiped is dead, according to Tillich, because He has been conceived as *a* Being instead of being-itself or being-as-such. But the fact that we mourn His death is evidence of His Resurrection, so to speak. For the need to believe betokens a psychological and metaphysical hunger for a cosmic security which can only be found by relating oneself to the power of Being. Tillich accepts Feuerbach's dictum that the secret of theology is to be found in the nature of man—but a nature conceived not merely psychologically but ontologically, according to which our individual selves are part of the Universal Self or Ego which is the Teutonic correlative of being-as-such. The secret of the Power of Being is the Cosmic Egoism from which our egos are painfully separated—and in which we find peace and security when our egos are dissolved and reintegrated. For all his talk of God as an "unconditioned transcendent," Tillich's God is the all-in-all of pantheistic spiritualism.

Just as for David Strauss and Feuerbach the God-Man is not *a* man but man, humanity, not an individual but the *Gattung* or species, so, for Tillich, God is not Yahweh, Baal, Zeus, or Odin but what all beings of ultimate concern have in common. He is right in understanding that what all beings have in common cannot be another being any more than what all men have in common is another man. But he does not see that it makes no sense to ask what all beings have in common, since that would give us an Essence or definition or common predicate.[1] And this is fatal to his position for two reasons: first, an essence or definition is not an ontological entity or being of any magnitude whatsoever, and second, to be intelligible, an essence or definition must itself be differentiated from something else—it must be a species with differentia of some genus —whereas Being, according to Tillich, is all-inclusive.

Strictly speaking, even on Tillich's own view, "the unconditioned transcendent" is ineffable. The considerations which lead him to identify it as a referent of religious symbols would justify us in characterizing it as "the unconditioned immanent" since God is in all things, nothing is outside His Power. Tillich admits that the validity or truth of religious symbols which speak of the personality of God is derived exclusively from the nature of human experience, and not from the nature of the referent. Ontologically it is false to say that God is a Person or has personality.

All this bears directly upon Tillich's atheism. Let us look away

60

from the difficulties of understanding what is meant by "the un-conditioned transcendent" or "the unconditioned (anything)" as either an identifying or descriptive expression. For every other thing we know or can conceive of, *is* related to, or dependent upon, something else. We can perhaps make sense of the expression as a way of observing that there is always more in the world than what is said about it, that the universe of discourse is presupposed by every object of discourse and can not itself be a term in any first-level sentence which identifies a thing, quality, or event. What relevance has this to any man's belief in God? One does not have to accept the pragmatic maxim in order to hold that for the pur-poses of religious belief, an ontological statement about God should make some difference to religious practice or commitment. Whether God exists or does not exist, whether he is being-itself or not being-itself, should have some bearing upon the character of religious belief and behavior—even if the effects are not so momentous as in the case of Dostoyevsky's characters. Since we can only know God through religious symbols, and since the validity and truth of these symbols can in no way be judged by any ontological fact but only by human experience and its needs, why do we require the ontological reference at all? It would seem that ontological statements are no more relevant to the adequacy and truth of religious symbols than the laws of logic. The great difference between them is that, whereas no one can meaningfully deny laws of logic, the whole of ontology with its vocabulary of Being is an unnecessary intellectual construction which adds not a whit to our understanding of the world or to religious experience. In Tillich's sense, to say that God as being-itself does not exist is to be guilty of a contradiction. If this is so, then the statement is purely analytic. It tells us, at the most, no more than, using his own terminology, that "Something is." Sub-stitute nature, the universe, the totality of things, or any similar expression for God as being-itself and denial of its existence gives the same result. This indicates that, even if we play the word game of classical ontology, we cannot do justice to the historical and psychological facts of religious belief and experience, especially in the Western tradition. For in that tradition, atheism was often identified with the belief that the world existed from eternity and was not created out of nothing by God.

When the religious man asks: "Does God care for me?" "Did He create Stalin and Hitler too?" "Does He see into all our hearts and judge us accordingly?" he assuredly refers to God as *a* Being who exists in such a manner that it is not self-stultifying to pray to Him. With amazing courage Tillich boldly says that the God of the multitudes does not exist, and further, that to believe in His existence is to believe in an idol and ultimately to embrace superstition. God cannot be an entity among entities, even the highest. He is being-itself. In this sense Tillich's God is like the God of Spinoza and the God of Hegel. Both Spinoza and Hegel were denounced for their atheism by the theologians of the past, because their God was not *a* Being or an Entity. Tillich, however, is one of the foremost theologians of our time.

I must confess that at certain moments I find Tillich's approach to religion attractive as a kind of moral strategy. For if God is not an entity or a being but being-itself, no religion truly oriented to Him or It could be persecutory. All religions would be equal in their sense of stuttering inadequacy as they sought to articulate that which was beyond articulation. Full of humility and awe before the Power of Being, they would revise or reinterpret their religious symbols in order to express the highest moral reaches of human experience. They would seek more explicitly than in the past to devise symbols which would integrate rather than disintegrate human personality. They would turn to the findings of modern psychology, sociology, and moral theory for leads and material rather than go adventuring on an impossible quest for being. They would provide aesthetic and emotional supports for the various types of humanisms and ethical culture whose rituals are so often dreary and funereal. Religion would forever cease its warfare against science and remove its "no trespass" signs from the roads of intellectual inquiry into the mysteries of mind and spirit.

62

The attractiveness of Tillich's approach is reinforced by the weariness induced by continuous criticism of his ontological incoherence. One feels that refuting him is like punching an eiderdown or fencing with a ghost. There is no sense of resistance. On the many occasions on which I have polemized against him, with my usual mildness and restraint, he has always replied with manifest sincerity, "I agree with everything you have said," and I have found myself embraced as a fellow religionist crusading for the Holy Grail of Being. I know that if he were excommunicated as an atheist by his congregation, as were so many religious thinkers before him who held views which were much more orthodox than his, I should rush to his defense. Even though I am unable to join him, why not leave him as a beneficent Trojan horse in the citadel of the idol worshippers?

I find these reflections disarming but in the end remain unconvinced. It may be that I am too literal-minded and old-fashioned, prepared to pay too high a price for clarity. But I am not really persuaded that Tillich's ambiguities can get the idol-worshipers out of the temples; there is some evidence that his ideas provide the rationalizations for those to remain who would otherwise have left. No matter how religion is reconstructed, there will always be a difference between the approach of a secular, rational, and ethical humanism to the problems of man and society and the approach of religion. History cannot be disregarded so lightly. The language of religion carries with it a mood of acceptance and resignation to the world as we find it, which tends to dissipate the mood of social change and reform. As Tillich uses this language it is, where intelligible, harmless and sometimes morally edifying. But others use his language to express the very supersititions he fears.

In the end, the question of religious truth cannot be evaded. Tillich himself does not evade it. But when God is identified with being-itself, it permits evasion by those without his great courage and integrity. I do not belong to that school of pragmatism, which has discredited its name, which believes that where man's place in nature is concerned, the warmth and light radiated by the beaming countenance of a cosmic confidence man is to be preferred to the stern and cheerless visage of the truth about man's tragic estate.

## NOTES

1. See my "The Quest for 'Being,'" *Journal of Philosophy*, L (1953), 709–31, reprinted with some changes and additions in *The Quest for Being: and Other Studies in Naturalism and Humanism* (New York: St. Martin's Press, 1961).

# 8

## ULTIMATE CONCERN AND THE REALLY ULTIMATE

*by John E. Smith, Yale University*

To say what religion is has proved to be the most difficult of tasks. For one thing, religion seems very close to us and therefore it appears as something both obvious and transparent; it belongs among those realities and experiences which we do not bother to analyze on the supposition that we know them fully enough already. But, as Hegel pointed out so forcefully, what is familiar is least likely to be known by us in a clear and cogent way.

The analysis of religion presents us with a peculiar difficulty at the outset. In order to do full justice to the phenomenon in its generic form, we must characterize it in a way broad enough not to exclude any relevant form; on the other hand, if we succeed in such a characterization, the result is likely to appear so general that religion seems to be trivialized and emptied of any differential meaning such as might serve to distinguish it from other aspects of life. There is the added difficulty that when we take religion in its generic sense we are implying that *every* man is "religious" and we are indulging in what has been described, somewhat mockingly, as "conversion by definition." We must see whether it is possible to deal with this problem without having to abandon the attempt to express religion in its universal or essential nature.

Religion in some sense belongs essentially to human life as is shown by its presence in every civilization of which we have record. It is, adapting one of Dewey's expressions, a generic trait of human existence. The question is: what is the meaning of religion in this form and how is it related to individual life?

If religion belongs to the structure of human existence, we may expect to find it as a permanent aspect of experience, for experience is the realization of existence. It is necessary to say a word about experience. We should understand experience not in the narrow and mentalistic sense characteristic of traditional empiricism, but rather in the broader sense indicated by Dewey and others. Experience is primarily a fund of meanings and knowledge possessed by beings with memory and the ability to use language. It is a product of intelligent interplay between human selves and the world in which they exist; all experience presupposes a being who has it and a concrete world or environment within which it is to be had. Experience is not confined to the objects and events, the qualities and the relations of which may be said to form its body or content; it has, in addition, aspects or dimensions rooted in the concerns and purposes of the selves in which experience is realized. We do not merely ask: "What did he see?" or "What did he encounter or suffer?," but "How did he take it?" "Why does he act as he does?" The how and the why of our experience go along with the what; we must be careful lest we ignore the dimensions of experience because of exclusive preoccupation with observing its content. Life in the world has its aesthetic, its moral, its political, and its religious dimensions. Our immediate problem is to describe the religious dimension.

What is there about an experiencing being and his life in the world which can be described as religious? The religious dimension means the concern for the ultimate ground and goal of existence. In addition to the special concerns which go to make up a life plan or career—concerns for this or that limited goal or activity—man asks about the purpose of his own being and the totality of his experience. Every self has a concern for this total meaning, and within this concern there is implied a question about ultimate foundations. The question and concern may direct the self to many different religious objects in the quest for fulfillment, but the serious putting of the question and the manifesting of the concern constitute religion in its generic aspect. Whatever the particular fulfillment, every self shows its concern to find what is for that self an ultimate or final good which gives purpose to all the lesser activities of life. This is the sense in which we can speak of the religious concern as "ultimate," for no other concern has the same final importance, and the preliminary concerns derive their meaning or purpose from the ultimate concern and not the other way around.

We can consider the well-known religious traditions as well as our picture of the so-called primitive religions and show how this conception of religion adequately interprets the historical record. The religious dimension of human existence is correctly described as concern for the ultimate ground and goal of existence; religion is, as Tillich has expressed it, the ultimate concern. The question arises, however, as to whether this description exhausts the meaning of religion. Two difficulties suggest that it does not. First, the description appears to make everyone into a religious person, a consequence which goes hand in hand with a dilution or weakening of the concept, and secondly, it appears to place too much emphasis upon the human side of the relationship and to neglect the religious object. Both problems are important; for present purposes we can deal only with the first.

When we describe religion as ultimate concern we are leaving out of account the many different objects upon which this concern has been focused and the ways in which it is at the same time overcome and fulfilled. There have been many objects of ultimate concern—wealth, fame, country—and within the positive religious traditions there has been a considerable variety of conceptions of the religious object. But the final question is whether our ultimate concern is fixed on the Really Ultimate or upon some lesser object which, being finite, must be regarded in the end as an idol. Not every person does in fact fix the Really Ultimate as the object of his concern, and indeed not every person has in fact acknowledged and committed himself to the Really Ultimate as that self-grounded power which overcomes his ultimate concern and fulfills it. Concern means involvement and participation, but it also means uneasiness and the awareness of not possessing; where we are concerned, there is the danger of losing, there is the risk of failure. Positive religious faith is more than concern; it means acknowledg-

67

ment of the Really Ultimate as the religious object or power which overcomes concern and fulfills it at the same time. Though it is part of human life to have an ultimate concern and to quest for its realization in the acknowledgment of *some object or other,* the structure of human existence does not determine that every man will in fact have acknowledged the Really Ultimate as the object of that concern. Every man participates in the religious dimension and every man must come to some terms with the question implied in ultimate concern; not every man specifically acknowledges what is Really Ultimate. Everyone has a god or gods; not everyone acknowledges God.

With the distinction between the religious dimension of life and positive acknowledgment of the Really Ultimate, we are able to resolve the problem with which we set out. Every man is "religious" in the sense that it is part of human life to have an ultimate concern and to seek its fulfillment in some way; not every man is "religious" since it is not the case that all men do in fact acknowledge the Really Ultimate.

The distinction between the two senses of the religious poses a related problem. If it is illegitimate to convert men by definition, it is equally illegitimate to settle the problem of the inescapability of religious faith solely in terms of what people *say* they do or do not believe or accept. A man's relation to faith in the Really Ultimate is not settled merely by attending to what he may say about himself and his religious convictions. It is, after all, easy enough for the self-styled atheist to put an end to all discussion merely by saying that he does not believe in or accept the Really Ultimate. But just as pragmatism has taught us to be dubious about identifying the possession of a conviction with its verbal expression, we must be just as suspicious about basing lack of conviction merely on the statement that one does not have it. Conviction, faith, and belief are all implied in action. We may want to ask what is implied (apart, that is, from what is said) about the nature of reality by the fact that every man has an ultimate concern. As philosophers we may speculate about the significance to be attached to the fact that this concern is pervasive. We may want to argue that ultimate concern cannot be what it appears to be unless it also includes the presence of the Really Ultimate. Such a line of argument would take us beyond the strictly religious situation to metaphysics, but it would not be sufficient for those rejecting the argument merely to *say* that they have nothing to do with the Really Ultimate. A problem remains as to the further determination and interpretation of the religious dimension of existence. To what extent does it point to the Really Ultimate even if the existence of ultimate concern cannot be used as a premise from which to support the reality of God?

# 9

## THE COPERNICAN TURN
## OF THEOLOGY

*by Jacob Taubes, Columbia University*

The discussion that ensued around the problem of the nature of religious symbols gained momentum when the chairman, Professor Hook, mentioned Feuerbach's critique of religion as a possible source for Tillich's theology and philosophy. Does the ghost of Feuerbach wander about undetected below the surface of contemporary theological discourse? Professor Tillich in answer to this question acknowledged Feuerbach's influence on his philosophic and theological program and even stated that Feuerbach's analyses and conclusions determined his first moves in the realm of theology. It may therefore not be entirely idle to ask in what way Tillich's theology meets the challenge of Feuerbach's critique. Does Tillich's theology settle the account with questions that have been raised, and with the conclusions that have been reached, by Feuerbach?

The congruence in the enterprise between Feuerbach's critique and Tillich's theology is indeed striking. Certainly Feuerbach's analysis of religion is critical in its intention. But, it may be observed, its intention is critical only in relation to the supernatural, not to the human, element in religion. Feuerbach's critique of religion is not simply reductionist, reducing theology to anthropology. While bringing down theology to the level of anthropology, Feuerbach exalts anthropology to the level of theology. Feuerbach and Tillich further agree in denying the fantastic projection of theology in order to affirm the religious essence of man. They may differ in the analysis of the essence of man, but they agree in relating the attributes of God to the essence of man.

Feuerbach charted the course of history of Christianity as a progressive realization and recognition of the anthropological root of theology, unveiling the essence of man as the mystery of theology. He drew the distinction between the Protestant and the Catholic phase of Christian theology by classifying Catholic doctrine and experience as "theocentric" and Protestant doctrine and experience as "anthropocentric." Catholicism has, according to Feuerbach, a supernatural or abstract God, a God who is other than human. "Catholicism has, both in theory and practice, a God who, in spite of the predicate of love, exists for himself, to whom, therefore, man only comes by being against himself, denying himself, renouncing his existence for self." Protestantism, on the contrary, has a God who at least practically does not have an existence for himself, but exists only for man, for the welfare of man. In a footnote, Feuerbach clarifies his intention by pointing to the general anthropocentric tendency of Christian symbolism. "It is true that in Catholicism also—in Christianity generally, God exists for man; but it was Protestantism which first drew from this relativity of God its true result—the absoluteness of man." [1]

Nevertheless, Protestantism, at least in theory, has retained in the background of this human God the old supernaturalist language. Protestantism seemed to Feuerbach a contradiction of theory and practice. He could therefore conceive of the reduction of the extrahuman or supernatural element in theological discourse to the natural and human realm as a liberation of Christianity in general, and of Protestantism in particular, from its fundamental contradiction. Such a reduction of Christian language seemed to Feuerbach to unveil the truth of its meaning, and, finally, this reduction seemed to him the necessary, irrepressible result of Christian history.

The shift from the Catholic to the Protestant theological rhetoric, which Feuerbach had observed seems to me not merely an internal process of theological language but part and parcel of the Copernican revolution that forged a new image of the world and of man. The Ptolemaic frame provides man with the clear notion of the vertical axis of the universe. Man can divide between below

71

and above in a concrete manner. Since the metaphors of the vertical axis have their analogy in the external order of the cosmos, man's vertical vocabulary is not yet reduced to the level of mere allegory. The Ptolemaic earth has a heaven above itself. And, therefore, whatever happens on earth is only a shadow of the heavenly realm. In the Middle Ages the principle of analogy expressed man's experience of a correspondence between the below and the above, the natural and the supernatural, which was integrated into the hierarchical cosmologic architecture of reality. Analogy is, at this stage of human consciousness, not merely a name for a philosophic method diluted and emptied of all concrete meaning, as in modern scholasticism, that artificially transplants the principle of analogy into a climate where it cannot flourish. The Copernican revolution not only overthrew an old astronomic theory, but actually destroyed man's dwelling in the cosmos. The Catholic Church was right in attacking the Copernican theory, sensing that the new cosmology indeed threatened the correspondence between the earthly and heavenly orders. It is true that the Church later compromised with the new cosmology under the pressure of an "enlightened" public opinion. Only under this pressure did the Church conceive the possibility of a cosmology that explicitly denied the correlation between the above and the below and implicitly destroyed the correspondence of the natural and the supernatural. It is well to be reminded that only when Catholic doctrine could no longer oppose the Copernican theory as a scientific perspective did it try to minimize its importance to that of a mere astronomical statement. In reality, however, the Copernican revolution shattered human experience of hierarchy, the heavenly as well as the earthly. In the Copernican universe, "above" and "below" become mere metaphors that are no longer rooted in the external order of the cosmos. In the Copernican universe the earth no longer reflects heavenly perfection. The vertical axis disappears, and above and below can no longer be genuinely distinguished. This shift in the cosmological pattern is at the root of the anthropological stanza of modern theology and metaphysics.[2]

It is a fundamental but seldom recognized fact that since the Copernican revolution theistic religion stands without a cosmology and is therefore forced to retreat into the domain of man's inwardness. Granted that even medieval religious language does not lack in hints that heaven may be inside the human heart, there is still a great difference whether the image of heaven is internalized on the basis of an established cosmological correspondence or whether the internalization has no possible reference in the external order of things and thus becomes a metaphor without root. If the cosmological order presupposes the division between heaven and earth, then a bold statement that heaven is in man's heart translates the cosmological order into an *ordre du coeur*. But if the *ordre du coeur* has no correlative in the external order of the cosmos, its language only proves that heaven is lost.

Feuerbach saw in this shift from Catholic to Protestant theology, from the supernatural to the natural rhetoric, the liberation of Christianity from its contradiction, and the reduction of religious language to its truth as the necessary result of Christianity. But at this end station in the evolution of Christian symbolism he no longer could concede an independent realm of theological discourse. Tillich, who shares Feuerbach's basic premises and who consciously partakes in the Copernican turn of the modern mind, considers, however, the style of theological rhetoric possible.

How does theology become possible after Feuerbach's critique? How does Tillich reach the first base of theological discourse on premises shared with Feuerbach concerning the symbolic nature of religious language? While for Feuerbach *all* statements about God are symbolic, Tillich makes a special case for *one* statement, lifting it from Feuerbach's critical bracket. "The statement that God is being-itself is a nonsymbolic statement." It is true, Tillich continues, "after this has been said nothing else can be said about God as God which is not symbolic." [3] Thus, the special status of the onto-theological statement allows Tillich to reach the first base of a theological discourse and, consequently, to construct a system of theology based on a principle of correlation. Which elements does Tillich correlate in this theological discourse? Tillich correlates the ambiguities of human existence with the ground of an unambiguous realm of being. This correlation between being and the ambiguities of human existence bypasses, however, the cosmos (or, more precisely, the problems of natural theology).

But is theological discourse in general, and systematic theology in particular, still possible in this anthropocentric circle? Are Feuerbach's premises a good omen for a theological enterprise? We can understand why dialectical theology was driven by Feuerbach's challenge into the opposite direction. Karl Barth, in a memorable essay, concedes that Feuerbach has become "a thorn in the flesh of modern theology, and perhaps will continue to be so: so long as the relation to God is not unconditionally inconvertible for us, and does not remain so under all circumstances, we shall have no rest in this matter." [4]

An analysis of the structure of dialectical theology is surely beyond our present scope. Suffice to say that the "change of direction" from the "deity" of God to the "humanity" of God [5] (in spite of Barth's rigorous insistence on the irreversible sequence: first divine, then human) repeats in one generation of theological thought the cycle Feuerbach describes in his analysis of the entire history of Christian symbolism: a small replica of the grandiose process of the humanization of God unfolding in the Christian language. At this stage the difference between Tillich's theology of correlation and Barth's Christocentric humanism is greatly diminished.

We may sum up our analysis of the condition of contemporary theological discourse in general, and Tillich's theology of correlation in particular, and state our thesis concerning Christian religious symbolism in form of a historic recollection: Tillich's strategy proves that the split into a left and right wing among the disciples of Hegel is still the paramount event in the philosophy and theology of the last hundred years. The academic and literary schools of pragmatism and existentialism surely do not contradict this observation. Nor does Kierkegaard's solipsistic meditation on anxiety and nothingness go beyond the limits of Hegel's dialectic. In the split between the disciples of Hegel, Tillich takes the direction to the "right" when he interprets the secular consciousness as the estranged consciousness of man that should seek its ultimate reconciliation in the holy community. He sides with the theologians among Hegel's pupils who constitute the academic tradition of Hegelianism. Hegel himself, however, and with him Feuerbach, Marx, Kierkegaard, and Nietzsche, interprets the Christian consciousness as the unhappy, torn, and estranged consciousness of man. Kierkegaard only tried to defend man in his torn and estranged consciousness; the others, however, tried to go beyond it and mark, each in a different way, experiments of a post-Christian age. Our thesis is stated in form of an historical collection. For if we do not recall the origin of our condition we are bound to perpetuate it beyond hope to gain new territory.

## NOTES

1. Ludwig Feuerbach, *The Essence of Christianity,* trans. George Eliot (New York: Harper Torchbooks, 1957), p. 337.

2. For further elaboration of this question see Jacob Taubes, "Dialectic and Analogy," *The Journal of Religion* (April, 1954), XXXIV, 2, pp. 111 ff.

3. Paul Tillich, *Systematic Theology* (Chicago: University of Chicago Press, 1951), I, p. 238 f.

4. See Karl Barth's introductory essay in Ludwig Feuerbach, *The Essence of Christianity, op. cit.,* p. xxiv (originally a portion of a lecture on the history of modern theology given in 1926 at Muenster).

5. See Karl Barth, *The Humanity of God,* trans. John Newton Thomas and Thomas Wieser (Richmond, Va.: John Knox, 1960), pp. 37 ff.

## 10

# DARKNESS OR LIGHT?

*by Vincent Tomas, Brown University*

According to what Professor Tillich has presented at this conference (I will not refer to any of his other works), all symbols —historical, artistic, and religious—have the following characteristics: 1) figurative quality, 2) perceptibility, 3) innate power, and 4) acceptability as such. I will comment on the first and third of these. For the sake of concreteness, I will consider them as characteristics of artistic symbols, to wit, paintings bearing the title *The Crucifixion* or other actual examples of religious art. My aim is similar to Professor Alston's. I should like, if possible, to get clear the respects in which Professor Tillich's view deviates from what we would pre-analytically accept as true about symbols. Only then would one be in a position to decide whether or not the deviations are justified.

## I. The Figurative Quality of Artistic Symbols

According to Professor Tillich, *The Crucifixion* will have figurative quality if "the inner attitude which is oriented to the symbol (i.e., to the painting) does not have the symbol itself (i.e., the painting itself) in view but rather that which is symbolized in it (i.e., the crucifixion on Golgotha)." That is to say, *The Crucifixion* has figurative quality relatively to a spectator of it if, while looking at it, what the spectator has in mind is not the content of the picture but what it may be taken to be a picture of, namely, an event not here and now perceptible which took place in Jerusalem more than 1900 years ago.

That pictures can have figurative quality is something much discussed by aestheticians and deplored by modern artists. Invariably, they resort to metaphors when they attempt to describe it. Thus, when for a spectator a picture functions as a symbol, he is said to be attending to something "outside the picture" and not to what is "in the picture." In his "Ten O'Clock" lecture, James McNeill Whistler accused John Ruskin of encouraging people to "look through" a picture at the subject of it, as if pictures were windows through which we can see something outside. Professor Tillich himself speaks of the "transparency" of symbols.

Under what circumstances might Grünewald's *Crucifixion* function for us as if it were a window which we look through at something outside of it? Professor Tillich suggests an answer. According to him, "Devotion to the crucifix is really directed to the crucifixion on Golgotha . . ." If the "inner attitude" of the spectator is *devotional,* not aesthetic, if he approaches Grünewald's altarpiece as if the latter were inviting him to contemplate the crucifixion on Golgotha and not Grünewald's *Crucifixion,* then Grünewald's picture for him has figurative quality. If, on the contrary, the spectator's attitude is aesthetic, then for him the picture has no figurative quality. For then he will have only the "symbol itself" or what is "in the picture" in view. He will not look "through" the picture but only "into" it. And then the object he will have in mind will be *the crucifixion depicted by Grünewald,* not the crucifixion on Golgotha.

Some aestheticians contend that an important difference between the devotional attitude and the aesthetic attitude is the following. When we take the devotional attitude first towards *The Crucifixion* by Grünewald, next towards one by Perugino, and then towards one by El Greco, the object we have in mind is in each case the *same*: the crucifixion on Golgotha. Only the windows, so to speak, are different, and (allegedly) we do not see the windows. But when we take the aesthetic attitude towards these pictures, the object we have in mind is *different* in each case. In the crucifixion depicted by Grünewald, against a profoundly gloomy and stark background, the body of Jesus hangs very heavily on the cross. Both Jesus and the cross are being pulled towards earth.

In the crucifixion depicted by Perugino, Jesus does not hang at all. He exists, with the cross behind him, midway between heaven and earth, in a world where all is poetic, bathed in light, and serene. In the crucifixion depicted by El Greco, against a tempestuous background, Jesus and the cross both soar upward.

We feel, when we aesthetically see these *Crucifixions,* that each has its own spiritual message. The Grünewald does not express the same thing as the Perugino, and neither expresses the same thing as the El Greco. What each expresses it is difficult, perhaps not possible, to formulate exactly in words. Yet, were we to make the attempt, we would not feel inclined to choose exactly the same words to formulate the message of each picture. Whatever the right words might be, we are inclined to think, there is not one and the same set of words which is right for all three.

Suppose, now, that you have a serene and sunny faith, untroubled by the problem of evil, and that for you the crucifixion on Golgotha, while symbolizing, as Professor Tillich would say, the redemptive action of God and in the end the object of ultimate concern, is nevertheless an episode which occurred in this best of all possible worlds. If you were given the job of choosing one of the three *Crucifixions* we have mentioned to be a symbol of the crucifixion on Golgotha, knowing that it was to be used to direct the attention of devotees to the crucifixion on Golgotha, which would you choose: the Grünewald, the Perugino, or the El Greco?

You would, of course, under the supposition that you have a serene and sunny faith, choose the Perugino. If you were untroubled by the exalting heights of mysticism or the depths of a tragic sense of human destiny, you would pass over paintings entitled *The Crucifixion* which express these heights or depths in favor of one that is serene, sunny, and pervaded by an atmosphere where no winds of ill-omen blow. (As Ruskin pointed out, a *Crucifixion* by Perugino takes place in the Garden of Eden. Only in the Garden of Eden, where no winds of ill-omen blow, do such slender trees grow so straight and so tall—and in the foreground there is the "tree" of the crucified Christ, from which he does not

78

really hang. Everything is for the best in Perugino's best of all possible, serene, and sunny worlds, including even the crucifixion on Golgotha.)

Now, suppose that you were asked to *justify* your choice of the Perugino as a symbol of the crucifixion on Golgotha. Would not your justification consist essentially in the claim that the Perugino is a visual embodiment of what you believe to be the "meaning" of the crucifixion on Golgotha? And if someone objected to your choice, would not his objection consist essentially in the claim that Perugino failed to capture the "true meaning" of the crucifixion—that, for example, unlike Grünewald, he sentimentalized it? To justify the use of a work of art as a religious symbol, that is to say, it is necessary that there be some independent conception of what it symbolizes, with which the content of the work may be compared with a view to deciding whether it is an adequate, or at least an appropriate, symbol or not.

This point will perhaps be made clearer by the use of another example. In *Acts* 9:3–4 we read: "And as he [Saul] journeyed, he came near to Damascus: and suddenly there shined round about him a light from heaven: And he fell to the earth, and heard a voice saying unto him, Saul, Saul, why persecutest thou me?" What do we make of these words? That is, what do we think really happened on the road to Damascus? That a miracle took place? That Saul had an hallucination, a "natural," albeit a very moving, experience? Or is our view rather that while on his way to Damascus Saul must have fallen upon the earth, but we don't know why or what this signifies, if anything, for the salvation of our souls? All three views are possible.

Suppose we take the first view—that on the road to Damascus Saul came into miraculous contact with Jesus. Will we not then find that Ruben's *The Conversion of St. Paul* (Munich), every square foot of which insistently proclaims "Miracle!" is a much better symbol of Saul's conversion than Caravaggio's picture of the same name in Santa Maria del Popolo in Rome? When Caravaggio's picture is taken to refer to the incident on the road to Damascus, its "message" amounts to this: "Saul fell upon the

79

earth—the rest is mystery." Clearly, the figurative quality of the Rubens is not the same as that of the Caravaggio. Since one points to a miraculous event, while the other does not, they cannot be regarded simply as "two different treatments of the same subject" or as being like two transparent windows through either of which we are able to see exactly the same view. The Rubens and the Caravaggio differ not only stylistically; *qua* symbols they differ theologically as well. Hence I am in entire agreement with Professor Alston when he says that "in practice religious symbols function against the background of a complex system of beliefs." This system not only furnishes the material for the necessary identification of what religious symbols symbolize, as Professor Alston says, but it is in terms of it that we justify the use of one particular symbol rather than another.

## II. The Innate Power of Artistic Symbols

I am not certain what Professor Tillich means when he uses the expression "innate power." But in the light of what precedes it would be natural to say that the Perugino has an innate power to convey a certain idea of the crucifixion on Golgotha that the Grünewald does not have, and that the Grünewald has an innate power to convey a different idea of that crucifixion. Professor Tillich seems to mean more than this. He states that symbols, unlike mere signs, "participate in the power of that which they point to" and that they are "connected to their objects." The only example he gave of such connection was, "The symbol participates in the majesty, for example, of what is symbolized."

This may mean, in the case of artistic symbols, that "what is in the picture" expresses or objectifies certain characteristics of the object "outside the picture" it points to. Thus, the superhuman majesty of the Byzantine *Madonna and Child Enthroned* (Mellon Collection) might be said to participate in, i.e., to convey to the beholder, something of the superhuman majesty of the Mother of

God. But if this is so, we are in no position justifiably to assert it unless we know or have good reasons for believing that super-human majesty is an attribute of the Mother of God. Moreover, we do not come to know nor do we find good reasons for believing that there is a Mother of God and that she is superhumanly majestic merely by looking at the *Madonna and Child Enthroned.* Any argument for the conclusion that we can do so would also be an argument for the conclusion that merely by looking at pictures we can come to know or find good reasons for believing that there are unicorns and that they are delicate and graceful. Before me now is a reproduction of one of the unicorn tapestries in The Cloisters in New York City. It has, if we wish so to speak, an innate power to symbolize a delicate and graceful animal with one horn. But it is in no way literally connected to such an animal, nor can it participate in the delicacy and grace of such an animal, for there is not, and never was, such an animal. If one uses this picture as a symbol of a unicorn, the unicorn that is "in the picture" cannot participate in the delicacy and grace of the unicorn "outside the picture" that it then points to, for there is no unicorn outside the picture.

Here we have revealed an ambiguity in the expression "points to" that Professor Tillich does not seem fully to appreciate. All symbols, as he correctly observes, "point beyond themselves," but this pointing is intentional. The object pointed to may not exist.

## III. Religious Symbols

Professor Tillich contends that a chief difference between religious symbols and other symbols is that they point to what concerns us ultimately—to the ground of our being and what determines our ultimate destiny. *The Crucifixion, qua* religious symbol, points to the crucifixion on Golgotha, which at the same time points to the redemptive action of God, which in turn points beyond God Himself to what concerns us ultimately. Thus, in the

presence of the Grünewald altarpiece we may, if we are not idolatrous, receive what Professor Tillich calls "a true awareness" of
the object of our ultimate concern. I think I understand this
doctrine, and I am not here concerned to deny it.

But to this Professor Tillich adds the doctrine that what concerns us ultimately is unconditionally beyond the conceptual
sphere. There can in principle be nothing in any *Crucifixion,* or in
any conception of the crucifixion on Golgotha or of the redemptive
action of God, which is in any respect adequate as a representation
of the object of our ultimate concern. Hence, "The criterion of
the truth of a [religious] symbol naturally cannot be the comparison of it with the reality to which it refers, just because this
reality is absolutely beyond human comprehension."

If we reflect upon the joint assertion of these two doctrines,
they are seen to be self-contradictory. If there can be a true awareness of the object of our ultimate concern, the latter cannot be
*absolutely* beyond our comprehension. And if that to which religious symbols point is indeed *absolutely* beyond our comprehension, then there can be no symbols that provide a true awareness
of it. At best, they are all purely indexical. They turn our attention
in a given direction, toward something we know not what. And
that is all. In that case, for all we can tell, they point toward
darkness, not towards light; toward something malignant, not
friendly; toward something like a sadistic schoolmaster, not like
a loving father; toward something utterly abominable, not holy;
toward something we ought to hate and despise, not worship. A
strange conclusion this is indeed for a theologian who has faith
in the good news of Christianity to allow himself to arrive at!

# 11

# THANK GOD, GOD'S NOT IMPOSSIBLE

*by Paul Weiss, Yale University*

From almost the beginning of our careers, and surely throughout, all of us live in a bipolar world. On the one side there are the robust space-time objects of common sense, whose meaning, roles, adventures, and values we have more or less mastered. Those objects are in part the objects of sound perceptions and steady experiences; they are also in part the products of social conventions, prejudices, and opinions. The world of common sense is at once real and artifactual. It would be foolish therefore to dismiss it, as Descartes did; it would be equally foolish to accept it without question, as G. E. Moore did.

Over against the world of common sense, there is a vague, almost amorphous, ineffable area which sometimes awakens hope, but more often arouses terror and fear. It is because we are aware of it that we can be so sure that no matter how much we now know, we do not know everything; that no matter how strong we are, we know that man is puny and inadequate; that no matter how immersed we are in daily affairs, we know that our daily world does not exhaust reality. We point to it in our tragedies; we speak of it in our metaphysics; we cherish it in our religions. He who denies its existence must content himself with accepting as ultimate the conventionalized world of common sense and what he can abstract from this. He will be unable to affirm that man and all of his works—scientific, political, speculative, ethical or aesthetic—are imperfect, or that justice has never been fully done to ethical and aesthetic ideals. Most shocking, he will be unable to grasp the import of art, to understand what privacy is, to acknowledge potentialities and, therefore, scientific laws. No one of these is a common-sense fact. No one of them, to be sure, reports the nature of the dimension which transcends the area lying beyond the objects of daily life, but all of them are grounded more or less deeply in it.

Following the lead of Plotinus and Spinoza, some modern thinkers take the common-sense pole to be a derivative from the other. Existentialists, such as Sartre, and Intuitionists, such as Schopenhauer and Bergson, take the world of common sense to be an appearance or expression of it—the Existentialists supposing that the real is ultimately individual, the Intuitionists taking it to be cosmic in nature and reach. But the world of common sense is social, much larger than the individual and much smaller than the cosmos. Both Existentialists and Intuitionists do less than justice to the reality of the evidences on which their own theories depend. Not only do they push the works of engineering, economics, and politics into the limbo of illusion, but inevitably they do this to the reading and writing of their own books.

Their opponents, the modern Analysts and Positivists, reverse this stress. It is their desire to treat what is outside the area of common sense as derivative from it, as secondary, unintelligible, or trivial. It is no surprise to find these thinkers baffled when they try to understand what is meant by obligation, worship, dispositions, possibilities, substance and the like, for these not only refer to what is outside the reach of common-sense methods or interests, but are presupposed in any understanding of what common sense comprehends and does. The desire to know the truth, the willingness to submit to the outcome of disciplined inquiry, the capacity to learn or to construct theories, the ability to read and write books, and, as was noted above, the surety that no one knows all there is, or knows anything existent with absolute certainty, depend on their tacit acknowledgement that there are powers not now manifest or evident in common-sense actions, meanings, or objects.

Most of the towering figures in the history of thought have insisted on the reality of both dimensions, and most have analyzed or qualified one or the other to produce such combinations as the Platonic Receptacle and a realm of Forms, the Aristotelian common-sense substances and a First Mover, the Kantian phenomenal world and a kingdom of ends, the Hegelian theses and the Absolute.

Both dimensions need analysis and clarification. It is the task of science to purge the common-sense world of conventional accretions and to provide a systematic understanding of the result, while politics, social, and mechanical engineering tell us something of the way in which common-sense items can be effectively used. Metaphysics stands somewhat on a par with theoretical science, religion with politics and engineering, in their treatments of the other dimension. Metaphysics asks, among other things, whether or not that dimension constitutes a single, undivided realm; what the nature of its components and actions are; and what bearing it has on the world of common sense. Religions, in contrast, seek to make contact with it, to interplay with it in an effective way.

Most metaphysicians have recognized that the realm which lies outside our daily world is not one undivided reality but in fact three—a domain of ideal possibility, a cosmic dynamic space-time, and a unitary, excellent being. It is traditional to take the first two to be interior to or dependent on the third, but I think Whitehead is essentially right in holding that all three—which he calls a set of eternal objects, creativity, and God—are on a footing, all equally real and basic. But whether one accepts the position of the classical thinkers or not, it is of utmost importance to realize that they, no less than others, take "God" to refer to a specialized, delimited or clarified expression of the reality which lies outside the world of common sense. That reality is omnipresent; all of us are aware of it, at least dimly, throughout our days. We can use the name "God" to designate it. If we do we refer to what necessarily exists. But if we use "God" to designate some supposed specialized form of that reality, we cannot be sure that we are naming an existent. The specific religions, since they are concerned with the latter, are tinged with dubiety. A religion which freed itself from the specifications characteristic of the extant religions would free itself from the possible error that haunts them all. But it would not be a religion unless it acknowledged that that reality interplayed with us and this world of ours.

Were a metaphysician able to show that there is no possible way in which the ultimate dimensions of reality, no matter what they were called or how they were specified, could interplay, he would show that religion is but theology, and that particular religions are merely hosannas of hopes or social ceremonials. But a dialectical, systematic study of what is reveals, I think—apart from all concern with religion—that ultimate realities, though independent and irreducible, affect, restrict, qualify, and support one another. It is this fact to which I think Professor Tillich does not give sufficient attention.

I am almost tempted to withdraw the last sentence, for it is very hard to know exactly what Professor Tillich affirms. Sometimes he speaks as though there were some specific object or occurrence in our daily world about which religion, as we know it, inevitably pivots. At other times, he speaks as though Christ and even "God" were only symbols of a higher reality, of a "God beyond God." He therefore gives good ground for those who call him an "outsider," a "non-Christian." His difficulty arises perhaps because he does not always clearly distinguish between what a freed religion requires and what his own Christianity demands of him. When he concentrates on the nature of religion as such, as a philosopher should, he forgets what he should have remembered from his Christianity: that God makes a difference to the world. When he attends to his Christianity, as a confessed Christian should, he happily multiplies miracles—which he calls "revelations"—so as to be able to do what this theology does not allow.

There is something parochial in the insistence that one can get to God only through the avenue of some such book as the Bible, the Gospels, or the Koran, or some such event as Moses on Mount Sinai, the Crucifixion, or the life of Buddha. This Professor Tillich, the philosophic theologian, has seen and said again and again. Apart from revelation, there is no warrant for insisting on these as the most appropriate means for symbolizing God. It is possible to symbolize him by means of the Communist Manifesto or a piece of dirt. This Professor Tillich seems almost ready to affirm. But what he does not make clear is his appreciation of the truth that not all symbols are on a footing, and that even apart from all revelation it is possible to recognize some to be better than others. Some things are more open than others to the influence of exterior realities; some things mirror what lies outside them better than others do. The Communist Manifesto not only tempts us to turn away from ultimate reality to attend to a state or society, but it distorts some of the signal features which God can be shown to possess. We find it hard to find God when we attend to human suffering, pestilence, injustice. But the difficult is not identical with the impossible. God can be symbolized by means of any of them, once it is recognized that he is radically different from them in being, nature and value. This, of course, we do not know unless we know that God exists and what he is like.

The fact of God's existence as an ultimate reality, follows necessarily, as Hartshorne has remarked, from an adequate concept of him. But—as he has not sufficiently noted—this concept must first be reached by going through something like the teleological and cosmological arguments. Once we have that concept, however, we have a principle in terms of which we can understand what things are most receptive to him, distort his nature least, mirror him best, and thus allow one to symbolize him most satisfactorily. It tells us to take the excellent, unified, creative, value-preserving—in short, a virtuous, aesthetically sensitive man—to offer the best image of God.

Were there no God, I have elsewhere tried to show, there would be no self-identity, no persistent past, no realization of what is really possible. Moral responsibility, history, prescriptions would all sink into unintelligibility. No one, therefore, should be so glad that there is a God as one who would like to live a full life in a common-sense world. He need not believe that God created the world, or that God engages in any particular act, here and now, directed at any particular result; but he must believe that there is a reality over against our daily world and that the two interplay, thereby making a difference to one another's being and action. A man has faith so far as he believes that what he most clearly sees to be good in this world is a simulacrum of the goodness of God. But he is never sure of this until he has a knowledge of what God is like. And this he can get only speculatively, which is to say only as the necessary outcome of a systematic account of whatever else there is. In the end this means that a living faith in a God is a half-denying, half-doubting, constantly rearticulated attempt to bridge the gap between what we daily are and know and what we dimly discern beyond. And since these two interact, it is a faith which constantly finds new objects and events that can make God's nature and intent evident, at the same time that it finds that it must re-express and reassess God's being and actions.

Faith is unshakable, not because it is dogmatic or stupid, but because it spans the gap between ourselves here and a reality beyond us. That faith is made possible only because there is a constant reciprocal determination of each by the other. We begin our careers with faith; we oversharpen it and overspecify its terminus in the course of our lives. We end by wrongly denying that God must constantly reconstitute himself and reorder the world at the same time that it reorders itself and varies in the way it qualifies him. But once we look beyond specific religions, with their practical concern for salvationally helpful truths, we will be able to see more clearly the reality which not only gives to our daily world some of the features it persistently exhibits, but which makes religion possible, and faith inescapable.

To give the name "God" to any part, or all, of the reality outside our daily world is but to underscore the fact that (a) there is an interplay between the two poles; (b) though all objects here, therefore, bear the marks of that reality's presence and power, some more readily reflect its nature or more readily allow one to move toward it than others do; (c) men should open themselves up to the transcending reality by using as symbols those objects which least distort its known nature; (d) those who make use of poor symbols are religiously insensitive while those who use their most cherished symbols to refer to something other than it are idolators. Among the latter is many a man who spends his time in church, denies himself, prays, or follows out some long-established ritual. The God men acknowledge in this part of the world must blush if he hears what such men say of him; he is surely mortified if he attends to what philosophers think of him; he evidently hides as soon as a linguist, a philosopher of science, or an analyst looks for him. Fortunately, behind him or any other supposed God there is an ultimate inescapable being which is irreducibly real, and effective here and now, no matter what men say, think, or do. That being, if cherished, is 'God the father,' Yahweh, the light of light, who necessarily is, and who makes possible any God a particular religion might focus on.

# PART II

## The Nature of Religious Faith

# 12

## ON THE NATURE OF FAITH
### by H. Richard Niebuhr, Yale Divinity School

The word "faith" (or its apparent equivalents) as used in common language—whether English or some other Western tongue —has no such definite reference that we can move directly from word to phenomenon and seek to elucidate the structure or the idea or the nature of the thing signified. Even if we confine ourselves to the use of the word in the languages of Western religious societies—in particular to the Christian churches which use the word most frequently—we can find no such agreement about its reference that would entitle us to assume that there is some one simple phenomenon properly called "faith" or "Christian faith," the nature or idea of which can be analyzed. Under these circumstances it is necessary to begin any inquiry into "faith" with an effort at semantic clarification and then proceed, if possible, toward phenomenological analyses and to the question of the relationship among the various phenomena or data referred to by means of the word (with its synonyms, analogues, and antonyms) in the common languages of various communities.

Unfortunately, semantic studies in this field are strangely inadequate. In theological circles much attention has been given in recent years to the meanings of the word "love," to the relations among such distinguishable phenomena as are designated more precisely by "agape," "Eros," "storge," and "philia"; to the structure and dynamics of "love" as a composite of "self-love," "neighbor-love," "God-love," etc.; to the confusions that have arisen in both popular and theological discussions of the "nature" of love and of moral directives to love, because of lack of discrimination in the use of terms and the accompanying lack of understanding. But no comparable inquiries seem to have been made in the case of "faith." Too many discussions of the word and its meaning seem to proceed on the basis of the prejudice that there is one proper meaning of the word or that some one phenomenon in human existence represents the "real" meaning of "faith." Nor are philosophical discussions of faith, insofar as I have encountered them, more helpful on this point than are the theological. Under these circumstances I must ask my readers to consider the following analysis of the meanings of faith as a preliminary venture, based upon a rather sketchy knowledge of the languages and the usages of our Western communities.

I wish to distinguish primarily between two sets of meanings, which for shorthand purposes only I shall designate as the Greek and Hebrew meanings, recognizing that if these designations are taken too seriously historical, as well as other, errors are bound to ensue.


*I.*


In the first set of meanings the word "faith" is used in contexts in which such other words as knowledge, opinion, conviction, apprehension, sight, etc. frequently occur. Its synonym is "belief." "Faith" is contrasted or otherwise related to "knowledge," "logic," "vision," "experience," as in such sentences as "holding something to be true has three stages: opining, believing (Glauben) and knowing" (Kant); or "we walk by faith, not by sight" (Paul); or "faith is understanding's step, and understanding is faith's reward" (Augustine); or "there is a state of mind that is neither wavering or uncertain opinion, nor yet knowledge, and for this state I can find no other name in our language than belief" (A. E. Taylor).

One may note the following special meanings under this general head of "faith" as designating something that is like knowledge or sight and yet is to be distinguished from it.

a) Faith refers to that understanding of things which a person holds and uses (more or less) without having direct relation to what he asserts to be true. It is the "knowledge" which one has at secondhand, so to speak; it is accepted as a basis for action because others, in whose directness of "vision" or "experience" or "understanding" of things one has confidence, have communicated their "knowledge" to the one who believes or has faith. In the New Testament, reference is made to faith in this sense in such statements as "Now Jesus did many other signs in the presence of the disciples which are not written in this book, but these are written that you may believe (pisteuete) that Jesus is the Christ, the Son of God," etc. (John 20: 30–31). Faith, in this meaning, refers to what we accept from others. The others may be eyewitnesses of events; they may be experts who have interpreted common experience in accordance with certain rules; they may be a community which has communicated to the believer certain dogmas or presuppositions of the common enterprise of knowing and acting. The distinctive element in faith in this meaning is not that it is characterized by a certain degree of assurance as compared with knowledge, but the indirectness of the relationship of the one who believes to that which he believes. He may even have a greater degree of assurance about the reliability of what he has been told than about the reliability of his own more or less immediate experience, as when he relies on a scientist's explanations of a natural phenomenon more than on his own immediate impression and interpretation. Faith in this meaning is what is distinguished from knowledge when knowledge means immediacy of relation to that about which an assertion is made.

b) With this meaning of faith—as that which is accepted on the authority of others—a second meaning is frequently confused. Faith often means a subjective feeling of greater or less assurance about the probability that a proposition that something is the case will be verified. It is contrasted with and related to other degrees of assurance-feeling, as in Kant's and Taylor's explanations about faith and knowledge. The term knowledge in these contexts also refers less to directness of relation than to a degree of assurance-feeling. "I do not have faith that there is a God," said a physicist;

"God is a fact." The word "fact" in such a statement probably means "certainty," "assurance."

The difficulty with this use of the word "faith" seems to be that there can be neither unanimity nor exactness in our designations and definitions of subjective assurance feelings. There are degrees of assurance-feelings among men without a doubt; but it is difficult, if not impossible, to compare them and there is no agreement about what name to attach to various degrees, even if those degrees could be measured by some instrument. The measure we commonly use of the degree of assurance present in a person is his willingness to act upon his opinion or conviction or faith or knowledge; the measure of his assurance may further be assessed by considering the amount of venture capital that he invests. But by what name are we to designate a high degree of assurance, and what other subjective states (or intellect or will, for instance) are normally or "justifiably" accompanied by feelings of high assurance? In theology, no less than in common usage, there seems to be confusion on these points, as it argues about "dead faith" and "faith informed by love," about historical and "saving faith," etc. Assurance-feelings and assurance-actions are doubtless present and important in human existence, and in religion we are very much concerned with them, but their relation to the other phenomena to which faith also points is not greatly illuminated by using the "basket-word" faith or by distinguishing between different "kinds of faith" as though we were dealing with species of one genus.

c) Faith may refer in the cognitive context to the state of mind (apart now from all reference to accompanying assurance-feelings) which is associated with the acceptance of dogma, not now necessarily as proposition communicated by the authority of experts, etc., but as first principle, as the accepted starting point for a way of reasoning or interpreting. In this case faith is contrasted with knowledge in the sense that the latter term refers to a process of reasoning, to a logical method. For instance: "The premises of science are called postulates. . . . Their ultimate validity is never assured. Being postulates which can only be verified through their consequences, and having, therefore, only the tentative validity of assumptions, their acceptance requires more than correct knowledge of facts. It requires a *commitment,* an espousal of unproved postulates often called axioms, which logically speaking, is of precisely the same nature as what we call *faith* in religion" (Henry Margenau).

d) Faith refers to a kind of direct apprehension which involves the activity of personal functions other than the senses and epistemic reasoning. The reference here may be to the "reasoning of the heart," or to "feeling" when "feeling" means an activity with more objective reference than "emotion," as in "feeling of absolute dependence"; it may be conscience; it may be a kind of totality of the apprehending self that apprehends as a psycho-somatic-rational-spiritual personal whole. "Faith" means "personal knowledge." The emphasis is differently distributed by different investigators. I think there is similarity between Whitehead's account of scientific faith and J. H. Newman's account of religious, specifically Christian, faith. "Faith in reason," writes Whitehead, "is the trust that the ultimate nature of things lies, together in a harmony which excludes mere arbitrariness. . . . The faith in the order of nature which has made possible the growth of science is a particular example of a deeper faith. This faith cannot be justified by any inductive generalization. It springs from direct inspection of the nature of things as disclosed in our own immediate present experience. . . . To experience this faith is to know that in being ourselves we are more than ourselves." It is "to know" a system of things as including both "the harmony of logical rationality and the harmony of aesthetic achievement." (*Science and the Modern World,* p. 27). For J. H. Newman, religious assent is a function of the whole person confronting a totality: "Christianity is addressed, both as regards its evidences and its contents, to minds which are in the normal condition of human nature, as believing in God and in a future judgment. Such minds it addresses both through the intellect and through the imagination; creating a certitude of its truth by arguments too various for direct enumeration, too personal and deep for words, too powerful and concurrent for refutation. Nor need reason come first and faith second (though this is the logical order), but one and the same teaching . . . elicits one complex act both of inference and assent." (*Grammar of Assent*, concluding paragraph).

e) Finally, there is the meaning of faith present in such a term as "the faiths of mankind," and frequently in "the Christian faith," where faith means a world view, a theory of the world and of human history, a grand orientation of the self or community within its space and time.

I do not wish at all to contend that these various meanings of "faith," as related to, yet distinguishable from, "knowledge," ever occur in our common usage and thought without overtones of the other meanings, but simply that these different *motifs* occur and that they all refer to actual phenomena in human experience; that, moreover, contentions about the meaning of faith or of "true faith" or "the true meaning of faith" would become more fruitful if they were more largely directed to the phenomena.

## II.

Discussions about the meaning or the nature of faith are, however, complicated even more by the use of the word in other contexts. In these contexts faith is not related to knowledge but to mercy, love, hope, joy, peace, etc. It is a quality or characteristic of persons in interpersonal relations. (1) One of the meanings in these contexts is that of *trust*. To have faith is to believe *in,* to count upon or rely upon another, particularly on another person as one who has made promises or has bound himself in covenant relations to the person who has faith in him. It is this meaning of faith which Luther especially emphasized, and in doing so seems to have been in harmony with the Hebrew Scriptures with their emphasis upon trusting in God.

(2) The second meaning of faith in these contexts is closely associated with the former: faith is faithfulness, loyalty, reliability. Faith is something that is kept; it is the resolute abiding of a person

by his promises and commitments. In modern times the only thinker who seems to have developed this meaning of faith to any considerable extent is Josiah Royce, but he did so without using the word. (Rebecca West's *Meaning of Treason* also belongs to the literature on trust-fidelity.)

It seems inadequate, however, to say that faith in the interpersonal context now means trust and now faithfulness. The difficulty which we encounter in discussions of faith that move within this sphere of interpersonal meanings is not that they employ the word ambiguously but too univocally, as though faith in interpersonal life were either a trusting or a being faithful. Luther, for instance, related faith as trusting in God to faith as believing the truth of propositions or theories, but had little to say directly about faithfulness as part of the structure of faith, though of course it was evident to him that trust upon the part of man was the counterpart of faithfulness in God. Yet it remains true that in the tradition of thought which follows Luther faith tends to be equated with trust.

I would suggest that an analysis of the *phenomenon* of "faith" as a characteristic of interpersonal life (together with its negative forms of unfaith, distrust, disloyalty), leads us to a recognition of a structure in which trust and loyalty (or *fiducia* and *fidelitas*) are in reciprocal relations, yet not in the simple reciprocity in which trust on the part of a self responds to the loyalty of the other to this self, but rather in that more complex pattern in which fidelity is related not to one term only but always to two; it is faithful to both the trusting self and to the common cause (to use Royce's term). This pattern or structure of interpersonal faith may be illuminated by means of illustrations. A ready one is offered by the reciprocal relations of fidelity and confidence in a community of knowers. Our interpersonal confidence in one another in such a community represents, in the first place, a reliance on the other's faithfulness to companion selves, that *he* is not using his knowledge for the purpose of deception. We "keep faith" with one another in this sense by not abusing our knowledge for the sake of gaining power over each other. But confidence rests no less on our expectation that the others whom we trust are devoted to a common cause, to which we may give the large name of "truth." Illustrations may be taken from all other interpersonal communities, from family to international society. (Cf. for instance Erick Erickson's discussion of the development of basic trust in the infant in his *Childhood and Society*). In analyzing the structure or nature of faith in this sense we are involved in the examination of a dynamic interpersonal process in which there are not two terms simply, but three—the self, the other, and the cause; and in which there is not one response (that of trust in the faithful, for instance) that maintains the structure, but where two responses are called for, trust and loyalty; and these two responses move in two directions— toward the other and toward the common cause. With such a structure of interpersonal faith in mind we shall then be able to distinguish among the various pathological forms of faith, not only as distrust of a faithful other, or as trust of an unfaithful other, but also as treason to a cause and as betrayal of the one who is faithful to the cause, etc.

## *III.*

Among the tasks which an inquiry into "faith"—which would allow us to speak ultimately of the "nature of faith"—needs to pursue more fully than our rough approaches to the question have permitted, the following seem important to me:

(1) A fuller inquiry into the relation of "religious faith" to faith as we find it in its interpersonal forms in the common life. There is a tendency even among such careful workers as are represented by Bultmann (see his article *Pistis* in *Theologisches Handwoerter-buch zum Neuen Testament*) to draw a sharp dividing line between the idea of "religious faith" and faith in secular relations. (This may be connected in Bultmann's case with his strongly individualistic existentialism.) If it is true that faith in the sense of trust and fidelity to cause and representatives of a cause is an

inescapable element in all personal existence, then the question about faith is not whether one has it or not but in what form one has it, whether for instance in pluralistic, or closed-society heno-theistic, or universal form and what the implications and consequences of each form are.

(2) A second task is the dispassionate attempt to elucidate the sources and the meanings of those large symbolic patterns in human minds which represent their sense of "being in the world," which are the background and the ultimate assumptions (thought unanalyzed) of their reasonings and apprehensions. We deal here with the "faith" or the "myth," not of religious believers only, but of all men and all times. Further, we need careful analysis, especially in theology, of the relation of these large patterns of interpretation to our explicit postulates or dogmas.

(3) An inquiry into the relations of interpersonal "faith" to noetic "faith." This, of course, is an ancient problem on which much thought has been expended. But new approaches are possible in our time, I think, as we abandon the attempt to deal with forms of "faith" as though they were species of one genus, as we make use of the fuller historical and psychological knowledge available to us and also employ new methods. It might, for instance, be rewarding for our understanding were we to construct model types of "faith" in which we did justice to the polarity in our existence of interpersonal trust-loyalty with theoretic orientation. This would shift, at the same time, the focus from the old intellection-will (or fact-value) dualism in which the problem has usually been set, and also move away from the effort to establish one normative form of faith. It may turn out that there is a distinctive type of human "faith-attitude" which moves from the giveness of personal existence in trust-loyalty relations to inferences about the larger world or about what must be the case; and another, relatively distinct type which, beginning with a theory (however gained—through authority, or "vision"), moves toward inferences about the personal life and its conduct.

(4) As a counterpart to the first task I suggest that theology and philosophy alike have the task of examining more carefully

the place of those various phenomena designated by faith (belief in authority, degree of certitude, acceptance of postulates, personal knowledge, trust, loyalty to cause, etc.) in that great syndrome we call religion, and in which such other phenomena as the sense of the numinous, the feeling of absolute dependence, etc. are to be distinguished and not immediately equated with faith.

(5) Finally, as a theologian, I see a task before us which consists in raising a question about the relations of the "great Religions" to each other in another form than is customary when they are set alongside each other as species of one genus, that genus being "faith," usually in the meaning of world view. Do they indeed represent alternative solutions to the same problem, or are they, in their historical beginnings at least, answers to different questions, cures for different evils? Is it perhaps true that the Judaeo-Christian movement is fundamentally directed toward the reconstruction of human faith as fidelity-trust in universal community, while Islam, though not irrelevant to the trust-fidelity—treason-distrust pattern of life, is directed primarily toward something else, and Buddhism to still another human dilemma. At all events I question that the easy use of the word "faith" in contrasting the "faiths of mankind" with each other does justice either to the uniqueness of Christianity or to the meaningfulness of other orientations of men in the universe, other forms of monotheism or monism.

I have thus not elucidated the "nature of faith" but have shown myself to be subject to the "faith" of our times, namely the confidence that analysis will lead to clarification, and that clarification will not end in chaotic pluralism but lead onward to the understanding of how all things hang together in a trustworthy universe, which is the cause of the faithful God.

## 13

# REFLECTIONS ON
# "ON THE NATURE OF FAITH"
*by Gustave Weigel, S.J., Woodstock College*

It seems to me that we are indeed fortunate that Professor Niebuhr has brought out for us the semantic difficulties involved in a discussion of faith. He has admirably outlined the different meanings assigned to the word and, rather than say more, he is willing to plant the question in its diversity. On reading Niebuhr, I could not help but think of a definition of faith given in the fifth century by Faustus of Riez which embodied most of the ideas which Professor Niebuhr has presented with such clarity. Faustus says:

> There is no evidence that a man believes in God unless he piously hopes in him. To believe in God, then, is to seek him with fidelity and pass over to him in complete love. I believe in him, therefore, is to say: I profess him, I worship him, I adore him, I give and pour myself totally into his command and lordship. In the reverent profession of faith are contained all the services due to the divine name. [Faustus of Riez, *De Spiritu Sancto*. C.S.E.L., 21, (Engelbrecht) p. 103, 11. 10–20.]

Just before this lengthy definition of faith, Faustus also refers to *fides catholica* which in the context means the orthodox faith and it is concretely the Apostles' Creed. For Faustus this verbal formula is *uirtus ueritatis,* dynamic truth. Explicitly and implicitly, all the elements of Professor Niebuhr's linguistic analysis are contained in the reflections of the fifth-century theologian. In other words, Professor Niebuhr's analysis is true to the Christian tradition on the subject of faith. And let us remember that it is precisely Christianity which has made much of faith and given tremendous significance to the word. Something of its high relevance is already to be found in the Hebrew writings called the Old Testament, but it was Christianity which developed the notion. Beyond the Judaeo-Christian tradition the word faith is not so religiously important. To an ancient Greek or to a modern Hindu, the word would not immediately suggest religion.

In the Catholic tradition the complexity of the term faith is simplified. According to Catholic thinkers from the 12th century onward, faith is considered in a double light. It is a *process* which is a complex of actions and conditions, and it is also a *single act* generated by the process and initiating a new series of actions. As a single act it is an intellectual assent, and therefore an achievement of truth. It belongs to the order of knowledge; it is an epistemological concept. The other elements which combine to produce faith, or after its achievement manifest it, are treated under other headings; e.g., hope and love, as found in the famous triad, faith, hope, and love, which in their unified totality are also called faith in an extended use of the word. Professor Niebuhr has pointed this out when he referred to faith made living by love.

For the Catholic, faith is man's first commitment to God. There is no valid religiosity before faith has been achieved, though there is indeed a previous preparation in man for its achievement. All valid religion thus supposes faith as an intellectual act which is simultaneously an orientation of man toward the revealing Lord.

Needless to say, this basic commitment implicitly contains an epistemology. Intelligence is conceived as a perceptive power which can transcend the finitude of the universe with which men are in empirical contact. There is simultaneously a recognition that this capacity of human gnosiological endowment cannot be excited into action except by a supernatural stimulus, internal and external, from the transcendental God who is necessarily considered as personal, where the notion of personality is understood not in logical univocity but rather in symbolic analogy.

The Catholic gives to the act of faith a privileged position. Its affirmation is primatial, and all other judgments must conform to it. It is not considered to be the first principle from which all other

104

statements are deduced, but it is a negative norm for comparison. Whatever contradicts the affirmation of faith is promptly rejected. This rejection need not be and, in fact, never is total. On the Augustinian principle that there is no error without its nucleus of truth, the Catholic believer who is a philosopher or scientist will examine the contradicting statement precisely to discover its truth in order to give it an adequate expression in thought and word. Faith is conceived as positive and not as negative—but in every case it is primary and normative. It is for this reason that Catholic thinkers, in utter consistency with their faith, can engage in the meditation of the philosophy of any historical school: Platonism in the days of the Patristic theologians, Aristotelianism in the Middle Ages, positivism during different stages of the Renaissance, and existentialism in our own time. Philosophy is considered to be a legitimate Christian enterprise. It will not and must not be derived from faith, but on the other hand, by reason of the Catholic's inner commitment, it must not deny it.

Given his notion of faith, the Catholic does not consider it to be subject to the criticism of a naturalistic philosophy because such a philosophy by its basic postulates is already an act of faith in the impossibility of the supernatural. What is more, the Catholic theology on faith supposes that it cannot be the subject of an investigation by direct empirical introspection. The nature of faith must be known through the only possible source which depicts the act, and this source is the revelation itself. Naturally and empirically, the act of faith is not discoverable, and it can be known only in faith itself. Quite literally, the Catholic cannot strictly know that he has made the act of faith. He only hopes that he has made it, and he judges its presence on moral grounds through a judgment of prudential wisdom. Nevertheless, the theologians have made studies about the nature of faith and they use psychological and epistemological categories in their work.

According to the theological description of faith, the act is the result of a divine stimulus on intelligence and will, two powers which, although radically capable of the act, yet need an immediate action of God to give them the formal capacitation for belief.

Without such divine influence the act cannot be brought forth. The act brings with it the highest possible intellectual commitment of the greatest possible certitude, involving the readiness to place it in value above every other conceivable human good. The true believer is ready to die for his faith. He is willing to relinquish all rather than abandon his belief. Yet he also knows that his assent is not dictated by evidence. There is no evidence for the truth to which he adheres in his credence. His motive for assent is the glimpse involved in the apperception that the object of faith is wrapped up in an apperceived divine invitation to accept the truth. The act of belief is made a function of man's vital encounter with the basis of all truth. Such an encounter does not give vision though it does arouse an aconceptual awareness of divine presence. Since there is no perception of the truth itself, it is necessary that the will imperate the assent because the necessitating influence of evidence is absent. Since faith is an intelligent assent, it is a mental judgment and adequately expressable in verbal propositions.

From this description it is quite clear that faith is not an act of reason. Yet the Catholic theologians insist that it is a reasonable act. By this they mean that the believer has grounds pervious to the native structure of the mind whereby he feels morally warranted in making his act of faith. The presentation of these grounds in discourse is called an apologetic of faith. It is well to remember the goal of apologetic. It does not wish to prove the proposition of belief. There can be no rationalistic proof for that. The aim of apologetic is to show that the assent of faith is a morally prudent action. It is not an action of whim nor an arbitrary fiat.

Catholic understanding of faith is far more detailed and precise than its counterpart in other religions. In Protestantism, faith is usually portrayed as warmly mysterious so that it is considered impossible and indecent to go into it with the surgeon's scalpel. In the Protestant conception, the strictly intellectual content of the act of faith is by no means denied, but the insistence is always on the voluntary elements in it: trust, decision, and confidence. For Protestantism in general the high value of faith is its confident adherence to the inwardly encountered God. Catholics do not deny this element, but they make it a factor of the process of faith rather than of the formal act itself.

It will be seen at once that the Catholic gives primatial importance to truth. It is truth which he wishes to achieve and, in his faith, truth is considered to be the first good which man must pursue. Truth, of course, is an ambiguous term. The Catholic sees at least three meanings for the word. The first and fundamental meaning is reality itself. That is the objective and substantive truth. The mental achievement of reality makes a judgment true. Finally the faithful communication of this achievement makes man a truthful speaker. In such a position there is the implicit affirmation that reality in itself is grasped in the intellectual enterprise. The grasp is not merely a consciousness of self reacting to the universe of stimuli. The grasp is of the reality which originates the stimulus. Sheer empiricism or Kantian phenomenalism are epistemological stands utterly uncongenial to Catholic theology. There is, indeed, an a priori assumed in Catholic thought, but this is not a mere formalism, it is rather a dynamism. In the act of knowledge the thing itself is grasped in and through the formation of concepts and judgment. The judicative assent is not to the union of concepts but rather to the object to which the concepts refer. This is, of course, a strong realism but it is not naïve. It rests on a phenomenological analysis of the living act of judgment. The Catholic theologian believes that the fruit of such analysis will show not only the formal structure of judgment but also its latent dynamism. The judgment is far more than a mental structure. Above all, it is a nisus outwards; toward the real itself. The real is not achieved in its ineffable individuality and concreteness but rather in its general intelligible structure.

In the history of Catholic theology this epistemology, which is a rational effort and not a theological enterprise, was formed in the light of the theology of faith. Quite literally the Catholic theologians constructed an epistemology which would satisfy the needs of their theology. They merely insist that though historically theology brought forth a philosophy, the philosophy is legitimate and valid in its own right. Many non-Catholic philosophers are not convinced that this is so. Such a position depends on one's own conception of philosophy, and no dialogue will be able to settle the issue. One must begin somewhere, and there is a voluntary element in the selection of the point of departure.

This paper has been sketchy. I wished to build on the semantic analysis proposed with genuine adequacy by Professor Niebuhr and go beyond it. In going beyond it a single development of the idea of faith was presented in hurried outline. I think that most Catholic theologians would accept it, at least in its substance. I do not think that non-Catholic Christians would subscribe to it, or if they did so, they would make serious reservations. The upshot of the matter is that Professor Niebuhr and I have not offered to the gathering a theological concept of the nature of faith which would be acceptable for all thinkers who are concerned with the nature of faith. This is regrettable from one point of view, but from another point of view it may be advantageous because it can provoke a real discussion of interest and fruitfulness.

# 14

## SOME MEANINGS OF "FAITH"
### by Gail Kennedy, Amherst College

In deference to the spirit of the age, Professor Niebuhr has taken the semantic approach to his subject. This is in itself a topic of sufficient complexity to pre-empt the time, so that at the end of his paper he confesses he has not elucidated the "nature of faith," but hopes that this preliminary analysis will lead to clarification of the issues. Granting that such an analysis is indispensable, I had perversely expected that he would deal, as he has in his book *The Meaning of Revelation*, with substantive issues. The difficulty in discussing the paper he has presented is that virtually all of my disagreements with him must be over matters of fact, since the questions raised are those of a proper usage of the term within the various contexts in which it is employed.

Professor Niebuhr is cautious and diffident in his approach. He offers his analyses as merely a rough sketch and warns us that in practice the meanings he discriminates may fuse in the sense that as employed in one context they may express overtones of their use in another. However, the analysis is made according to a straightforward logical arrangement. I am afraid that this schematic approach leads to a specious clarity, one that makes the various usages more distinct and independent than they are.

This is where the first of my difficulties with his paper has its source. Professor Niebuhr puts broad meanings of the term "faith" into two groups derived respectively from Greek and Hebrew usages. In the first set "faith" is a noetic term. "Its synonym is 'belief' "; it designates "something that is like knowledge . . . and yet is to be distinguished from it" (p. 94). The other set of meanings "is not related to knowledge but to mercy, love, hope, joy, peace, etc." In this context it is used to denote "a quality or characteristic of persons in interpersonal relations" (p. 98).

The first of the intellectual meanings he states as follows:

> Faith refers to that understanding of things which a person holds and uses (more or less), without having direct relation to what he asserts to be true. It is the 'knowledge' which one has at secondhand, so to speak; it is accepted as a basis for action because others, in whose directness of 'vision' or 'experience' or 'understanding' of things one has confidence, have communicated their 'knowledge' to the one who believes or has faith" (pp. 94–95).

I take it that this meaning is the one Locke had in mind when he defined faith as "assent to a proposition . . . upon the credit of the proposer." [1] Under his second group the first of the meanings Professor Niebuhr describes is that of *trust*: "To have faith is to believe *in,* to count upon or rely upon another, particularly on another person as one who has made promises or has bound himself in covenant relations to the person who has faith in him" (p. 98).

Now, what is the difference between these two meanings? Are they distinct? Professor Niebuhr in illustrating the first gives the example of someone relying on "a scientist's explanations of a natural phenomenon more than on his own immediate impression and interpretation" (p. 95). The example is not, to me, entirely clear. If, as a reasonably well-educated person, I accept the scientist's explanation as more reliable than my own, in what sense am I assenting to a proposition on the credit of its proposer? The example as given seems to imply that the relation between the scientist and myself is impersonal. In this case, however, am I not really judging the competence of the proposer? And in making this judgment I am not relying on the scientist at all but on my own opinion of his competence. In this case the reasons that impel me to credit the proposer are reasons which do not, *ipso facto,* involve any element of faith. It would, therefore, be irrelevant and inappropriate for me to say that my conclusion is due to my faith in the scientist. On the contrary, it is presumptively based on my knowledge of his competence.

Let us take a related case where something properly called faith might be involved. Suppose my physician tells me that I have a heart disease and that the best treatment of my particular illness is a regime of rest, diet, the administration of certain drugs, etc. Now I may well have some reasonably good evidence of my physician's competence and honesty, but it is hardly on the basis of that opinion alone that I will assent to his propositions. Surely, in this instance there is an interpersonal relationship of mutual trust. And is it not appropriate now to introduce the word "faith" because this trust is a characteristic of the situation? If this be so, how can we distinguish two genuinely separate meanings of the word "faith," one intellectual, the other interpersonal?

Intellectual conviction, as such, Professor Niebuhr would agree, is not faith; and blind belief, if we call it faith—"the Führer can do no wrong"—is pathological. I do not see how the distinction between the two first meanings in these respective sets can be maintained. Does not every instance in which it would be *appropriate* to say that faith is assent to the proposition on the credit of its proposer involve an element of trust? And in this particular example, at any rate, the relation of the physician to his patient, is there not *also* a reference to the second of the meanings which Professor Niebuhr distinguishes as characteristic of interpersonal relations, namely, a common cause? Obviously, the physician-patient relationship is one of mutual concern with the disease. Perhaps, during the discussion, Professor Niebuhr will give us two examples in which this distinction between "faith" as related to knowledge and "faith" as expressing trust is maintained, even though each of them have overtones derived from the other kind of meaning.

The second definition in Professor Niebuhr's first set is "a subjective feeling of greater or less assurance about the probability that a proposition that something is the case will be verified" (p. 95). I am not entirely clear about Professor Niebuhr's discussion of this meaning. Would he agree with me that there are

**111**

contexts in which the term "faith" is inapplicable no matter what the degree of assurance-feeling? If the weatherman is himself convinced that come next Tuesday we'll have snow, is that a matter of faith? Is it even suitable to assert that a gambler has faith the horse he is backing will win? I take it that the term "faith" would be appropriate where St. Paul's formulation, "the assurance of things hoped for, the conviction of things not seen (Heb. 11:1 [R.S.V.]), is properly applicable.

It is clear that there are degrees and kinds of assurance-feeling about the probability of different types of statements. What is needed here is a criterion which will differentiate those cases to which Paul's definition, or one similar to it, is relevant. Professor Niebuhr would, I think, agree with me; yet he does not advance, even tentatively, this criterion. Of course, there will be overlapping and uncertain instances, but without some kind of standard the second meaning in Professor Niebuhr's first set remains obscure.

The third meaning in Professor Niebuhr's first set is: "the acceptance of dogma" as the "starting point for a way of reasoning or interpreting" (p. 96). To illustrate he quotes a statement by Professor Margenau that scientific inquiry "requires a *commitment,* an espousal of unproved postulates often called axioms, which logically speaking, is of precisely the same nature as what we call *faith* in religion" (p. 97). This, it seems to me, is a false analogy. When the mathematician declares that certain propositions must be accepted without proof as a necessary condition for the demonstration of another group of propositions, no act of faith is involved. And when the physical scientist asserts that certain propositions are assumed by him as a necessary condition for the construction of hypotheses that he can submit to experimental test, it is still irrelevant to use the word "faith." The physical scientist need believe in his propositions only in the sense that they are assumptions useful for his purposes. He is a fallibilist who is ready to amend or revoke them when further inquiry shows that they are inadequate to these purposes. Surely the term "faith" is used for a different sort of commitment. Faith implies, as in Paul's definition, an assurance of things hoped for that is different in quality. Who would say: "In order to establish these doctrines of a religion, I must assume the truth of certain antecedent propositions, but I am a fallibilist and shall abandon them if subsequent experience should convince me that they are not tenable. Upon those antecedent propositions I base my faith"? It is clear that there are degrees and kinds of assurance-feeling about the probability of different types of statements. Again, what is needed is a criterion which will differentiate those cases to which Paul's definition is relevant. Professor Niebuhr has not given us one.

The fourth meaning of the first set is "a kind of direct apprehension which involves the activity of personal functions other than the senses and epistemic reasoning" (p. 97). This meaning would apparently include what Pascal intended when he said: "We know the truth not only from reason but also from the heart. It is in the latter way that we apprehend first principles which reason, since it here plays no role, cannot attack." [2] In this case also, Professor Niebuhr, by juxtaposing quotations from Whitehead and Newman, implies an analogy between an imputed faith of the scientist and religion. It is true that scientists have often said their research was intended to disclose latent harmonies in the universe. Whitehead's "faith in reason" expresses a belief that is held by many scientists, but in expressing it he is not speaking *as* a scientist. Nor need one be a scientist to have that faith. Stoics and Christian Scientists, among others, also "trust that the ultimate nature of things lies together in a harmony which excludes mere arbitrariness. . . ." And it is the same Whitehead in the same book, *Science and the Modern World,* who remarked fifteen pages earlier in the same chapter on the origins of modern science that:

> Galileo keeps harping on how things happen, whereas his adversaries had a complete theory as to why things happen. Unfortunately the two theories did not bring out the same results. Galileo insists upon 'irreducible and stubborn facts,' and Simplicious, his opponent, brings forward reasons, completely satisfactory, at least to himself. It is a great mistake to conceive this historical revolt as an appeal to reason. On the contrary, it was through and through an anti-intellectualist movement. It was the return to the con-

113

templation of brute fact; and it was based on a recoil from
the inflexible rationality of medieval thought.[3]

Scientists do not need faith that nature exhibits "a harmony which
excludes mere arbitrariness"; they merely need to believe that their
methods of inquiry will enable them to solve many problems—that
it is possible for a human being to discover laws even for such
arbitrary, or "irrational," phenomena as the behavior of photons,
genetic mutations, and the phantasmagoria of dreams. This relief
does not depend upon Pascal's reasons of the heart or upon any
other sort of feeling. It is an assurance based upon prior success.

The final meaning in Professor Niebuhr's first group, since it is
merely denotative, a use of the term to designate the historic
"faiths of mankind," needs no comment. And I have no disagreement with what he says about his second group of meanings, those
referring to characteristics of interpersonal relations.

I have pointed out what I believe are certain defects in Professor Niebuhr's classification; but is it also incomplete? Where, for
instance, should one place the definition given by Tillich, "Faith
is the state of being grasped by the power of being-itself"? [4] If
anywhere, this definition would come within the fourth meaning of
Professor Niebuhr's first set; yet *his* definition, "a kind of direct
apprehension which involves the activity of personal functions
other than the senses and epistemic reasoning," does not, apparently,
allow for a passivity of the subject, "the state of being grasped,"
which is for Tillich the dominant characteristic of faith.

Perhaps I am reading this into it, but the tone of his paper, particularly in his description, at the end, of three inquiries he thinks
essential before we can answer the question What is the nature of
faith? leads me to think he would agree that the semantic approach hasn't gotten us very far. Though "faith" *is* one of the
weasel words, are we really so uncertain about its varieties of
meaning? "Faith" is not, I think, a term seriously infected with the
intricate ambiguities of usage characteristic of many important
words. It should not be hard to settle most of our doubts or disagreements about the correct meaning of this term. The serious
difficulties in the way of an adequate understanding of the *nature* of

faith are encountered when we ask, What precisely is the relation of knowing to believing?—a question not at all about words and their uses.

With this expectation, I repeat the questions:

(1) Is the word "faith" ever applicable to the acceptance of a proposition upon the credit of the proposer *unless* trustfulness is also an ingredient of the situation? (2) What criterion is needed to differentiate those cases where one can properly call a feeling of assurance that a proposition will be verified an act of faith from otherwise similar cases where the term would be inapplicable? (3) In what cases, if any, is it appropriate to say that one exercises "faith" in accepting a group of postulates? (4) Why should it be supposed that the scientist must necessarily be sustained by some sort of faith as he proceeds with his inquiries? (5) And finally, are Professor Niebuhr's two sets of meanings complete? Do they include all important uses of the term?

# NOTES

1. *Essay Concerning Human Understanding,* IV, xviii.
2. *Pensées,* Art. XXII, 1. "Nous connoissons la vérité, non seulement par la raison, mais encore par le coeur; c'est de cette dernière sorte que nous connoissons les premiers principes, et c'est in vain que le raisonnement, qui n'y a point de part, essaye de les combattre."
3. *Science and the Modern World* (New York: The Macmillan Company, 1925), pp. 11–12.
4. *The Courage to Be* (New Haven: Yale University Press, 1959), p. 172.

# 15

## THE LOGIC
## OF FAITH AND BELIEF

*by Raziel Abelson, New York University*

It is a hallowed cliché to say that faith is beyond or independent of rational knowledge. But I think that a careful study of the logic of statements employing the word "faith" will show that, like most clichés, this one too is largely false. The motive for placing faith out of the reach of argumentative assault is fairly obvious. Throughout the history of Western religion, people have used "faith" as a label that forbids further inspection of the contents it marks, in the way that government officials sometimes stamp "classified—top secret" on documents that would, if made public, reveal bureaucratic blunders. It will not be my purpose to discredit all claims of faith, but, on the contrary, to protect genuine faith against debasement by counterfeits. But it will turn out that the price of such devaluation of the currency is rather high. The price is that the evidence for a claim made in the name of faith must be made available for public inspection. I shall argue that, if religious discourse is to achieve the minimum level of clarity necessary for effective communication, it must permit a rational assessment of the cash value of its concepts.

Various efforts have been made by theologians to immunize faith against infection from rational doubt. In the main, such efforts have been of two general types: the identification of faith with non-rational belief, and the reduction of faith to emotional states. Catholic theologians, from St. Augustine to Etienne Gilson, have tended to define faith as unprovable belief, i.e., belief accepted on the authority of the church or the Gospels, and independent of empirical evidence. Augustine's (and Anselm's *credo ut intelligam,*

Tertullian's *credo quia absurdum est,* Bernard of Clairvaux' *credo supra rationem* ) and Aquinas' "truths of faith and truths of reason," while expressive of different views of the exact disparity between faith and reason, agree at least in regarding faith as nonrational belief.[1] On the other hand, Protestant theologians have tended to employ "faith" primarily as a name of an emotional state, rather than a mode of belief in certain propositions or "articles." The emotional state of faith is sometimes identified with loyalty, trust, a sense of commitment, a feeling of reverence for the holy, or, as Dr. Niebuhr suggests, a combination of all these states. I do not mean to suggest that Protestant theologians deny altogether the cognitive claims of faith, but only that, with some notable exceptions such as fundamentalism and the dogmatics of Karl Barth, they place much more stress on the emotional concomitants of faith.[2] Similarly, it must be noted that Catholic theologians, in stressing belief, do not by any means deny that faith also involves emotion. It would be a serious oversimplification to sum matters up by saying that faith is an affective state for Protestants and that it is nonrational belief for Catholics. It seems to be something of both, for both groups, but in different degrees.

I think that the main source of the unending dispute between proponents of faith and defenders of reason lies in the tenuous relation between the cognitive and noncognitive implication of the claims made in the name of faith. It is, therefore, important to clarify this relation so as to disclose in just what ways the claims of faith can be evaluated and which claims, if any, can be granted immunity from rational challenge. A careful examination of typical uses of "belief" and "faith" may help us to unravel the many overlapping strands that link these concepts, so that we can see more clearly how they fit smoothly together and why they so often kink up into the hopeless snarl that evokes, in the mind of the impatient positivist, the image of what Alexander did to the Gordian knot. Let us ignore for the moment the specifically religious use of "faith" and "belief" and consider their uses in everyday discourse.

Recent studies of ordinary language have brought philosophical attention to an odd but highly significant feature of epistemic expressions such as "know," "believe," and "faith," a feature which is lost sight of when one concentrates on the *substantives* "knowledge," "belief," and "faith," instead of the *verbs,* "know," "believe," and "have faith." The verbs in question have a different logic when used in the first person than when used in the second or third person. When I say, "I know that it will rain" or "I believe that it will rain," I assert the proposition that it will rain. I thus make a claim to the truth of the proposition that I say I know or believe. Again, when I say, "You know that it will rain" or "Smith knows that it will rain," I am also claiming or asserting that it will rain. However, when I say, "You believe that it will rain" or "That witch doctor has faith that it will rain," I am *not* making any claim to the truth of the proposition that it will rain. Thus "I believe that it will rain, but it won't rain" is self-contradictory. So is "Smith knows that it will rain, but it won't rain." But, "You believe that it will rain, but it won't rain," or "That witch doctor has faith that it will rain, but it won't rain," are perfectly consistent and indeed often true.

This striking difference between the logic of the first person use of "believe that" and "faith that" and the second or third person uses can be explained with the aid of J. L. Austin's notion of the performatory function of language. The first person use is not descriptive, but performatory. When I say, "I believe that it will rain today," I am not describing myself or reporting a fact about myself; I am performing an act, the act of making a declaration of belief. But when I say, "Smith believes that it will rain today," I *am* describing Smith or reporting a fact about him. This explains why I can be mistaken when I say, "Smith believes. . . ," but not when I say "I believe. . . ." In the latter case I can, of course, be insincere (I can be making a spurious declaration, like an oath taken with one's fingers crossed), but I cannot be in error.[3] Yet, one may wonder, if I cannot be mistaken in declaring my belief, how then can I be asserting the truth of the proposition I say I believe? If "I believe that p" asserts the truth of p, and p is false, why is "I believe that p" not false as well, just as, when p is false,

"I know that p" is likewise false? The answer to this puzzle is, I think, that while "I know that p" entails that p is true, "I believe that p" does *not* entail that p is true. In other words, the belief claim to the truth of p is not as definite and complete as the knowledge claim to the truth of p. The belief claim is a *tentative* claim, rather than a categorical claim, in the way that an option or a deposit paid on a commodity is a tentative claim to that commodity. By "tentative" I mean that the claim is incomplete and therefore subject to withdrawal or cancellation. If I say, "I believe that it will rain today," and its does not rain all day, then my belief declaration is cancelled, just as, if I pay a five-dollar deposit on an overcoat to be held for one week and I do not show up within the week to consummate my claim, then the force of my deposit is nullified, but not falsified or in any way discredited. However, if I say, "I know that Citation will win this race" and Citation does not win, then my knowledge claim is not cancelled or withdrawn. It remains as a false and discredited claim, like a check marked "insufficient funds." I can be regarded as intellectually dishonest or at least as irresponsible if I make such knowledge claims frequently. The performatory analysis of "know that" and "believe that" as claims, rather than descriptions or reports, thus explains why "I know that p" is discredited by the falsity of p, while "I believe that p" is merely cancelled.[4]

Second and third person uses of "know" and "believe" have been shown by Austin and Urmson to be derivative from and dependent on first person uses.[5] E.g., "Smith believes that p" means that Smith is prepared to say, "I believe that p." Thus the first person, performatory use is primary, and the descriptive use is derivative.

The performatory analysis of these expressions helps to make clear that knowledge and belief (and faith) are not emotional states or psychic entities of any kind. One does not *have* knowledge or beliefs as one has money in his pocket, an ache in his heart, or joy in his soul. To "have" knowledge or to "hold" as a belief is simply to be prepared to *say* "I know that . . ." or "I believe that. . . ," and thus to be prepared to make, in the case of

119

knowledge, a categorical claim, and in the case of belief, a tentative claim to the truth of a proposition.

While "I believe that p" makes only a tentative claim to the truth of p, the claim may be more or less serious. The seriousness or "weightiness" of the belief claim is measurable by the strength of the evidence one is prepared to give when challenged to back up his claim. When we ask, *"Why* do you believe that p?", we challenge the believer to show us his credentials for his claim, as a storekeeper may challenge a customer who wishes to make a deposit on an overcoat to produce documents that validate his civic and financial standing. Nevertheless, we sometimes admit explicitly that we do *not* have backing for our belief claims, as when I say, "I admit that all the evidence is against Jones, but I still believe that he is innocent of the theft." The introductory clause "I admit that . . ." serves as a warning that the belief claim has no *present* backing. But in such cases, we expect the backing to be forthcoming. If I say, "Despite the evidence to the contrary, I believe that Jones is innocent," I imply that the proof of his innocence will be found eventually. "I know the evidence looks bad for Jones, so far. But wait and see. There is more to this case than meets the eye, I can assure you." Here the belief claim is tentative, not in the way of a deposit (incomplete payment, subject to cancellation), but more in the way of an I.O.U., that is, a promise of payment or validating evidence in the future.

Many philosophers, beginning with Bain, Peirce, James, and Dewey have emphasized another aspect of belief claims, namely, their behavioral commitments. Gilbert Ryle, in *The Concept of Mind,* explains beliefs as tendencies to act in certain ways, so that, on his analysis, "I believe that the ice is thin" means that I will not skate on the ice in question or, if I do, I will skate very cautiously.[6] Stuart Hampshire, who also emphasizes the behavioral implications of belief, calls this use of "I believe that" a "declaration of intention." [7] I do not think this pragmatic interpretation of belief is adequate, although there is obviously some basis for it in fact. But it cannot account for all the facts, such as the fact that we frequently use "I believe that" in a purely theoretical way, as

120

when we say, "I believe that in sixty million years, the earth will fall into the sun," or "I believe that Sacco and Vanzetti were innocent." If there is any behavioral commitment in these declarations, it is at most a linguistic commitment to continue to *assert* the proposition believed. On the other hand, it seems unlikely that we ever use "I believe that p" *merely* to declare our behavioral intentions without also making a truth claim. Even when we use weaker formulations such as "I imagine that p" or "I have a hunch that p," we assert the truth of p, although rather feebly and with explicit warning of probable cancellation.[8] The behavioral commitments of "I believe that p" are, in fact, dependent on the degree of firmness with which we mean to assert p. If I say, "I firmly believe that this mushroom is nonpoisonous," and I refuse to eat the mushroom, I can be suspected of insincerity. But if I merely say, "I am inclined to believe that it is nonpoisonous," or "I have a hunch that it is nonpoisonous," I clearly do *not* commit myself to acting as if the mushroom were edible. Thus, *disclaiming* behavioral commitments is the very function of qualifying expressions like "inclined to believe," "hunch that," etc. These considerations indicate that "I believe that" is primarily a more-or-less tentative truth claim, and only secondarily a commitment to action.

Let us now consider the relation between "I believe that" and "I have faith that." Like "know that" and "believe that," "faith that" makes a claim to the truth of the proposition which it introduces. But like "believe that" and unlike "know that," it warns the listener that the claim it is making is not supported by conclusive evidence and is therefore subject to future cancellation. Yet unlike "believe that" and more like "know that," it makes a firm and definite commitment to *action* relevant to the truth of the proposition it asserts. If I say, "I have faith that this parachute will open," I am promising to rely on this parachute when necessary. But if I say, "I believe that it will open," I may be urging someone else to try it out and be unwilling to try it myself, without being guilty of insincerity.

An interesting difference of function between "I believe that p" and "I have faith that p" is that the behavioral commitment of

"faith," unlike that of "believe," is constant and therefore independent of the strength of the truth claim being made for p. It is
inappropriate to say "I have faith that p" when I have plausible
reasons for asserting p. I would not say "I have faith that this
parachute will open" unless the parachute looked old or torn, or
in some way gave cause for doubting its effectiveness. Yet despite
the weakness of the truth claim, (i.e., despite the implicit admission
that the evidence is against the truth of what I am claiming) "I
have faith that . . ." expresses a very strong commitment to action.
Any refusal to act in a way relevant to the truth of the proposition
introduced by "I have faith that . . ." may be taken as evidence
of the insincerity of my declaration of faith. This is probably what
leads Dr. Niebuhr and most theologians to regard faith as a stronger
state of certainty than belief. But to speak of "certainty" here is
misleading. The *truth claim,* as we have seen, is not stronger, but
weaker, in the case of "faith that." It is the behavioral *commitment*
that is stronger. This has nothing to do with intellectual certitude,
but only with willingness to take a risk, as in the case of the
habitual gambler who knows that the odds are 100 to 1 against a
certain horse winning the race, but bets his bundle on just that
horse in the "faith that" Lady Luck will favor him. I do not think
that anyone is so irrational as to have a strong *belief* without
plausible evidence (although we are often mistaken in what we
*take to be* plausible evidence). Now the expression, "faith
that . . ." functions as a disclaimer of plausible evidence for (and
sometimes even as an admission of strong evidence against) the
proposition whose truth it asserts. Consequently, any declaration
of the form "I have faith that p" is contrary to reason, although it
may be perfectly sincere. Where "faith that" is concerned, we must
judge Bernard of Clairvaux to have been right as against Abélard,
when Bernard argued that faith is not grounded on reason. (But I
shall argue later that Abélard was right with respect to a different
kind of faith, namely "faith in." Had the issue been less political,
they might have worked out a satisfactory compromise.)

It is, I think, this disclaimer of reason involved in "I have
faith that" which leads many Protestant theologians to regard

122

faith as an emotional state. But we have seen that, if we take "I have faith that p" as the paradigmatic use of "faith," then faith cannot be an emotional state anymore than beliefs, knowledge, or hunches are emotional states. These concepts are substantives derived from what Urmson calls "parenthetical verbs," whose function is to make a more or less firm, and more or less complete, truth claim for the propositions they introduce. (In the case of "faith that," as we have seen, the function of committing oneself to a course of action takes precedence over the assertive function, but the assertive function remains.) Of course, there is always an emotional *background* for making such truth claims, and a particularly intense emotional background for declarations of faith. I would not say, "I have faith that I will survive this operation," unless I were in a state of intense emotion (the emotions being fear, because the odds are against my survival, and hope, because I have confidence in medical science and the competence of the surgeon). But the emotions that *motivate* a declaration of faith are not *reported* by the declaration, since a declaration is not a report. To put it in another way, "faith" does not *denote* an emotion, anymore than "hunch" does, in "I have a hunch that Citation will win the race." There is no special emotion called "faith," but only the fear and hope ("desperate hope," one might say) that motivate one to declare, "I have faith that things will turn out well." Perhaps the most exact way to describe faith, in this sense, is to say that it is a *decision,* occasioned by the presence in one's soul of both fear and hope—a decision to act on one's hope and defy one's fear, although the reasons for fear may be more rationally potent than the reasons for hope. "Faith that" is thus an essentially irrational decision, but when made sincerely, it is admirably courageous.

I have argued that a declaration of "belief that" is, primarily, a more or less tentative truth claim and, secondarily, a more or less definite commitment to action, while "faith that" is an extremely weak truth claim, disclaiming any reliable backing for itself, together with an extremely firm commitment to action. Both are to be distinguished from knowledge claims and also from

123

self-descriptions, including reports of one's emotional state. I have also tried to show that "faith that" declarations are essentially unreasonable, since they are courageous and sincere in direct proportion to the evidence *against* the truth of the propositions they affirm. Another way of putting this is that faith is related to risk; the greater the risk one is prepared to take, the more profound and serious is his declaration of faith. One must admire the courage of a man who is prepared to take an overwhelming risk, but one cannot put much stock in his practical intelligence.

But this is not all that there is to be said about the relation between faith and belief. We have been considering only the "cognitive" uses of these concepts. That is, we have examined the uses of "believe that" and "faith that" as parenthetical verbs, introducing propositions to which they make some kind of truth claim. But there is a second important use of the concepts of belief and faith, a use which is nonpropositional and makes no truth claims at all. We frequently say that we believe *in* or have faith *in* people, capacities of people, social policies, or even inanimate objects. Now it seems to me that these uses of "belief" and "faith" have a very different logic and must be evaluated separately.

"Believe in" and "faith in," like "believe that" and "faith that," have a performatory function in the first person use and a descriptive function in the second and third person uses. However, their logic is in other respects quite different. They take, as their grammatical objects, not propositions, but persons, capacities, policies, or things. We say, "I believe in Jones (or in Jones' honesty)," "I believe in Dr. Smith (or in Dr. Smith's surgical competence)," "I believe in trial marriages," or "I believe in jet airplanes," and we sometimes say that we have faith in the same things. Both "I believe in X" and "I have faith in X" declare my intentions toward X and thus commit me to certain modes of action with respect to X. They also presuppose fairly intimate personal experience of X, and they express approval, support, or commendation of X. The differences between "I believe in X" and "I have faith in X" are not essential for our study of religious claims, and so I shall indicate them summarily: (1) "I believe in X" does not always imply a risk, whereas "I have faith in X" does. (2) "I believe in X" is frequently, if not always, less definite in its commitment to action than "I have faith in X." One usually declares one's faith in some person or thing in a situation in which a dangerous action of entrusting oneself to the object of faith is clearly indicated, e.g., when I am about to undergo an operation from which few have recovered, I might say, "I have faith in Dr. Smith (or in his surgical competence)." I am more likely to say, "I believe in Dr. Smith" in a less hazardous context, such as a parlor conversation, where no specific action is clearly at issue. Similarly, one is more likely to say, "I believe in God" in a theological discussion, but "I have faith in God" when one is critically ill, or when one is preparing to abandon a sinking ship. (3) A "belief in" declaration is often more ambiguous than the corresponding "faith in" declaration. In saying, "I believe in God" I may mean various things. I may mean that I believe that God exists, or that I am willing to entrust myself to His care ("faith in"), or that I intend to enforce and follow His commandments (this last is a declaration of allegiance, like "I believe in the Constitution of the United States"). The ambiguity and indefiniteness of "belief in" declarations make them useful vehicles of equivocation. One can piously profess his belief in God and escape intellectual responsibility for producing evidence for his belief while also escaping moral responsibility for any commitment to obey the divine commandments, because of our (and perhaps his) uncertainty as to just what his declaration amounts to. I shall, therefore, say no more about "belief in," after noting that it is often suspiciously equivocal, and I shall concentrate on its more straightforward partner, "faith in."

"Faith in," unlike "faith that," often appears to be both serious and reasonable. Its seriousness is a function of the risk one commits himself to taking, while its reasonableness is a function of the degree to which one's personal experience of the object of faith justifies "putting one's faith" in it or in him. I do not need *faith* in Dr. Smith to go to him to be treated for a cold. I need faith to undergo a dangerous operation. I do not need faith in Jones's honesty to lend him five dollars, but lending him a thousand is a different story. On the other hand, my faith in Dr. Smith is reasonable if Dr. Smith has cured patients when other doctors have failed. My faith in Jones is reasonable if I have known him for years and found him consistently honest. But if I met him only yesterday and I lend him a thousand dollars today, then he is a talented confidence man and I am a fool. The two criteria for evaluating "faith in"—namely, seriousness and reasonableness—thus seem to vary inversely. The more *reason* for my faith, the less real risk I incur, and conversely. Perhaps, if I have conclusive reasons for my faith, it is even inappropriate to call it "faith." Yet we do speak of faith in doctors or faith in science, and surely we have rather conclusive reasons based on long experience for faith of that sort.[9] I would suggest that the reason we still use "faith" in such cases is that what appears as a small and therefore reasonable risk from within the personal knowledge of the one who has the faith often looms as a great and, therefore, unreasonable risk from outside. To one who has little personal knowledge of medical science or of airplanes, undergoing surgery or flying in a jet will seem enormously risky. Consequently, we can say that such faith is serious—judged from without—and reasonable—judged from within. But if we are applying both criteria from within the standpoint of adequate personal knowledge, we might say, "It isn't a matter of faith, it's plain good sense to trust Dr. Smith (or jet planes)." At this point it may be of interest to note that one who declares faith in God is *not* likely to explain that his faith "isn't really faith, but just plain good sense." But a refusal to say this would amount to an admission that his faith is not very reasonable.

It is time now to connect all the loose ends of this discussion by applying our conclusions to the evaluation of religious claims. Let us consider first religious declarations of "belief that," such as "I believe that God exists, that He is three persons in one substance," etc. We have found that "belief that" declarations, if they are to be candid in their truth claims, should be accompanied by qualifying expressions when the evidential backing for the belief is weak or nonexistent. Thus, if one cannot give evidence for his religious beliefs, he should, if his language is not to be misleading, say, "I am inclined to believe that God exists and is a Trinity," or "I have a feeling that God exists," or, if one means to make a firm commitment to action together with a weakly supported truth claim, one should say, "I have *faith* that God exists."

I have argued that "faith that" declarations are always unreasonable because they commit one to actions predicated on the truth of propositions for which there is either no evidence or strong evidence to the contrary. "Faith in," on the other hand, *is* reasonable when grounded on adequate personal experience. Thus the Protestant stress on "faith in" God (based on one's personal encounter with God, and rendered by the Latin, *fide*) would seem to qualify as more reasonable than the Catholic stress on "faith that" (*credo*). However, the Protestant concept of faith presents a special difficulty. If one's faith in God is to be reasonably grounded on one's Encounter with God, then this Encounter must be a real event and not just an abstract symbol of one's religious emotions and commitments. One must *really* have encountered God. And yet the evidence for the real occurrence of such Encounters, according to modern theologians, can only be appreciated *through faith*. Those who lack faith cannot hope to encounter the divine object of faith. This seems to get us into a methodologically vicious circle, such that we cannot reasonably have faith without first having the Encounter, and we cannot have the Encounter without first having faith. Things were simpler in Biblical times when Elijah could demonstate the reasonableness of his faith to the heathens by bringing rain that was observable to the faithful and faithless alike. But perhaps the modern theologian would say that faith and its ground in the Encounter occur simultaneously, so that one need not have one *before* the other. But the trouble with this explanation is that one must accept *it* on unreasonable faith. For belief in the simultaneity of reasonable faith and its experiential ground is surely not itself a reasonable conclusion from experience. All our experience of life leads us to believe that reasonable faith in something must be grounded on a good deal of *prior* experience of the object of faith. The veteran paratrooper has reasonable faith in parachutes. The experienced animal trainer has reasonable faith in the power of animal psychology. I can have faith in neither. But I can and do have such faith in my dilapidated old car, which I have learned to trust over many years. However, I cannot persuade those to whom I offer it for sale to share my faith. Indeed, it would be quite unreasonable for them to take the risk of purchasing it.

Since "faith in," to be reasonable, must be based on long experience of the object of faith, and since "faith that" is always contrary to reason, one is forced to conclude that religious faith is never reasonable faith. Is it then always serious faith? This, we have seen, would depend on the magnitude of the risks that the faithful are prepared to take. Pascal, in his famous discussion of the religious wager, argued that it is the *atheist* who takes the greater risk. Thus if Pascal was right, then the faith of the atheist is more serious than the faith of the theist. But I am inclined to think that Pascal was wrong. It seems to me that the saintly man of faith, who genuinely renounces all the pleasures of this world in the hope of something better after death, takes just about the greatest risk conceivable. Such a man must therefore be recognized to be the most serious—but, alas, the least reasonable—of us all.

# NOTES

1. Cf. Augustine, *Sermons* XLIII; Bernard de Clairvaux, *De Erroribus Abailardi,* C, 1, 1055–60; Aquinas, *Summa Theologica,* I, 1, art. 2; see also the article on "Faith" in the *Catholic Encyclopedia* (New York: 1913), V, 752–53: "Non-Catholic writers have repudiated the idea of faith as an intellectual assent and . . . fail to realize that faith must necessarily result in a body of dogmatic beliefs."

2. In his authoritative essay on "Faith," in *A Handbook of Christian Theology,* eds. Marvin Halverson and Arthur A. Cohen (N. Y.: Meridian Books, Inc., 1958), p. 128, John Dillenberger defines faith as follows: ". . . the concept of faith should be confined to the living confidence and trust in God which results from . . . the experience of His active presence." But on p. 129 Dillenberger adds: "In

various degrees an emotional element is included in religious experience but it cannot be reduced to emotion. . . . Just as reason and will are included, so is the concept of knowledge. . . ." Characteristically after *confining* faith to the emotions of confidence and trust, this distinguished theologian then *stretches* it to include belief and even knowledge. The Catholic stress (or stretch) goes the other way.

3. Cf. J. L. Austin, "Other Minds," in *Proceedings of the Aristotelian Society,* Supp. Vol. XX, reprinted in A. Flew (ed.), *Logic and Language* (Second Series), (Oxford: Basil Blackwell, 1953), pp. 123 ff.

4. Austin, whose analysis I have drawn upon, (*op. cit.*) denies that a knowledge claim is always discredited by disproof of the proposition it asserts. But I think that it is not discredited only when we have good reason to think an "honest mistake" was made (note that it is a mistake, all the same). Such cases of exculpation are, I think, like suspended sentences. It seems to me clearly false to say "Ptolemy *knew* that the sun revolves around the earth," but correct to say that Ptolemy's *mistake* was more intelligent than the correct guesses of some of the Pythagoreans.

5. Cf. Austin, *op. cit.*; J. O. Urmson, "Parenthetical Verbs," in A. Flew (ed.), *Essays in Conceptual Analysis* (New York: St. Martin's Press, 1956), pp. 192 ff. Many of the points made in this paper are based on Urmson's illuminating discussion.

6. Cf. G. Ryle, *The Concept of Mind* (New York: Barnes and Noble, Inc., 1960), pp. 133–35.

7. Stuart Hampshire, *Thought and Action* (New York: Viking Press, 1960), p. 159: "A man who with apparent sincerity professed beliefs upon which he never acted . . . would be said to be holding these beliefs in words only, but not truly believing."

8. Cf. Urmson, *op. cit.,* pp. 201–203, on such qualifying expressions.

9. In his essay in this volume, Professor H. R. Niebuhr approvingly quotes H. Margenau and A. N. Whitehead stating that scientific faith and Christian faith are equally nonrational. It seems that scientists, as well as theologians, frequently overlook the fact that our faith in science is based on long and highly successful experience with it. Yet they, of all people, should know better!

## 16

## RELIGIOUS FAITH
## AND SCIENTIFIC FAITH
*by Raphael Demos, Harvard University*

Mr. Hick has spoken of the 'circle' of Christian faith. There
is a sense in which I agree with him and another in which I feel
that his statement is dangerous. No basic doctrine, religious or
scientific (or appearing in common sense), is immune from philosophic criticism, from Socratic questioning, from Cartesian doubt.
It is the business of philosophy to examine, for instance, not
only the religious beliefs in the existence of God, in free will,
and in immortality, but also the common-sense beliefs in the
existence of physical objects and of other persons, and the scientific
conceptions of causality and law. Until the very recent past, all
philosophers have regarded *all* basic belief as their province;
they have recognized no 'circle' into which they might not penetrate;
no 'No trespassing' sign has stopped them; there have been no
fences over which they did not jump.

But there is another sense of 'circle' which makes Mr. Hick's
use of the term justified. Science, no less than Christianity, operates
with certain beliefs which may be called premises or presuppositions; that is to say, both of these disciplines are based on beliefs
which are ultimate in the sense that (a) they are not demonstrable deductively, and (b) they are not verified by sense-experience. If we take the meaning of 'reason' to consist of these two
criteria, then we can say that the presuppositions of both science
and Christian doctrine are without rational justification. Such ultimate beliefs may, therefore, be called articles of faith.

In developing my points, I hope the reader will forgive me if
I repeat what I have written elsewhere. Religionists are accused

by secularists of accepting the proposition that God exists without rational demonstration and without evidence; so they are called dogmatists. I will answer the charge by admitting the first part while demurring to the second. There is a difference between premise (or presupposition) and dogma. A premise is not necessarily a dogma; it may become one when the believer does not proceed to inquire into his belief, when he is not even aware that it is a premise.

As for the scientists—and their fellow travelers, the philosophers of the naturalistic school—they, too, have their ultimate commitments and, as often as not, are not even aware that they have them, thus meriting the charge of dogmatism. The pot has been calling the kettle black. Both the scientists and their fellow philosophers have recourse to faith, if by faith we mean the acceptance of belief without evidence, demonstrative or empirical. (Faith = "The vision of things unseen," *Epistle to the Hebrews*.) Such a statement may seem a willful paradox on my part. Surely, it will be asked, unlike religious people, scientists rely on evidence for the hypotheses which they accept? Granted. The question remains as to the stipulation of what constitutes evidence. For example, the criterion in science for the acceptance of a theory is confirmation by the senses, not by the imagination, not by feeling. Yet all three alike are modes of conscious experience. The selection of only the first as relevant to evidence is the outcome of a decision. Take images: there is no intrinsic difference between sense-data and images. In order to establish a relevant difference, Berkeley made the point that sense-data display a regularity of sequence, that they obey 'natural laws,' whereas images do not. This distinction cannot hold water for a moment. No psychologist would admit that the appearance of images is not governed by laws, however complex these laws might be, and although largely undiscovered as yet. Dreams, no less than waking experiences, have their regularities. Berkeley's 'natural laws' are defined as those laws which govern 'ideas of sense,' while 'ideas of sense' are defined as those which obey these laws. Berkeley has argued in a circle.

It will be objected that what is given to sense has the special

131

privilege of being common property, whereas what is imagined or felt varies from person to person. But this is to *assume* that inter-subjectivity is a necessary criterion for the acceptability (reality?) of a datum. Democracy consists in the submission of the whole to the decision of the majority; if the scientists choose to adopt the political principle of democracy in their own operations, it is their own affair. But that is no reason why the mystic's or the poet's private visions should be disqualified from citizenship in the realm of cognition.

Here we touch on another basic belief—namely that other persons exist with whom we can share our sense-experiences. (By a person I mean a being who makes a contribution to the pool of sense-experience.) Now, I know of no proof for the belief in the existence of other persons. There is a further complication. On the basis of the criterion of intersubjectivity, I know that my sense data are veridical, that is, because they are shared by others. I know this to be a fact because the other persons so report to me. Thus, I hear them saying that they see the same green color on the fruit which I see. But how do I know that I have really heard, not just *imagined* that I have heard? Because, other persons too have heard the same voices; I have *really* heard them saying so because others report . . . and so on.

It is a platitude that several theories may be consistent with sensory evidence; in choosing one among the many theories, the scientist must appeal to still another criterion: simplicity and elegance, otherwise known as Occam's razor, which shaves off the complexities of theories. But who is Occam that we should worship him? In the modern world we deny the divine rights of kings. Leaving aside this (mixed) metaphor, why assume that only the simple theory is true? It may be that the Creator of the cosmos was extravagant, like a painter who does not spare his brush strokes.

It is obvious that common sense accepts the trustworthiness of memory; it is not so obvious, yet equally true, that science, too, proceeds in a like fashion. Descartes went further and maintained that even mathematics relied on memory. As he said: When the proof is very long, I cannot hold all the steps before my mind at the same time; I have to rely on my memory that I have proved the earlier steps in the argument. Mathematical belief cannot be certain unless one has evidence that memory is trustworthy. Descartes found this evidence in his belief that our various mental faculties have been given us by God, and that God will not deceive us.

As a scientist, I observe an experimental result in the laboratory. But time is passing; in fact, I have left the laboratory, and now I no longer observe the result. Instead, I *remember* that I saw. Memory plays a greater role than any other factor in what is loosely called scientific observation. Observations are remembered observations. Let us suppose, however, that the scientist, concerned about the weakness of his memory, puts his results down on paper; now he relies on written reports. But then our scientist must remember that he himself has written the report; otherwise it might be a hoax played on him.

As just noted, Descartes justified his trust in memory by recourse to a God who will not deceive; other philosophers have justified memory by noting that there is a convergence in its disclosures. I will not dispute the validity of these attempts as a justification of memory; my point is the simple one that a person still has to *remember* the justification or the proof of the trustworthiness of memory. And in thus remembering, one is already trusting one's memory while engaged in justifying its trustworthiness. Or one might say: I have trusted memory in the past and it has worked. Good, but one must remember that it has worked.

The appeal to the past, just cited, involves an appeal to the inductive principle. Science makes its generalizations and formulates laws on the basis of this principle. As Hume has conclusively shown, this is a principle which cannot be justified by evidence of any sort; he called it a habit, I will call it a premise. In his reply to Professor H. Richard Niebuhr, Professor Kennedy says that the scientists "merely believe that their methods of inquiry will enable them to solve many problems," concluding that "this belief does not depend upon Pascal's reasons of the heart. . . . It is an assurance based upon prior success." But how does Mr. Kennedy know that the fact of prior success justifies an expectation of suc-

133

cess in the future? Of course, he is assuming the principle of induction.

Some positivists have, in a way, restated Hume; thus Von Mises has written (referring to his account of induction): "All of these propositions are supposed to be merely descriptions of the hitherto observed ways of research. . . . We are dealing primarily with a description of the characteristic features of scientific activity."

I take this to mean that the rules of induction are the scientist's rules of the road. The scientist drives his car on the right, but then the Christian is entitled to his own different rules—he drives his car on the left. The scientific tribe has its custom (Hume's habits); so have other tribes other customs. For instance, the Polynesian natives explain certain events by referring them to the evil eye; their authority is not the scientist but the medicine man. Von Mises describes the characteristics of scientific activity; the description of the animist's activity is different, and that is all there is to it.

But, the opponent might say, surely science is not magic. This is indeed so true as to be a platitude; neither is religion the same as science. But if one goes on to say that science and science only reveals what is the case, we have a right to challenge him: "By what right do you assume that knowledge can be secured only by conformity to scientific criteria?" The statement which equates science with knowledge is an unacknowledged premise, and therefore a dogma.

It will have been noticed that the basic commitments in science concern its procedures and its criteria for the acceptability of a proposed belief. And now we are driven back to Professor Hick's concept of a 'circle' with a vengeance. There is the circle consisting of the scientific faithful, of the scientific tribe. Scientists have their customs, their mores, their morality of intellectual behavior. Science, then, is a branch of morality. Now, according to the positivist, an ethical sentence is not a statement but a recommendation. And since science is a department of ethics, then, scientific sentences are no more than recommendations too, and my tribe might recommend otherwise.

134

Should the positivist, putting on the mantle of the pragmatist, say that science works, he must answer the question, works to what end? For success, for salvation, for salvation in this life or in the next? Any pragmatism presupposes some theory as to what things are valuable. Thus, science assumes the value of prediction (but how do we know that there is a future to predict?). Thus, the scientist has his preferences, and preference is a *feeling* for something. Plato excluded the poets from his Ideal State because they relied on feeling rather than on reason. In turn, the positivists exclude Plato from the Ideal State of cognitive discourse because, so they say, his ontology is an expression of feeling. Now the positivists must be excluded too because their criteria are expressions of feeling.

To return to induction. The scientist assumes the universal application of the principle of explanation. Supposing, for instance, that our scientist is confronted with a datum which he cannot explain; will he say: here is a brute irrational fact? No, indeed. He will say: give me (or my successors) time and the explanation will be found. So does a Christian, confronted with human misery, still say that God is good and that everything will turn out all right in the long, the very long, run. Job said: though He slay me, yet will I trust in Him. So does the scientist say: though the facts slay my expectations yet will I trust in my principles. Both the Christian and the scientist are willing to stand by their conviction, not only beyond but also contrary to the evidence. And in a curious way, they are both saying the same thing: the cosmos will not deceive us.

In concluding, I must clarify my views further in order to avoid misunderstanding. I do not mean to say that, because a belief is a presupposition, it lacks cognitive worth. I do not mean that the premises of science or the premises of Christianity are not true or are not knowledge. Not being a positivist, I do not hold that the criteria for belief in science are a matter of custom, of how 'we do things.' I believe that the criteria of science are valid, that the body of scientific statements is (approximately) true, just as I believe that the body of Christian doctrine is true, again only to a degree, given that we are finite human beings. But I think it is nonsense to say that while science is a matter of reason, Christian doctrine is a matter of faith; both have their basic commitments (faiths) and both strive to establish rational structures upon these foundations. I think it is nonsense to accuse Christianity of dogmatism while proclaming the spiritual chastity of science. May I remind the reader of the following statement by Whitehead: "Science has never shaken off the impress of its origin in the historical revolt of the late Renaissance. It has remained predominantly an antirationalistic movement, based upon a naive faith." It is easy for us today, as we look many centuries back into the Middle Ages, with their almost Gothically intricate Christian formulations, to see that these statements rest, ultimately, on faith; and that their arguments can persuade only those already converted. But because science is of the present and because science is an ever-expanding movement, it is more difficult to discern its limits, to realize that it also has its ungrounded beliefs. Science, being the greatest intellectual power today, tends to overwhelm and to blind us to the fact that the 'evidences' for scientific ideas can be persuasive only for those who are already converted. All this, I think, will become more evident to human beings of a later and a metascientific epoch.

But it is not enough to show that both science and Christianity rest on presuppositions. The labeling of a statement as an article of faith should not mean the giving of free tickets to superstition for admission into the theater of thought. There is the problem, then, of distinguishing true from false faith—one acknowledged in the Scriptures, as when they warn us against false prophets. Magic and animism, on the one hand, must be kept out of the halls of science, and Christianity, on the other. How to judge the good from the bad, how to distinguish the true from the false faith; science from antiscience, true from false religion—here is a problem demanding solution. However, this is not a problem for the present essay.

# 17

## FAITH, LANGUAGE, AND
## RELIGIOUS EXPERIENCE: A DIALOGUE
*by Arthur C. Danto, Columbia University*

> *Enwrapt in misty cloud, with lips that*
> *stammer, hymn chanters wander and*
> *are discontented.*
>
> Rig Veda, X, 82.

A: The conflict between science and religious faith! Fancy raising *that* old ghost. I thought by now we were all agreed that religious language, like scientific language, has it own validity in the contexts in which it is appropriate to use it. And since the contexts are different, a conflict could hardly arise. Except trivially, one doesn't celebrate Mass in the laboratory. Nor measure mass in the cathedral.

B: That notion of validity may be valid at Oxford. But not here. I'm glad the issue was raised. I believe there is a conflict, and your pun only clouds it over. As if religion were merely a matter of performing rituals! Surely some religious utterances mean to state a truth, and so undertake to do the job which scientific sentences, by common consent, are meant to do. So, in principle, a conflict can arise—even if the conflicting sentences are uttered in laboratory and cathedral respectively.

A: You surely wouldn't want to say that every so-called scientific sentence asserts, or means to assert, a truth: scientific sentences do all sorts of jobs. But considering only those sentences which do mean to do this job—they can conflict with religious sentences only if they are about the same things. But I would deny that this is ever the case.

B: There is nothing which scientific sentences cannot be about. There are no limits set for science in point of subject matter.

# Religious Experience and Truth

And simply as a matter of fact, scientists and religionists have talked about the same things.

A: Oh, there may well have been such disputes. But these arose only because each party misrepresented the scope of his own discipline. You, apparently, are victim to the same delusion. What do you mean by "faith," for instance?

B: One might do worse than use the old notion of which Professor Hook reminded us: to have faith is to hold for true a belief for which there is insufficient evidence. I may have great confidence in some hypothesis, and believe very strongly that experiment will bear me out. But, quoting Nietzsche, "Strong faith proves only its strength, and not the truth of what is believed in." [1] I have no right to assert my hypothesis until I have other than subjective grounds for doing so. But religious people act as though they had such a right. I'll bet you would drop your language-game immunities fast enough if you had sufficient evidence for any of *your* beliefs!

A: In fact we have evidence, *strong* evidence, but you are doubtless too narrow to regard it as such. But what in general can you mean by "sufficient evidence?" If we set our standard of "sufficient evidence" sufficiently high—none of our beliefs after all admit of perfect certainty—everything becomes faith, for everything we believe is now based upon insufficient evidence. And it would be wholly arbitrary on your part to specify a degree of confirmation such that any sentence confirmed to a lesser degree becomes faith. For I, with equal justification, could specify an upward revision. But anyway, the difference between scientific and religious beliefs cannot simply be a matter of differing degrees of confirmedness. The hypothesis to which you referred a moment back did not pass from religion to science in virtue of successfully passing tests. And should there have been a conflicting hypothesis which was disconfirmed when your hypothesis was confirmed, it would not thereby be relegated to religion.

B: No, but it would become a matter of faith if someone were to now hold it for true. By faith I shall mean holding a sentence true when there exists evidence which a reasonable man would regard as sufficient for holding its contradictory. We scientists relinquish our beliefs in such circumstances. But not religious people. There, if you like, is the difference between us.

A: I am not prepared to grant this as a characterization of *religious* faith, for which, as I said, evidence is available to those not hardened to reality. You are thinking of such cases as these, perhaps. A man has faith in his success when the world has written him off as a failure. Or in his wife's chastity when half the village knows her for a trull.

B: Exactly. And only consider, if I may play your game, the contexts in which we would say "I believe in . . ." or "I have faith that. . . ." We use such propositional attitudes only when a belief has been challenged, for purpose of expressing our resolve to go on believing. If there were something wrong with the evidence brought against us, or if we were privy to a fact unavailable to our challengers, we would simply say he was wrong and show why. Instead, we take a stand. Of course I can understand this. The man has his back to the wall, and to give up his belief will mean the collapse of his universe. But that doesn't make faith a rational thing. Rationally, we ought to face the facts and not persist in illusion.

A: It is a part of the concept of faith that a man's faith be *tried,* even that he should be alone in his faith. But there are martyrs in the history of science and religion alike. And let me point out that you and I try one another's faiths. Is it not true that you are committed in advance to stand by certain of your beliefs no matter what contravening evidence religion might bring forth?

B: You *want* to try my faith. But you are hardly likely to produce evidence in support of religious beliefs.

A: Why do you say that with such force? Is it not because, as a scientist, there are certain beliefs which you hold, and must go on holding, if you are to do science at all? Beliefs you would not *allow* to be abrogated? The conflict between science and religion is then a conflict between faiths. I have this in mind: you are antecedently committed to the view that there are no ultimate dark spots in the fabric of things, and that everything, in the fullness of time, must yield to scientific understanding and explanation. Einstein wrote: "The regulations valid for the world existence are rational, that is, comprehensible to reason." [2] And surely, to say that there must always be a natural explanation is to announce a creed? If I then insist that there are ultimate mysteries, even claim to be able to point them out, you would remain unshaken in your faith. Unless, indeed, you were to convert. For a conversion it would be—from one faith to another.[3]

B: I am a scientist, interested in finding solutions to problems I regard as genuine. I believe these problems admit of solution, though I may not be clever or lucky enough to find them. If I fail, the fault at least does not lie with the world, and I should hope sooner or later that my colleagues or our successors will do what I could not. If you refer to this, then, indeed, I have faith of a kind. And so perhaps has every scientist. It may even be true that had they not had this faith, science could never have arisen or advanced. But this would then be a psychological fact concerning scientists, or a sociological fact concerning science considered externally. For the "faith" is not part of science itself. You will not find "The universe is comprehensible to reason" listed amongst the sentences which together make up a theory in physics, or chemistry, or what science you will.[4] And even were you to insert it, say as an independent postulate, it would be inert, and play no logical role there: "A wheel that can be turned though nothing else moves with it, is not part of the mechanism." [5] As for the sentences which *are* part of the machine, no scientist is prepared to defend them come what may. Of course, a man might try very hard to make a favorite hypothesis stick. Like Priestley. But this, while possibly *his* faith, is not science's. I add, by way of an *ad hominem* remark, that you religionists don't, as a matter of fact, treat science as a faith amongst faiths. Have you not time and again given up beliefs of yours which conflicted with science (in *my* sense)? Do any of you seriously defend Genesis against geology today? Yet I have not seen any comparable readiness to retreat when conflicts arise between competing religions.

A: It is not quite true to say that they have been given up—

they have been seen in a new light, and interpreted so as to remove the alleged conflict.

B: But isn't that just the same thing as to have given them up? I mean, you obviously are not saying that Genesis is *true*. Where then does "interpretation" get you? Suppose P and Q are respectively scientific and religious sentences, that P and Q are incompatible, and that you accept P. Then let R be an interpretation of Q. If R is equivalent to Q, the conflict remains, for now R is incompatible with P, and hence false if P is true. If not equivalent, then R now turns out to be incompatible with Q. So either you remain in conflict with science, or you enter into conflict with the faith of your fathers.[6]

A: You miss the point. Genesis was literally false all along. People failed to see it for what it was, an ambitious metaphor. And a metaphor may be true though the sentence which expresses it, taken literally, is false.

B: All you tell me is that you have shifted ground since last century's controversies. And this just makes my point for me. There was no attempt, until science arose and threatened it, for religionists to decide that their canon was a tissue of metaphor. But up to that time there were plenty of opportunities to concede this, since there were plenty of conflicts between religions. In those days you condemned your opponents as heretics or worshippers of false gods. I won't push you on the fact that there are inconsistencies even within your own canon.

A: I want to grant your point and then go on to show how little comes of granting it. Consider this analogy. The camera showed (as Socrates' mirror should have done) that representation was not a sufficient condition for art. Kandinsky showed that it was not even a necessary condition. The essence of art lies elsewhere, and works qualify as artistic independently of whether or not they are representational. The old masters thought differently, but they produced art in spite of not quite understanding what they were doing. So with my forebears. They mislocated the essence of religion and felt themselves obliged to defend every sentence of the canon. The Bible contains religious truth independently of

141

whether it contains literal truth or not. The Genesis controversies had the valuable consequence of making us see this fact.

B: Non-objective religion! You then give up making cognitive claims? The issue goes by default. I win.

A: Not quite. My fundamentalist forebears, well meaning as they were, erred in feeling they must pitch their faith where they did. They might, as I, have given Genesis up and retained their faith intact. Genesis tells a lovely story, and makes a point, but it is bad cosmology and worse geology. But lest this, like illusions in epistemology, threaten every claim to empirical knowledge, I will go further. I will concede that every sentence in the Bible which can possibly conflict with science is to be given up. The Bible, of course, contains a number of true statements, and I understand that it has become a valuable tool for the archeologist. But even such literal truths as there may be are dismissed by me from the body of faith: consider it expunged of whatever sentence science may confirm or disconfirm.

B: That's it, is it not? What do you plan to do, now that religion is finished?

A: It's not finished, only purified. And there still remains a conflict between you and me, though not between science and religion. We believe in, and our faith rests upon, the occurrence of a miracle. Thus: "The Eternal has entered the time-series and become Temporal." [7] I don't suppose science denies this? The denial of it is not included amongst the sentences which make up theories in physics, chemistry, or whatever you regard as science. Nor would it do to list it as an independent postulate, so to speak. For it would not be part of the machinery. To be sure, it is a terribly dark thing I refer to, and utterly incomprehensible to reason, and so conflicts with the belief (dare I say "faith"?) that "the universe is comprehensible to reason." But this you have conceded not to be part of science. We have each effected a purgation. I have cleansed religion of everything which might fall within the province of science. And you have purged science of whatever might clash with religion—including the very principle I would have thought to have animated your entire enterprise. Or do you want to reconsider, and relocate "the universe is comprehensible to reason" within the body of science? In that case, as a scientist, you must stand ready to relinquish it upon discovering dark spots in the universe. Which you now must allow as possible, if only to save your belief from vacuity.

B: You would not really want me to take it back into science. For then, by *your* criterion, you would have to give up your belief in dark spots. For this would now rest upon a claim which would, by my fiat, fall within the province of science. But I need not make this move. For your belief happens to conflict with logic, which I consider part of science. Indeed, you make it very easy for me. To say that something is eternal is to say that temporal predicates are inapplicable to it. It is self-contradictory then to say that something is both temporal and nontemporal. And please spare me any pious reference to life as being bigger than logic and God as being bigger than both. You can't turn your back on logic. You may be irrational enough to believe in what is impossible, just as Tertullian was insane enough to believe in what is absurd. But impossibility (and absurdity) are given content, after all, by logic. Had you no commitment to logic, you would not have what to believe. The question is why you want to be so perverse.

A: It only *sounds* impossible. But that is because our understanding here is limited. Our faith is that this is what *happened.* But we don't know how or why. We see as through a glass darkly.

B: The fact is that you don't understand *what* you believe in. We scientists at least know what we mean when we assert something, and then we try and find out whether it is true. You seem to work reversely: first you take something for true, and then you hope to find out what it means. Suppose a friend and I are trapped by the proprieties into sitting through a lecture in Turkish. My friend afterwards tells me that every word of it was true. I commend him on his knowledge of an exotic language, but he disclaims such knowledge: he *hopes,* he says, someday to understand Turkish. I call him either weird or silly. But now I think I know what faith is, or at least religious faith. It is not, as I thought, to hold onto a belief in the teeth of contrary evidence.

143

For apparently nothing can count for or against a proposition, the meaning of which we do not know. How then *could* there be a conflict between science and religion? Faith is a matter of defending an incomprehensible proposition.

A: You show your shallowness. The language is, and must be, paradoxical. It makes plain by not making plain. Its purpose is to show how exceptional and how awesome a thing it is which we worship. The paradox is *there,* at the heart of things. Christ was human, and fully so. And he was fully divine as well. Temporal *and* eternal. Ordinarily, of course, "is human" and "is divine" are contrary predicates, and contrast with one another. But contrary predicates are both true of Jesus. Or Krishna, if you are a Hindu. Or Buddha if you accept the *Lotus Sutra.* Christ is a paradoxical entity. I accept logic everywhere but here, and my acceptance of it helps to throw the entire world into contrast with the dark spot at its core.

B: I don't understand a word you say. And neither do you.

A: "It is the duty of the human understanding to understand that there are things which it does not understand, and what these things are. . . . The paradox is not a concession but a category, an ontological relation between an existing cognitive spirit and an eternal truth." [8] So wrote Kierkegaard—who incidentally helped do for religion what Kandinsky did for art.

B: We should have to change our assessment of Kandinsky were we to discover that his paintings showed the world as he *saw* it. For then it would not be a case of nonrepresenting, which was to have been his contribution to the concept of art, but rather a case of representing the world abnormally. Enlarging rather than eliminating the subject matter. But that's inconsistent with what you said.

A: Nonetheless I like your point. Why not represent reaches of reality abstractly which cannot be captured via conventional imagery? Why not describe reaches of reality paradoxically when consistent language fails?

B: But your statement of the paradox begs an important question. The paradox arises only because both contrary predicates are allegedly true of Christ. One of these predicates is "is divine." But divine is a word I fail to understand. Nor can you simply say that to be divine is to be a paradoxical entity. For the paradox arises only because Christ is supposedly *already* divine: his being divine is *one pole* of the paradox. Notice that "is human" contrasts with many predicates. Grant me that it contrasts with "is vegetable." Then to say that something is a human vegetable is to posit a paradoxical entity, as you like to say. But surely you don't believe in every possible impossibility. Hence the object of worship here is doubly obscure. Once because paradoxical. But more basically, once because divine. The predicate which must antecedently be cleared up then is "is divine." What does it mean?

A: It is learnt by ostension. Except God revealed Himself the term would not be in the language. Christ was a divine being, Jesus an individual in history. Those who saw Jesus saw a divine being, given that Christ and Jesus were identical. Fa $\cdot$ a = b $\cdot$ ⊐ $\cdot$ Fb. Fa $\cdot$ a = b $\cdot$ ⊐ $\cdot$ Fb.

B: But not everyone apparently saw him as such. What did they fail to *sense*? You call him the Son of God. But you can't teach the meaning of the term by referring back to God, for the problem gets raised all over again. Think of a kind of Prince and Pauper situation: suppose someone were a replica of Jesus, only of merely human provenance. The visual experience of seeing Jesus matches the visual experience of seeing his counterpart, admittedly nondivine. Then divineness cannot be seen, for by hypothesis the visual experiences are identical. But then suppose this were the case for each sense modality. How then is divinity to be sensed and "is divine" learnt?

A: Divinity is sensed by the eye of faith. "The numinous cannot be 'taught.' It has to be awakened from the spirit." [9]

B: Ah, I thought we were going to get a behavioral criterion. I thought you were going to tell me Christ performed miracles but His replica could not.

A: The miracles were signs and portents of His divinity, toward which they pointed. But how should we really understand what was being pointed to only by means of signposts? No, they

145

may have helped cause men to be awakened to divineness. But they were not the object of the awareness. "Is divine" is primitive. It cannot be explicitly defined, and hence cannot be eliminated in favor of the garden variety of observational terms.

B: Could it not perhaps be *reduced*? Let N be a numinous predicate. And F and G observational predicates. Then we could say that if *a* is F, then *a* is N if and only if *a* is G.

A: You know as well as I that this doesn't eliminate N. You might just as well regard it as primitive.

B: Still, we would have a decisive test for numinosity if we could decide upon F and G.

A: We would not. If you put something claimed to be soluble in water which fails to dissolve, then this decisively tells against its being soluble in water. But here it very much would depend upon who was performing the test. You, lacking grace, might get a negative result. But the argument is silly. Numinosity is a manifest property.

B: I *could* get a decisive test providing N were allegedly manifest to somebody. I simply present him with *a*, and then *a* is N if he *says* it is. My only problem is to find a numinosity detector.

A: We call that trusting to authority. And for the bulk of mankind that is the best that can be done. We rely for our knowledge of the mysteries upon saints and prophets. Isn't that the gist of faith?

B: The gist of faith lies in believing that somebody knows what he is talking about. If that's what your faith is, I wish you joy. I prefer clarity. And I know that I haven't a clue as to what divinity means. For *me* there is a disposition on the part of certain entities to elicit "N" from those specially disposed to respond religiously to those entities. But "N" as yet means nothing more to me than that. How, for instance, am I to know whether or not they speak the truth when they say "N"?

A: Aren't you being rash in supposing them to be making an assertion, true or false, to begin with? It may simply be a kind of ejaculation, a wince upon being struck by holiness. Or better—it may be a contingent fact that they respond verbally at all. Instead they could fall prostrate. Or jump. Or clap their hands. And you, in their place, would perhaps not respond at all. Merely peer in puzzlement at their odd behavior or notice nothing out of the ordinary were they not present and reacting. That is, you would be lost and anaesthetic.

B: But could these inspired men not tell me afterward what they saw ("saw") when the reaction occurred?

A: That's just it. They *try*. But it is hard for them, and the words come out sounding paradoxical. For this reason I neglected to take up your point about canonical inconsistencies. Consider: "Grasping without hands, hasting without feet, he sees without eyes, he hears without ears." [10] It is the Self which is here referred to: "smaller than small, greater than great." The writer is not trying to be obscure. But this is the only way he can capture in words a concept which strains the rules of usage.

B: But what really does he *tell* me? Suppose I am told of a new theological discovery, namely that Brahma wears a hat. And then I am told that it is a divine hat and worn infinitely, since Brahma has neither head nor shape. In what sense then is a hat being worn? Why use *these* words? I am told that God exists but in a "different sense" of *exists*. Then if he doesn't exist (in the plain sense) why use *that* word? Or that God loves us—but in a wholly special sense of *love*. Or God is a circle whose center is everywhere and circumference nowhere. But this is then to have neither a center nor a circumference, and hence not to be a circle. One half of the description cancels out the other half. And what is left over but just noise?

A: But we after all speak in such wise even in normal circumstances. A man's wife dies after a long and painful illness. He says he is happy and unhappy at once. Does he contradict himself? I should think not. Or someone says he loves someone and he doesn't. Or that he can and he can't do something. Or that something is and isn't *F*. The conjuncts go together and don't cancel each other out. In a way, Cusanus's "definition" is a sophisticated stammer before the ineffable. The religious man's imagination is exercised in saying, by means of such expressions, what cannot

147

otherwise be said. For the object of his discourse cuts across what in ordinary experience are mutually exclusive categories. And hence is paradoxical.

B: I call that misplaced concreteness. Language may be paradoxical, but not the world.

A: On the contrary. The language is clear—providing we understand the mode of utterance appropriate here. It clearly depicts a mystery. And tries to draw our attention to the mysteriousness. That is the main use of religious language.

B: The issue between us looks clear now. But I cannot accept your analysis.

A: Only because of your faith that there are no dark spots.

B: But this is surely not a *religious* faith if you are right. For a religious faith is based upon believing in dark spots. That rules me out.

A: I should think it a dark spot indeed if the universe were such that it contained no dark spots. What a miracle it would be if the universe were comprehensible to reason! We are of one mind after all, you and I.

B: We are *not*.


## NOTES

1. Friedrich Nietzsche, *Human, All too Human,* I.
2. Albert Einstein, "Science, Philosophy, and Religion," reprinted in Phillip P. Wiener (ed.), *Readings in Philosophy of Science* (New York: Charles Scribner's Sons, 1953), p. 605.
3. John Wilson, *Language and Christian Belief* (London: The Macmillan Company, 1958), p. 64.
4. This point was made at the conference by Professor Sidney Morgenbesser.
5. Ludwig Wittgenstein, *Philosophical Investigations* (New York: The Macmillan Company), 271.
6. The argument here is particularly directed at the position of Averroes. See especially "A Decisive Discourse on the Delineation of the Relation between Religion and Philosophy," in *The Philosophy*

*and Theology of Averroes,* trans. Mohammad Jamil-ur-Rehman (Baroda: Gaiekwad's Oriental Series, 1929).

7. Emil Brunner, *Revelation and Reason,* tran. by Olive Wyon (Philadelphia: The Westminister Press, 1946), 294 ff.

8. Sören Kierkegaard, *Journals,* p. 633. Cited by S. R. Hopper in his essay, "Paradox" in *Handbook of Christian Theology* (New York: Meridian Books, Inc., 1958), p. 262.

9. Rudolph Otto, *The Idea of the Holy,* trans. J. W. Harvey (London: Cumberlege, 1950), p. 67. Cited in Ninian Smart, *Reasons and Faiths* (London: Routledge and Kegan Paul, 1958), p. 27. Smart's book ought to be quite widely read, not least of all because of his use of Oriental materials.

10. *Svetāśvatara Upanishad,* III, 19. trans. Max Müller, in Nicol Macnicol (ed.), *Hindu Scriptures* (Everyman's Library).

# ON FAITH

*by Ernest van den Haag, New York University*

In the Western tradition, it is probably most fitting to define religion minimally as belief in a God who is *sua sponte* involved in human destiny—almost but not altogether decisively (even Calvin admits: "Cadit homo Deo sic ordinante, sed suo vitio cadit.")—and has revealed itself to us to that extent. This being would be omniscient and omnipotent, or nearly so, and would have loving empathy with human fate and feeling—though his concern and providence "passeth all understanding," as does his ultimate nature. Nonetheless, he would do justice to us in the end and is "justly secret, but secretly just." Our traditional religion is at once explanatory and redemptory.

Scientists have long quarreled with religion. Essentially their argument is still threefold: 1) the religious hypothesis is not necessary and solves no problems (indeed, at best, it shifts problems further back); and 2) it involves great difficulties of its own for science; 3) God's existence is not demonstrated and, worse, not demonstrable according to ordinary canons of scientific proof. In addition, one might doubt, considering this world, that whatever God exists is omniscient, omnipotent, *and* benevolent. His wishes, moreover, which all religions ask us to follow, are in dispute—and no conclusive reasons for following them, if they were known, has been offered; it has not even been demonstrated that to do so would be fruitful in some intrinsic or extrinsic way.

How relevant are these objections? Demonstrability is required for scientific hypotheses, and demonstration is required for scientific conclusions. But since existence need not imply demonstrability (even though conversely demonstrability implies existence), why require demonstrability for nonscientific, for religious ideas as long as these do not aspire to become part of the body of science? Why reduce the universe to one dimension, the one that science—our senses and instruments aided by our reason—can grasp? Why make "truth" equivalent to "scientifically demonstrable at least in principle?" Do the scientists actually have the cosmos by the tail, or do they define the cosmos as that which they do have by the tail?

Nondemonstrability entails nonexistence only if we identify demonstrability with existence, but truth and demonstrability are not the same; at best their provisional identity is a methodological rule, a definition, useful only for one type of belief—science. It is misleading to extend such a rule without warning that one excludes from one's universe by definition that which is not science, i.e., religion *inter alia.*

That science qua science can do, and perhaps can do better, without religion is an argument against religion only if it be assumed that the world can, should, or must do without anything that science does not need or cannot use. But this seems an odd assumption. Religion need not allow its fate to be decided by the application of the canons of science. Since when is the value and the truth of poetic experience to be decided by its demonstrability according to scientific rules, or by its usefulness to physics? And yet do we not rightfully speak of the truth of art? Just as scientists in the past were right in not allowing scientific propositions to be judged by the application of theological canons, so now theologicians should reject the unwarranted extension of scientific jurisdiction to religion.

## De Fide Abscondita

Ultimately the beliefs of scientists rest on faith no less than those of the religious. The attempt to justify them—epistemology— is not in a much better state than the attempt to justify belief in

God. Both rest on faith—animal faith in the case of science, more human faith in the case of religion. The character and purpose of the scientist's belief, of course, differs from that of religious belief. It is precisely because of this difference that the claim of science to test religious faith by its own is no more valid than the claims of religious faith in the past to test science by religious principles. "God," Tolstoy said with magnificent ambiguity, "is my desire." That God may be no less than desire does not mean that he may be no more. That this "more," this fulfillment, cannot be demonstrated in ways that would satisfy the scientist means no more than that.

The scientist, to be sure, need not believe: he need only postulate fruitful hypotheses. Whereas, to be religious one must believe at the least 1) that God is and 2) that belief in God is fruitful. Does that mean more than that religion demands a faith that is psychologically—but not epistemologically—different from that of the scientists? For in religion the faith itself bears fruit; whereas in science faith in the postulates is not necessary for their postulation or for the harvest which is explained by them. Still they are postulated to explain, i.e., to be believed. Epistemologically, the postulation involves an act of faith—however provisional.

Religion certainly is not justified by saying science is not justified either. And within the religious framework—compounded of revelation, faith, and analytical reason as well as empirical observation—much remains to be done. But why do scientists and, even more, their philosophical apologists, so insistently demand that religion be justified scientifically, i.e., by acceptance first of the postulates of science—on faith—and then of its methods? Why is it inadvisable for religion to be based on its faith and advisable for science to be based on its?

It is true that the religious elaboration of faith does not actually carry us much beyond the brute fact that we require it. From a purely logical viewpoint, Occam's razor might indeed economize. But religion has functions beyond the logical. Logic at best is of help to these more important functions. The small logical economy that we can obtain by cutting ourselves off from religion would be

152

outweighed by all the nonlogical losses: aesthetic, social, and psychological. Indeed, the logical economy is small enough to be of interest only to a fanatic logic-miser who has made his parsimony into an article of faith.

## De Humana Servitute

When the scientist becomes a philosopher and tries to justify moral norms—even the simple one that scientists should pursue the truth, i.e., science (for the scientific definition of truth makes the terms nearly synonymous)—he appeals to an axiomatic faith that goes beyond his own pragmatic postulation. Even the fruitfulness for science of pursuing truth can be shown only by definition, and the moral value of fruitfulness only by the same regress which ends in revelation on the theological level. Further, a particular scientist might do better by faking his results, just as an individual may do better for himself at times by violating norms which he approves, justifies, or recognizes as socially useful and would not want others to violate. We may be "ethical" because of conditioning, but we can justify our ethic only by faith. When extended to include the unobservable—for the purpose of excluding it as nonexistent—scientific faith (besides being oxymoronic, for where it is faith it violates the defining rule of science) merely has the disadvantage of yielding no norms except the priority and the rules of truthfulness which define it. Thus, science as ersatz faith cannot even justify the activity scientists are engaged in or its rules. Though necessary, science can never be sufficient for norms, which however are necessary for it.

Since I do not see much immanent reason (as distinguished from motive) for doing good or even for upholding *"pacta sunt servanda"* or *"neminem laede,"* I think religion quite necessary, even if it be undemonstrable. *Do ut des* works in but a limited and insufficient way—however necessary it be. And I can discover no other justification (and motives ultimately require justification to remain effective) untainted by religious faith, be it howsoever hidden. Kindness, motivated aesthetically, or fairness and reasonableness, motivated ethically, are acquired characteristics all too replaceable by indifference or cruelty. The socially desirable qualities are more likely to be acquired and retained with superrational sanction. Ultimately there are not any rational ones. (I do not know what "supernatural" means.) Hence, the importance of finding transcendent reasons for goodness, i.e., for a value system that is socially viable. They may not suffice either but remain necessary. And they approach psychological sufficiency more than other justifications.

No doubt evil can be done in the name of religion as well as in any other. But reasons for doing evil are nearly infinite—any value system will do—and thus the religious reasons are hardly needed by the evildoer. And they are seldom used today. Isn't it an advantage, on the other hand, to have an appealing justification for good? For there aren't many, and religious belief seems to play an important role among those that still appeal to many people. To the religious, God, though symbolized by many things and the principle of all, is more than a principle and a symbol: God is that which is symbolized and that from which principles derive their raison d'être, as does life itself. Without God, life becomes meaningless; it loses its values; it becomes valueless. Many of the moral rules of the nonbeliever, too, derive from the faith which he no longer has. Will they be kept if that faith is altogether forsaken? And what will replace it and them? Whatever it is, it must be another faith. And I see no reason to believe that it will be a better, more effective, or more "scientific" one. The attempt, indeed, to make science into religion can but destroy its one actual article of faith: disinterested truthfulness. (I have tried elsewhere to indicate the futility of attempting to derive moral norms—rather than circumstances of application—from science, particularly psychology and the social sciences. See "Man as an Object of Science," *Science,* January 30, 1959.)

ERNEST VAN DEN HAAG

## De Ecclesia

If there is a God, organized religion, and political protection for it, might be useful but not indispensable. He could accomplish his purpose by other means. But if there were no God, organized religion would be indispensable: without God to make people believe in him and to prevent disaster, belief would still have to be maintained; without it, organized society based as it must be on a shared and justified ethos cannot continue. (At least it never has so far; and I see no substitute in sight that could be even remotely considered as an improvement.)

## De Deo Querendo

Jesus on the *via dolorosa* must have lost his faith. It would not have been much of a sacrifice for him had he walked that way to suffer and to die knowing it was all play-acting, knowing "I am God's son and will be resurrected." (It is because of this difficulty that the ambiguously "incarnated" nature of Jesus led to so many schisms.) No, he did not believe it, then. "My God, why hast Thou forsaken me?" This makes his a real and a great sacrifice: he died without hope of resurrection, in despair, to help us believe, to help us believe in redemption and thus to be redeemed by our belief.

Sacrifice is no argument for truth, but argument is irrelevant to faith in its beginning. Sacrifice is faith's supreme cause and ultimate effect. It is necessary if human society is to continue. And, in the long run, only religion does justify it.

## 19

# ON THE COGNITIVE IMPORT
# OF CERTAIN CONSCIOUS STATES

by *George Nakhnikian*, *Wayne State University*


Many people who suppose that religious beliefs are not capricious or arbitrary, that they are true—but not because of anything the sciences have to say about the world—take it for granted that some of our most poignant attitudes, responses, feelings and "experiences" either intimate or reveal outright just those vital truths which religion teaches. This epistemological assumption must be distinguished from another, a genetic hypothesis, according to which the feelings in question are the *source* of the religious spirit, even in those who reject all religious doctrines and illusions. The genetic hypothesis is for the psychologists to appraise. Freud provides an appraisal in Ch. 1 of *Civilization and its Discontents*. The epistemological thesis, on the other hand, requires philosophical appraisal, and it is my present purpose to provide one. The points I am about to make are obvious, and, I believe, matters of agreement among most philosophers. But they may be worth rehearsing for the benefit of those whose religious and theological talk seems to presuppose the epistemological assumption I am about to criticize.

The epistemological assumption is really two assumptions. There is first the unspoken claim that the feelings, responses, and the like are *grounds* for *defending* the truth of religious convictions. The second, which is restricted to the claims of the mystic, assumes that the feelings and responses *reveal* the truths of religion. In order to appraise these claims we need to locate and to elucidate the character of the feelings, attitudes, and the like mentioned by them.

That there are certain peculiarly poignant feelings, attitudes, responses, and "experiences" should be granted at the outset. Imagine a man contemplating the vast heavens on a starry night. The majesty, beauty, and immensity of the starlit night are such as to induce in the beholder awe, wonder, reverence, and even a sense of cosmic piety. The majesty, beauty, and immensity are supervenient properties, very much like goodness. Their attribution to the heavens is supported by pointing to the observable features of the panorama spread overhead. And the panorama's being awesome, wonderful, and capable of inspiring reverence is supervenient upon its beauty, majesty, and immensity. So far we have no reason to suppose that these attributes and their correlative moods, attitudes, and responses are singularly "religious." They are much more directly to be construed as aesthetic. The moods, attitudes, and responses can be those of an infidel, and he can correctly make the corresponding attributions to the panorama.

Their relevance to religion is a function of certain conceptual facts. "Awe," "wonder," and "reverence" are closely interrelated concepts. Let us concentrate on "awe." The primary contexts in which this word is used are in relation to people. We stand in awe of this or that man. He inspires awe because he is exceptionally stern, dedicated, purposeful, pure. We must think such things of a man in order to be awed by him. We may, of course, find out that he is not what we had believed him to be. But it is still true that before we knew the facts, we did feel awe. The point of importance is that having certain beliefs about a man is a logically necessary condition of our standing in awe of him. As the starry heavens are not a person, our awe of them is not in all respects identical with our standing in awe in the primary sense. Is the word "awe" in these two occurrences a mere homonym, or is there some principle of similarity in spite of the crucial difference? I think there is a principle of similarity. The starry heavens are austere and pure, impersonally austere and impersonally pure, to be sure, but the austerity of the heavens is more like the austerity of a man than either like the color of a rainbow or the levity of a fool. Perhaps it is this similarity that leads certain religions to anthropomorphize nature or aspects of nature and to worship the anthropomorphized

157

entity. The illegitimacy of this procedure is evident, if the above conceptual points are granted. The mistake consists of being misled by a conceptual similarity into overlooking a conceptual difference.

The situation is different with respect to the so-called "high" religions, such as the prophetic religions of the Judaeo-Christian sects. Leaving aside the special problems involved in the Christian belief in the divinity of Jesus, in the main, the Judaeo-Christian tradition distinguishes the proper object of religious awe from nature or any aspect of nature. The basic religious conviction here is that God is immaterial—a transcendent personality, the creator, sustainer, law giver, and judge of creation. How can this conviction be defended as being a true belief on the strength of such facts as the awe felt by the beholder of the starry heavens? There is obviously no problem about how it is possible to stand in awe of God if one already believes in God. Nor are we concerned with the psychological question as to whether or not such facts as feeling awe under the starry heavens induce the religious belief. The epistemological question is: given that a man feels this awe, and given that he believes in God, does the awe provide adequate grounds for defending the truth of the belief? Let us be perfectly clear as to the issues. Those whom I have in mind do not mean to say that religion is not capricious or arbitrary in the weak sense. If I profess a certain religion within a religious community, my beliefs will be neither arbitrary nor capricious insofar as I believe as a member of the religious community. But this is a weak sense of being neither arbitrary nor capricious. That which is neither arbitrary nor capricious by these standards may yet be false. The question then is this: is a feeling of awe under the starry heavens a ground for holding that the belief in God is true?

The answer is negative if the conceptual facts are such as we have so far described. But there are additional data. He who feels awe under the starry heavens may also feel a sort of gratitude or thankfulness. These would not be ordinary gratitude or thankfulness. I shall call them "cosmic gratitude" and "cosmic thankfulness." Between them and their ordinary counterparts there are similarities and differences. I can be grateful only if I believe that someone has done me a favor, and my gratitude is to that person. But cosmic gratitude cannot be to a person. No one in his right mind believes that a human being made the heavens for our gratification. Again, imagine a man who is suddenly struck by the sheer brute contingency of his ever having been born. He too might feel cosmic gratitude. What he feels cannot be directed toward any person. No one who has thought about it can be grateful (in the ordinary sense) to his parents for bringing *him* into the world, because his parents could only bring *a baby* into the world. They could not have had *him* in mind when they conceived a child. The conceptual point about gratitude and thankfulness is this: they presuppose a belief that someone has done us a favor, a kindness, a good turn, while cosmic gratitude and thankfulness may arise in the absence of such a belief. An atheist cannot (logically) be grateful if he does not believe that someone has done him a good turn, but the same atheist can have a feeling of cosmic thankfulness. The feeling of cosmic thankfulness is like the feeling of thankfulness minus the belief that someone has done us a good turn. In place of that belief there is an inclination to grant that if anything existed to bring about this (the starry heavens, my birth) in a providential way, it would be majestic enough to be the fitting recipient of my cosmic gratitude and thankfulness.

Psychologically, it is quite possible that a man who feels cosmic thankfulness may entertain the hypothesis that there is something, a superhuman personality, toward whom this thankfulness is properly directed. But the fact that I feel cosmic thankfulness does not imply that such a superhuman personality exists. Nor can the natural awe we feel under the starry heavens serve as a logically adequate ground for supposing that the natural feeling is evidence for the reality of a superhuman personality having the attributes necessary to merit cosmic awe. Thus, neither the feeling of cosmic awe nor the feeling of cosmic gratitude by themselves provide adequate grounds for supposing that the belief in God is true. And, because they fail for identical reasons, to suppose that they strengthen one another is like supposing that buying two copies of the same edition of a newspaper strengthens the probability of a

159

news item (the example is Wittgenstein's but the application is different).

The logic of the situation is very much like the one mapped out by Hume in the *Dialogues on Natural Religion*. Hume points out that there is no inconsistency in the argument from design. The argument, however, is weak, because the analogy on which it is based is weak. It is *conceivable* that the universe is the creation of a supreme intelligence. But the argument from design does not support the conclusion that the hypothesis is probable. Similarly, it is conceivable that our feelings of cosmic thankfulness and cosmic awe have a fitting recipient, but the mere fact of our having the feelings does not support the probability of the hypothesis. Again, following Hume's strategy, suppose we grant that the conceivability of the hypothesis alone is enough to hold that the belief in the truth of the hypothesis is not bizarre. But, just as in the case of the argument from design the hypothesis of a providential designer is not the only one which will explain the facts, so in the case of feeling cosmic thankfulness and cosmic awe, the hypothesis that there is a fitting recipient of the feelings is not the only one that will explain their occurrence. There are plausible explanations of how the design argument can take hold of the imagination, as there are plausible explanations of how the cosmic feelings arise under perfectly natural conditions. We are, therefore, not even in the position of having to grant that the religious hypotheses are the only ones that enable us to make sense of the force of the design argument on the one hand and of the occurrence of the cosmic feelings on the other. The force of the design argument lies in failing to take note of the weakness of the root analogies. The occurrence of the cosmic feelings can be explained in more than one plausible way. Freud's is one way.

A less controversial way is simply to describe in a common-sensical way what goes on in a specific context. When one of my daughters was a year and a half old, she just missed being killed by a car. It was on a Sunday. One of our good but talkative friends had brought her little boy to play with the children while she visited with us. We always kept the porch screen door locked in those days to make sure that the baby didn't walk out on the street. We were in the kitchen listening to the incessant chatter of our friend while the children played upstairs. Suddenly I had one of those sinking feelings that parents get when the children are unusually quiet. I rushed around looking for the baby. Nobody knew where she was. In a mild panic I rushed to the porch. The screen door was ajar. It had been left unlocked. At that moment I saw a neighbor walking to our front steps. She had the child in her arms. I must have looked badly frightened because she began at once to reassure me that the baby was perfectly safe. The neighbor described what had happened. The child was standing in the middle of the street looking up at the house tops. A car driven by elderly people had come to a stop just in front of her. Apparently they were waiting for her to get out of the way. In the meantime, another car, driven by some impatient youngsters, had come up behind the first car. The youngsters could not see the baby, so they impatiently zoomed around the first car. The baby stood still while this was going on. If she had taken two steps in the wrong direction at a certain moment, she would have been killed instantly.

I took the child in my arms. She was calm and happy, her usual self. She had no idea of what had happened. I thanked our neighbor for her kindness. But what I felt at that moment was a vast thankfulness which I could not appropriately express to any human being. So much could have gone so tragically wrong, yet the fact that nothing did go wrong was just plain luck. Had I retained the religion of my fathers, I should have thanked God in my heart, I should have gone to the nearest Armenian church to light a candle before the image of a saint, and I should have given the priest some money for the poor. But I could not do any of these things without feeling silly. I believe that even if I had not been brought up as a Christian, I would have felt the cosmic thankfulness which I have just described. It seems to me that to love one's child is to be disposed to feel this way on occasions such as the one I have been describing.

Not only is it a fact of experience that such feelings occur naturally, but it is also a fact that the sorts of conscious states I have been calling "cosmic" are peculiarly poignant and "vectorial";

they create in those who are in those states a need to find symbols adequate for externalizing them. One natural way of externalizing them is to use religious symbols referentially, i.e., as symbols which have appropriate external referents. This is what religious people do. The rest of us find other means of externalizing the inner states. Ever since the day I have recalled, I have felt a special tenderness for my child. When I see her sitting at the family table at mealtime, or when she comes home from school, I often reach over to stroke her hair, as if to say, "Thank you for being here." Also, what I am doing now, telling the story, is a way of externalizing what I feel. And the thought that someday she may read this is also a part of the process of externalizing.

The epistemological assumption, then, to the effect that certain special conscious states are grounds for defending the truth of religious convictions, though consistent, is not compelling. Nor can it gain in plausibility on the grounds that unless it were true we could give no adequate account of how the poignant and "vectorial" inner states can find adequate expression.

The second formulation, according to which these inner states *reveal* the truths of religion fares no better. First, it is a misuse of language (in the sense that no one could make out what was being said) to say that to *feel* cosmic awe is to *feel* God. Conceptually, God is not an inner state. Mystics talk this way. But we can make no sense of what they mean. Secondly, it makes sense to say that our eyes reveal the colors, shapes, and locations of the objects surrounding us. But it makes no sense to say that our eyes reveal to us providential design. Colors, shapes, and locations are conceptually distinguishable from providential design. Moreover, providential design, if it is a property of the world at all, must be a supervenient property. Its attribution presupposes that certain principles or criteria are satisfied. It is a higher order property than the properties revealed to us by observation. We cannot simply by looking at the world see that it is "finite." To "see" it as "finite" is already to "look" at it from the religious perspective. But, you will say, the mystic does not invoke his senses to support his claims. He reports his inner states as being the "experience" of God. However, he conveys this "experience" to us by saying such things as that he is in the presence of ultimate reality, an incomprehensible notion. Or he says that he is in the presence of a superhuman personality. He fills in details of the following sort, that he feels as he would be feeling in the presence of a person, only *this* presence is no ordinary presence. He is in ecstasy before this presence, an ecstasy which no ordinary human confrontation produces. But surely these reports do not entail or render it probable that there is something answering to the mystic's *interpretation* of his "experience." And to speak of his claim as an interpretation is not to beg any issue, for it is only by construing his claim as an interpretation that *we* can talk intelligibly. It has been suggested that perhaps the mystic's difficulties of communication stem from the fact that there is no language adequate for expressing what he means. But every model that we can provide as an illustration presupposes the possibility of making conceptual distinctions. But the mystic seems to be saying that the reality he "experiences" is in principle incapable of being conceptualized. This implies the logical impossibility of his *describing* to us *what* he thinks is revealed in the mystical state. This has two immediate consequences. One is that the mystical "experience" cannot reveal intelligible and communicable religious beliefs. The other is that the mystic's claims can have no epistemological validity. For the incommunicable residue, which is the heart of the matter from the mystic's point of view, cannot be discussed at all. "What we can't say, we can't say, and we can't whistle it either." We cannot philosophize about what we cannot say. This, in the final analysis, is the only philosophical statement we can make about it.

I take it as established, then, that the attempt to defend the truth of religious convictions by appeal to certain special conscious states is bound to fail. But there is another, and allowable, use which profounder strains in the Western religious traditions make of these conscious states. The *locus classicus* is the Book of Job. There the terrible vicissitudes that flesh is heir to are dramatically rehearsed. Cosmic thankfulness, cosmic optimism, and the other "cosmic" conscious states have their darker counterparts. Job expresses a

163

sense of cosmic despair, of cosmic isolation, something like what Christ felt on the cross when he said "My God, My God, why hast Thou forsaken me?" The evil in the world is no less present than the grandeur and majesty of things. In spite of it all, Job cannot but hope and have faith. Except for its Hollywood ending, which, in my opinion, detracts from the dramatic force of this great and truthful work of art, the Book of Job emphasizes Western religion's teaching that the sense of cosmic thankfulness and cosmic security ought to overcome the sense of cosmic despair and abandonment. From the religious point of view, this moral imperative cannot be proved, either with the help of science, or common sense, or by appeal to the special conscious states we have been examining. The moral imperative is ultimately rooted in the *faith* that the consolatory cosmic feelings are profounder revelations of the cosmic order than their dark and desperate counterparts. Religion expresses this faith in the conviction that we are all in the hands of a loving providence. Inasmuch as this position makes no intellectually indefensible cognitive claims, and inasmuch as, for people conditioned in a certain way, this is the only way in which they can face life constructively, the rest of us are bound to respect the faith which sustains their lives, even though we cannot share it, even though we respond to the demands of human existence in our own different ways.

# 20

# FAITH

*by Richard Taylor, Brown University*

"Our most holy religion," David Hume said, "is founded on *faith,* not on reason." (All quotations are from the last two paragraphs of Hume's essay "Of Miracles.") He did not then conclude that it ought, therefore, to be rejected by reasonable men. On the contrary, he suggests that rational evaluation has no proper place in this realm to begin with, that a religious man need not feel in the least compelled to put his religion "to such a trial as it is, by no means, fitted to endure," and he brands as "dangerous friends or disguised enemies" of religion those "who have undertaken to defend it by the principles of human reason."

I want to defend Hume's suggestion, and go a bit farther by eliciting some things that seem uniquely characteristic of *Christian* faith, in order to show what it has, and what it has not, in common with other things to which it is often compared. I limited myself to Christian faith, because I know rather little of any other, and faith is, with love and hope, supposed to be a uniquely Christian virtue.

## Faith and Reason

Faith is not reason, else religion would be, along with logic and metaphysics, a part of philosophy, which it assuredly is not. Nor is faith belief resting on scientific or historical inquiry, else religion would be part of the corpus of human knowledge, which it clearly is not. More than that, it seems evident that by the normal, common-sense criteria of what is reasonable, the content of Christian faith is *un*reasonable. This, I believe, should be the starting point, the *datum,* of any discussion of faith and reason. It is, for instance, an essential content of the Christian faith that, at a certain quite recent time, God became man, dwelt among us in the person of a humble servant, and then, for a sacred purpose, died, to live again. Now, apologetics usually addresses itself to the *details* of this story, to show that they are not inherently incredible, but this is to miss the point. It is indeed *possible* to believe it, and in the strict sense the story is credible. Millions of people do most deeply and firmly believe it. But even the barest statement of the content of that belief makes it manifest that it does not and, I think, could not, ever result from rational inquiry. "Mere reason," Hume said, "is insufficient to convince us of its veracity." The Christian begins the recital of his faith with the words, "I believe," and it would be an utter distortion to construe this as anything like "I have inquired, and found it reasonable to conclude." If there were a man who could say that in honesty, as I think there is not, then he would, in a clear and ordinary sense, believe, but he would have no religious faith whatsoever, and his beliefs themselves would be robbed of what would make them religious.

Now if this essential and (it seems to me) obvious unreasonableness of Christian belief could be recognized at the outset of any discussion of religion, involving rationalists on the one hand and believers on the other, we would be spared the tiresome attack and apologetics upon which nothing ultimately turns, the believer would be spared what is, in fact, an uncalled-for task of reducing his faith to reason or science, which can, as Hume noted, result only in "exposing" it as neither, and the rationalist would be granted his main point, not as a conclusion triumphantly extracted, but as a datum too obvious to labor.

## Faith and Certainty

Why, then, does a devout Christian embrace these beliefs? Now this very question, on the lips of a philosopher, is wrongly expressed, for he invariably intends it as a request for reasons, as a means of putting the beliefs to that unfair "trial" of which Hume spoke. Yet there is a clear and definite answer to this question, which has the merit of being true and evident to anyone who has known intimately those who dwell in the atmosphere of faith. The reason the Christian believes that story around which his whole life turns is, simply, that he cannot help it. If he is trapped into eliciting grounds for it, they are grounds given after the fact of conviction. Within "the circle of faith," as one symposiast observed, the question whether on the evidence one *ought* to believe "does not arise." One neither seeks nor needs grounds for the acceptance of what he cannot help believing. "Whoever is moved by *faith* to assent," Hume wrote, "is conscious of a continued miracle in his own person, which subverts all the principles of his understanding, and gives him a determination to believe. . . ." It is this fact of faith which drives philosophers to such exasperation, in the face of which the believer is nonetheless so utterly unmoved.

The believer sees his life as a gift of God, the world as the creation of God, his own purposes, insofar as they are noble, as the purposes of God, and history as exhibiting a divine plan, made known to him through the Christian story. He sees things this way, just because they do seem so, and he cannot help it. This is why, for him, faith is so "easy," and secular arguments to the contrary so beside the point. No one seeks evidence for that of which he is entirely convinced, or regards as relevant what seems to others to cast doubt. The believer is like a child who recoils from danger, as exhibited, for instance, in what he for the first time sees as a fierce animal; the child has no difficultly *believing* he is in peril, just because he cannot help believing it, yet his belief results not at all from induction based on past experience with fierce animals, and no reassurances, garnered from *our* past experience, relieve his terror at all.

## Some Confusions

If this is what religious faith essentially is—if, as a believer might poetically but, I think, correctly describe it, faith is an involuntary conviction, often regarded as a "gift," on the part of one who has voluntarily opened his mind and heart to receive it—then certain common misunderstandings can be removed.

In the first place, faith should never be likened to an *assumption,* such as the scientist's assumption of the uniformity of nature, or what not. An assumption is an intellectual device for furthering inquiry. It need not be a conviction nor, indeed, even a belief. But a half-hearted faith is no religious faith. Faith thus has that much, at least, in common with knowledge, that it is a *conviction,* and its subjective state is *certainty.* One thus wholly distorts faith if he represents the believer as just "taking" certain things "on faith," and then reasons, like a philosopher, from these beginnings, as though what were thus "taken" could, like an assumption, be rejected at will.

Again, it is a misunderstanding to represent faith as "mere tenacity." Tenacity consists in stubbornly clinging to what one hopes, but of which one is not fully convinced. The child who is instantly convinced of danger in the presence of an animal is not being tenacious or stubborn, even in the face of verbal reassurances, and no more is the Christian whose acts are moved by faith. The believer does not so much *shun* evidence as something that might *shake* his faith, but rather regards it as not to the point. In this he may appear to philosophers to be mistaken, but only if one supposes, as he need not, that one should hold only such beliefs as are rational.

Again, it is misleading to refer to any set of propositions, such as those embodied in a creed, as being this or that person's "faith."

168

Concerning that content of belief in which one is convinced by faith, it is logically (though I think not otherwise) possible that one might be convinced by evidence, in which case it would have no more to do with faith or religion than do the statements in a newspaper. This observation has this practical importance, that it is quite possible—in fact, common—for the faith of different believers to be one and the same, despite creedal differences.

And finally, both "faith" (or "fideism") and "reason" (or "rationalism") can be, and often are, used as pejorative terms, and as terms of commendation. Which side one takes here is arbitrary, for there is no non-question-begging way of deciding. A rationalist can perhaps find reasons for being a rationalist, though this is doubtful; but in any case it would betray a basic misunderstanding to expect a fideist to do likewise. This is brought out quite clearly by the direction that discussions of religion usually take. A philosophical teacher will often, for instance, labor long to persuade his audience that the content of Christian faith is unreasonable, which is a shamefully easy task for him, unworthy of his learning. Then suddenly, the underlying assumption comes to light that Christian beliefs ought, therefore, to be abandoned by rational people! A religious hearer of this discourse might well reply that, religion being unreasonable but nonetheless manifestly worthy of belief, we should conclude with Hume that reason, in this realm at least, ought to be rejected. Now, one can decide *that* issue by any light that is granted him, but it is worth stressing that the believer's position on it is just exactly as good, and just as bad, as the rational sceptic's.

## 21

# ON THEOLOGICAL DEFINITION
*by Linwood Urban, Swarthmore College*

Religious writers and theologians are often accused of conceptual confusion on the grounds that they do not use words in the ordinary way. If this criticism meant only that theologians, or that religious language, stipulated different meanings for words used otherwise in ordinary discourse, it would not be a very severe censure. If differences in stipulation were all that separated religious language from ordinary language, it would be possible to provide a glossary of the special uses. Were a glossary provided, an individual might still be confused about the meaning of theological terms, but in principle he need not be. However, the point of the criticism does not lie in differences of stipulation, but rather in the fact that the religious writer intends to use some words with their ordinary meanings and yet does not employ the ordinary criteria whereby the correct uses of these words are established. When the theologian says that God is a person or is personal, he says that he means that God is like a human person. However, when he is asked to apply the ordinary tests by which we establish whether an object is a human being or not, he declines to do so. Under ordinary circumstances, we require that the object in question be a psychophysical organism which is capable of intelligent action and a high degree of abstraction. Yet the theologian insists that these criteria are not applicable to God because God is a Spirit. Again, when the theologian is asked to specify the meaning of the word faith, he sometimes says that faith is like the trust which men have in their doctors. "Trust," as often used, is a complex word, denoting not only a particular kind of feeling or attitude, but also a belief in the trustworthiness of the object of trust. However, when the theologian is asked to justify his use of "trust" as we ordinarily do—the person trusted acts consistently and is, therefore, reliable—he often declines to do so, saying instead that God's actions are not to be subjected to any yardstick of man. Since religious writers appear to employ different sets of criteria from the ordinary ones for testing their use of words, analytical philosophers often insist that these words do not have their usual meaning. However, this conclusion the theologian will not admit. Under these circumstances analytical philosophers conclude that many religious writers are confused.

Before we proceed further we must clearly state the question: Has the religious writer the right to claim that he is using words in their proper senses while employing alternative sets of criteria for justifying their uses? Two other related questions arise which are often confused with the first: Has the religious writer succeeded in setting forth his criteria in a sufficiently unambiguous fashion? And, has he shown that his words refer to something in the external world and not simply to states of mind and psychological events? These last are very important problems, and I believe that the real issues between the religious writer and the analytical philosopher lie here. If an analytical philosopher holds that much of theological discourse is meaningless because it fails to provide the necessary criteria and because it fails to establish nonmental references for its words, I would dispute his conclusion. But these are very different criticisms from the claim that the theologian is confused or that he gives improper meanings to his words. I shall not deal with the latter two criticisms in this paper, but shall restrict myself to showing that the religious writer has the right to assert that he is using words in their proper senses while employing alternative sets of criteria for justifying their uses.

A. Can words have the same meaning but have more than one set of criteria for justifying their usage? In one instance at least, the answer to this question is certainly yes. First-person and third-person statements about pain do not imply different meanings of the word pain no matter how different the ways of verifying them. When I say that I have a pain in my head, I justify this statement

171

to myself and others on the grounds that I feel a pain in my head. But when I say that George has a pain in his head, I justify this statement by reference to George's physical behavior. He grasps his head, he utters low moans, or he may take an aspirin. He may also say that he has a pain in his head. I infer that George has a pain in his head because I have noticed that when I have a pain in my head I often act as George does. To justify the statement that George has a pain, I make a causal inference, which I do not do in my own case. I do not infer from my own actions that I must be feeling a pain; I simply report what I feel. On the basis of the difference in the method of testing the application of the word pain, some philosophers conclude that I do not mean the same thing by the word pain in the two instances. In the one case, I mean that I feel a pain; in the other case, I mean that George acts in a certain way. However, this conclusion is extremely odd; for when I say that George is in pain, I do not mean that he is behaving in a certain way, but that he has a pain like the ones which I sometimes have. To put the matter another way, I am arguing that "pain" has the same meaning in both first-person and third-person statements, but that the evidence for concluding that I have a pain and that George has a pain are of different orders. I am arguing that only the criteria necessary for a simple recognition of pain ought to be considered part of its meaning. Inductive inferences used to give evidence for pain ought not to be considered part of its meaning.

B. Furthermore, casual inferences are not of the same status as simple recognition because they will not be able to justify the use of a word under all possible circumstances. Suppose we ask someone to justify his use of the word yellow. He would certainly satisfy us were he to point to yellow objects. He would also satisfy us if he reported that yellow was the color which appeared between green and orange in the spectrum, unless of course we had some doubts that he knew what the spectrum was. But in another world yellow might not appear between green and orange in the spectrum, but between violet and indigo. In that world, were he to point to yellow objects he would still satisfy us, but he would not satisfy us were he to report that yellow appeared between green and orange in the spectrum. The use of a particular causal inference to justify the use of a word depends upon the particular character of the empirical world in which the subject happens to be and is, therefore, subordinate to simple recognition. But we must argue this point with more examples. Let us do so with the word faith in theological discourse.

C. It is sometimes argued that every "believing in" presupposes a "believing that." This statement usually means that we must believe something about an object of trust in order to justify the use of "trust" in the ordinary manner. We must at least believe that the object exists. Hence it is argued that, when a religious writer uses the term faith to denote trust as an attitude or feeling apart from and not involving a "believing that," he is not only stipulating an unusual meaning for "faith" by limiting it to trust, but he does not even use "trust" in the ordinary way. The manner in which trust is thought to presuppose "belief that" is illustrated by a quotation from Erik Erikson: "The infant's first social achievement, then, is his willingness to let the mother out of sight without undue anxiety or rage, because she has become an inner certainty as well as an outer predictability." [1] It may well be that in our world "outer predictability" usually precedes "inner certainty." Thus it appears plausible to assume that, before we are ready to believe a man who professes trust for his doctor, we would want to know whether he thinks him a skilled practitioner. Were he to doubt seriously his doctor's ability, some would conclude that he was a liar, or a madman, or did not understand the meaning of "trust." Here we are not interested in whether he is a liar or a madman, but whether he is justified in saying that he trusts his doctor. We are not concerned with whether or not he is justified in trusting his doctor, but whether he is using "trust" properly.

I believe it proper to restrict the meaning of "trust" to "inner certainty" exclusive of "outer predictability." "Inner certainty," as attitude or feeling of trusting, can be established by simple recognition; "outer predictability" demands for its justification inductive inferences. We have already argued that for establishing the proper

173

uses of "pain" and "yellow" causal inferences are not of the same status as simple recognition. The same is also true for "trust." In another world "belief that" need not precede "belief in." It might be that only the sight of his mother was a sufficient condition for stimulating the infant's trust. It might also be that because the infant trusted his mother he was emotionally capable of noticing that she was fairly consistent in her actions. Furthermore, we might remove the cognitive element altogether. We might think of a world in which the relationship between inner certainty and outer predictability was the same as in the previous example, but in which the cause of one's trust was a structure of the brain. In such a world, it would not be possible to justify one's use of the word trust by reference to a prior observation because trust would be the necessary precondition for all observations. In such a world, it would also be improper to demand an object of trust or a belief that the object exists, because the feeling of trust is a necessary precondition for the discrimination of objects and for any beliefs whatever. At the same time, it would always be proper to assert that we were using the word trust as inner certainty in such a way that its proper use would be established by simple recognition.

D. I have urged this example because I believe that it gives us a different but important reason for separating the meaning of a word from inductive inferences employed to justify its use. Someday the theory of child development upon which Mr. Erikson's views are based may be discarded in favor of the view which I have suggested for another world. If this should happen, and at the same time "trust" be defined in such a way that it necessitates a "believing that," we should not be able to say that we trusted anyone. We could not do so because the necessary precondition for the correct use of trust would be lacking. It might be more convenient to define trust in such a way as to make it possible to express this new state of affairs without a new terminology or a redefinition of the word trust. The threat of new definitions may not be a serious one for psychology, but it is a different matter for religious discourse. In twentieth-century religious writing there is no universally accepted view concerning the relationship between trusting and "believing that." It is, therefore, less confusing to be able to state different theories with the same words and with the same meanings than to employ a new set of terms or a new set of definitions for each theory. In his paper Professor Niebuhr has shown that because of the multiplicity of uses of "faith" we cannot restrict its use sufficiently; but we can do so with the various synonyms for faith: trust, vision, believing that, etc. Part of the value of his paper is that it points out the need for such a vocabulary.

E. Let us take one more example. Martin Buber has been accused of conceptual confusion because he has stated that we can have an immediate awareness of God in an I-Thou relationship which has no element of I-it in it. By I-Thou Buber means roughly our relationship to persons; by I-it, our experience of things. We use things, but in using them we do not meet them in a personal encounter. We can, of course, treat people like things, but sometimes we meet them as other persons like ourselves. In this encounter there is an element of mutuality, of interaction, of what he calls dialogue, which is not an element of our experience of things in a use relationship. In a personal encounter, Buber believes, there need be no element of I-it. (Professor Buber has said that we can have I-Thou relationships with trees. This remark appears to vitiate the original distinction between I-Thou and I-it. I shall not deal with this problem here, since the issue is too complex to be treated in a short paper.)

It has sometimes been objected that, when we try to decide whether we have established an I-Thou relationship with another human being, we take our I-it experience of him into account. If he has shifty eyes, if he gives other indications by his actions that he does not trust us, we would use this evidence to conclude that we had not entered into an I-Thou relationship no matter what we might feel. We would take these actions as inductive evidence that the required mutuality had not been established. Clearly the religious philosopher wants to say that the I-Thou relationship to ordinary people is analogous to the I-Thou relationship with God. However, if it is true that the I-Thou of the personal encounter with other people depends for its verification on I-it experience, the

175

religious writer is equivocating when he asserts that he is still using I-Thou in the same way to apply to a relationship with God which has no element of I-it in it. It must have a different meaning because a different way of justifying its use is presupposed.

Many of the same issues of the two previous examples are present here, but the solution is somewhat different. There seemed to be no reason to deny that the proper use of the words pain and trust can be established at least in first-person statements by a simple recognition. The problem here is whether there are examples of simple recognition of I-Thou relationships which do not involve inferences from bodily behavior. Buber claims that there are. To make this claim is not to be guilty of conceptual confusion, because in another world it might be as Buber describes it. In another world we might be able to meet people in the way in which the mystic claims he meets God, or the way in which the extreme Realists claimed that we came to know the supposedly self-subsisting universals—by a purely mental cognition without the aid of any empirical experience. Even if this is a theoretical possibility, the more important issue is whether Buber can give any examples in this world where all inferences from bodily behavior are irrelevant.

F. Thus the analytical philosopher would say that this discussion has missed the point. He might admit that we have shown how the concept of pain is derived or how the I-Thou concept is to be formulated but say that we failed to show that there is, in fact, any alternative method to justify their uses from the ordinary ones. If these methods could be developed, he might be willing to agree that one particular causal inference is not to be preferred to another, providing that each is sufficiently reliable. In order to delineate this issue more exactly let us take another example. Let us consider the application of the word poison in the statement: This apple has poison in it. Let us further assume that the apple is impregnated with cyanide crystals. To one sufficiently trained, simple recognition would be adequate. He might cut the apple open and observe the crystals under a microscope. On the other hand, he might taste the apple. Or he might subject the apple to chemical analysis, or observe the behavior of an animal who had eaten some of the apple. These latter two methods involve causal inference. In other worlds, where the natural laws were different from our own, neither of these two methods might be efficacious; yet were this true, we would still conclude that the apple was poisoned with cyanide on the basis of the first test. However, even in this world, since each of these inferences does, in fact, have a high degree of accuracy, there is no reason to give one priority over the other.

G. Let us apply this conclusion to the justification of the use of "trust." If the argument up to this point is valid, the proper meaning of "trust" is a feeling of confidence. It may be that in this world there is no undifferentiated confidence, so that our trust is always in objects. Even Mary Baker Eddy, who is reported to have said, "I accept the universe," made it perfectly clear that certain aspects of our experience, pain and evil, were not possible objects of trust because they were illusions. Thus it is plausible to argue that since we have objects of trust, we must at least believe that the objects exist. If we want to know whether or not the adjective "trusting" is properly applied to a particular person's attitude, we can at least invalidate it if he does not believe that his objects of trust exist. But even in this world there are other inferences which will invalidate the application of "trusting" or "confident" to a particular person's attitude. We can observe the particular person's behavior. The behavior of the confident person can be distinguished from that of the fearful or timid person. Here again there seems to be no reason to give priority to one of these inferences rather than the other.

There is, then, no reason to demand that "believing that" be a particular requirement for even third-person statements about trust. Thus Kierkegaard uses the concept of trust properly when he says that the question of God's existence is irrelevant to the justification of faith in God. He has, of course, to justify the attitude of trusting confidence in spite of his refusal to consider any evidence which might bear on God's existence. He justifies the kind of faith which eschews evidence of the existence of God by holding that this kind of faith is admirable. I do not believe this kind of faith to be admirable. I fear the consequences of such faith. But Kierkegaard is not using "faith" improperly if it denotes only an attitude or feeling of confidence.

H. Furthermore, we can use much the same argument regarding statements about pain. Were telepathy an established fact, there would be available to us an alternative inductive inference for establishing the correct use of third-person statements about pain. If this were the case, in order for me to assert that George is in pain, I need only states of consciousness in which I am aware of George absent from me, present states of consciousness in which pain is associated with awareness of George, and present states in which I do not think about George at all and in which there is no pain. Under these circumstances there would be no reason to associate this pain with me or with every consciousness of George, but with George himself at this particular time. If it is still objected that I could not know that it was George having the pain until I had met George face to face, this objection would not hold. If I had had a telepathic consciousness of George before I met him face to face, I would be merely establishing which telepathic consciousness belonged with which body.

Here again its seems that we would be ill-advised to define our terms in such a way as to preclude alternative methods of justification. The more important question concerns whether telepathy of sufficient magnitude for this kind of inference is a fact or not.

I. Let us next consider Buber's statements about the relationship between I-Thou and I-it. Buber asserts that there is an alternative method for establishing the use of I-Thou. What he attempts to show is that the consciousness of an I-Thou relationship is prior to and necessary for forming the concept of I-it. He attempts to do so on the grounds that the element of trust which is a part of the I-Thou relationship is a necessary precondition for any knowledge whatever. Without this I-Thou, we could not take the world sufficiently into our consciousness to observe its regularity. There must therefore be an I-Thou consciousness which is simply recognized and not inferred. The interesting question is: Can he

178

establish this hypothesis? I do not find his arguments convincing. But to say so does not mean that he is guilty of conceptual confusion, but that he has failed to make his point.

J. Religious writers of stature generally attempt to establish alternative methods of justifying the use of words where required by their systems. The traditional arguments for the existence of God can be viewed as such an attempt. Those religious writers who repudiate the arguments and who believe that God addresses man in a self-authenticating revelation, often attempt to show that "being addressed" is properly descriptive of man's religious experience and that psychological interpretations of religious experience are unsatisfactory. A different kind of attempt is exemplified by Emil Brunner, who believes that every moral obligation is a command from God; he has an elaborate argument in which he attempts to demonstrate that the word command is properly applied and that other interpretations of our sense of duty are unacceptable. If the thesis of this paper is correct, it is trivial to object that religious writers claim to be using words in their proper senses while attempting to find alternative methods for justifying their uses. More fruitful questions for discussion between theologians and analytical philosophers are whether the religious writer has succeeded in presenting his criteria and methods of testing in unambiguous fashion and whether his words have reference to the external world.

## NOTES

1. Erik E. Erikson, *Childhood and Society* (New York: W. W. Norton & Company, Inc., 1950), p. 219.

## 22

# BELIEF AND ACTION
### by Michael Wyschogrod, Hunter College

Among the meanings of the word "faith" discussed by Professor Niebuhr in his suggestive paper is a "subjective feeling of greater or less assurance about the probability that a proposition that something is the case will be verified." Together with Martin Buber, he classifies this among the "Greek" meanings of the word, in contrast to the "Hebrew" meaning whose affinity is closer to the English word "trust" than to "believe." In the terminology of the Hebrew Bible, believing in God is not taken to mean believing in His existence or even in some proposition about His nature, but trusting that He will manage things properly even if it may not seem so at any particular moment. It would appear that there are no insuperable logical difficulties in translating any expression of trust into an expression of belief. Thus, the sentence "I trust John" may be translated into the terminology of belief as "I believe that John is honest" or "I believe that John will get us there." These beliefs may be held with varying degrees of intensity, just as one trusts another with some degree of intensity. The significance in the shift from an expression of trust to one of belief does not therefore seem to be one of cognitive content; it is a shift of existential stance. When I express trust, I am in the context of Buber's "I-Thou" encounter, while when I formulate the trust in terms of belief, I am doing the talking "about" that Buber locates in the "I-It" relationship. In formulating beliefs I view myself in the trusting relationship and formulate judgments about it, thereby transcending the trusting relationship toward a self-consciousness that is not easy to reconcile with the initial purity of the act of trust. This can also be expressed by saying that trust is the language of prayer, while belief is that of theology.

Be that as it may, Professor Niebuhr is fully aware that the "Greek" sense of the word "faith" raises many difficulties. These difficulties all stem from the fact that, as a feeling of assurance, an act of faith is a mental act and, as such, very difficult to define, much less to measure in any precise way. There is, first, the difference between knowing and believing. Here usage is diverse. Sometimes believing is contrasted with knowing in such a way that the former carries with it a sense of lack of conclusive evidence such that any use of the word, no matter how emphatic, is taken as an indication of uncertainty. This is the sense in which someone will say, "I believe (have faith) with all my heart that Jesus was God, though I cannot prove it." In another usage, no such distinction is made between knowing and believing. The former is taken simply as the highest degree of the latter, so that the assertion "I believe as strongly as I possibly can" is taken as synonymous with "I know." To me, this usage seems the more reasonable, since any attempt to draw a sharp cleavage between "know" and "believe" tends to produce a situation where we can only believe that we know, because to know requires the fulfillment of certain conditions which we can only believe, but never know, to be fulfilled. (This, for instance, applies to John Hospers who writes: ". . . we have two defining characteristics of knowing p. We know p when (1) p is true, and (2) we believe p to be true. Both of these are necessary conditions for knowing. In the absence of even one of them, the word 'know' would cease to be applicable." [1] According to this definition of "know," it seems to me impossible for anyone ever to be aware that he is knowing rather than believing, even when, in fact, he is knowing.)

Taking "know," then, to refer to the greatest possible intensity of "believe," the question arises as to what is the test whereby we can determine whether one does or does not hold any given belief. It is traditional to turn to action as that test. Thus, Descartes, in speaking of mankind, writes: ". . . in determining what their opinions really are, I ought to give heed more to what they practiced than to what they said. For, owing to the corruption of our minds, not only are few disposed to say all they believe; the act of thought by which we believe a thing is different from that by which we apprehend that we are believing it, and the one is often found without the other." [2] Similarly, William James, in a footnote to his essay "The Will to Believe," writes: "Since belief is measured by action, he who forbids us to believe religion to be true, necessarily also forbids us to act as we should if we did believe it to be true. The whole defense of religious faith hinges upon action. If the action required or inspired by the religious hypothesis is in no way different from that dictated by the naturalistic hypothesis, then religious faith is a pure superfluity. . . ." [3] These statements are of significance for both of the authors mentioned. In the case of James, in spite of the relegation of this comment to a footnote, we must not be misled as to its importance. It is actually the crux of his argument. If you believe the religious hypothesis, he claims, then your conduct will be different than if you do not believe it, and since the evidence is rather evenly matched, it is better to believe that hypothesis which is conducive to the better conduct. In the case of Descartes, the quoted comment assumes interest when read in juxtaposition with another comment appearing on the very same page. Speaking of his decision to suspend all his beliefs, he decides nevertheless to "obey the laws and customs of my country, adhering unwaveringly to the religion in which, by God's grace, I had been educated from my childhood. . . ." [4] Applying his own criterion for determining what someone's opinions really are, we would seem to be justified in being quite skeptical of his contention that he is, in fact, suspending all his beliefs when, by his own admission, this alleged suspension will have no effect whatsoever on his actions.

The point that both of these authors, and a host of others, make is that action, external conduct, is the proper measure of beliefs held. This, I think, is an erroneous opinion. The relation between a proposition referring to a man's belief and one referring to his actions is never one of logical entailment. No proposition in the form "x believes p" is ever contradictory to the proposition "x does c" where c is any given conduct. This is clearly the case with a large number of propositions whose relationship to conduct is not only not one of logical entailment, but remote in every other way. Thus, there is certainly no obvious conduct connected with holding the belief that the opinions attributed to Socrates in some of the later dialogues are not those of Socrates but of Plato except, perhaps, saying so; if that is to be interpreted as the conduct entailed by that particular belief, then the term "conduct" is being used broadly indeed (even that, however, is not entailed; it does not follow that because I believe something I must say or write so). But even in cases where the connection between belief and action seems less remote, it is still not one of logical entailment. The statement "x believes action y to be wrong" does not in any way entail "x will not do action y." Now, of course, it might be argued that if x does commit action y, he cannot possibly believe it really to be wrong. There is reason to believe that Socrates (Plato?) held this opinion. But surely this is a matter of definition. We can, of course, define belief in the wrongness of action y in terms of not doing y, but clearly this is nothing more than a stipulated definition —and one quite far removed from common usage at that. Normally, there is nothing extraordinary in saying that someone succumbed to temptation, which usually means that he did something he considers to be wrong.

Nevertheless, the feeling persists that there is a connection between beliefs held and conduct. It seems to me best accounted for on inductive grounds. There is nothing to prevent us from correlating what people believe with how they act. There is probably a higher correlation between the belief that drinking is immoral and abstinence from drink than between those who believe it not to be immoral and abstinence from drinking. But this must be established empirically. We may, therefore, be in for some surprises. It may be interesting to discover the kind of conduct with which belief in certain propositions correlates. Perhaps there is a high correlation between the belief that the proposition "Ideas have an independent existence of their own" is meaningless and the rate of divorce. However high any particular correlation may be, the relationship between the belief and the action is never one of logical entailment but only of inductive correlation. It follows from this that any inference from belief held to anticipated conduct, or from observed conduct to belief held, is convincing only to the extent that it is backed up with a body of previously obtained inductive information. This is precisely the defect in James's essay. I do not think that James can demonstrate that belief in the religious hypothesis dictates (in the logical sense) any determinable conduct. And, even more important, I do not think he can show that any given line of desirable conduct is possible only given the adherence to any particular belief. I think I have some idea of the kind of conduct James approved of, and it is rather clear that there are people who engage in such conduct without adhering to the religious hypothesis. It is, of course, possible that James is thinking here of an inductive correlation on the basis of which he would maintain that there is more likelihood that people who have the mentioned belief engage in the desirable conduct. But if this is so, he certainly makes no mention of such evidence, and he does not give me the impression that it is this kind of evidence on which he wishes to base his argument.

Once the relation between the domain of belief and the domain of action is considered not to be as intimate as is usually thought, a number of problems arise. There is the question as to what belief is. As long as belief is stipulatively defined in terms of conduct, or even if conduct is considered a significant index of belief, this problem does not become very acute. But if we reject the behavioristic solution, the question does arise in various forms. As far as we can see, the most likely answer lies in the direction of classifying the act of belief among the emotions. This is the position James takes in his *Psychology* when he writes, "In its inner nature, belief, or the sense of reality, is a sort of feeling more allied to the emotions than to anything else." [5] His point seems to be that to believe a proposition is to have certain kind of emotional feeling toward it. The evidence for this is, in the first instance, phenomenological. Then there is the indication of language. The Oxford Dictionary tells us that the roots of the modern word "believe" are the Teutonic word "galantrian," which means to believe, probably "to hold estimable, valuable, pleasing, or satisfactory," and the Aryan word "lubh," which means to hold dear, to like, whence also "love," "lief." The rootedness of the word in affective attitudes is, at the very least, suggestive. And, finally, when we view belief as an emotive attitude, a number of facts appear more understandable. Thus, for instance, it is not surprising that belief is susceptible of infinite gradations; the same is true of all emotions. Something similar is true of the sense of involuntariness we have toward our beliefs. To a great extent we do not "choose" our beliefs—they seize us. Nevertheless, we also feel that men are responsible for their beliefs. Very much the same dialectic applies to all emotions: though one does not usually decide to become angry or amused, one still exercises some control over these feelings, and it is, therefore, possible to blame someone for entertaining these feelings inappropriately. And, above all, we begin to understand how it is possible for men to believe and disbelieve the same proposition at the same time. If belief were fundamentally an action, this would violate the law of the excluded middle: one simply cannot do and not do the same action at the same time. But if belief is an emotion, the logical disjunction no longer applies. As John Wisdom puts it: ". . . for any minute understanding of people's spiritual states, laws such as 'If he loves he doesn't hate,' 'He can't think this and also not think it' become as much a menace as a help." [6]

The conclusion that seems to me to emerge from this is that, in discussing the relation between belief and action, we are dealing with two spheres of virtue: that of belief and that of action. Each possesses its own excellence and, presumably, to excel in both is ideal. But it is possible to believe well (to exercise the "emotion" of belief on true propositions) without acting well, and vice versa. It can, of course, be debated which of these two orders of virtue is the more important. Here, there seems to be a significant difference between the Old and New Testaments. For the Old Testament, revelation occurs through the Divine Will as Law. As such, Divine Law is directed to the regulation of action because it is only action that can be the object of legal regulation. With the incipient anti-nomianism of the New Testament, the emphasis shifts to the domain of belief and to salvation through faith. This division is not, of course, perfectly exclusive. Since both belief and action are always present in the human situation, neither the Old nor the New Testament can concentrate on one to the exclusion of the other. Judaism therefore has a literature on the "Duties of the Heart" while Christianity is concerned with "good works." But the test is specificity. Whereas Judaism elaborates in great detail a code of conduct and only rarely elaborates propositions of belief, the heart of Christianity is a proclamation of faith, while the elaboration of a code of conduct with any degree of specificity is never in the center of the Christian focus. Each faith thereby reflects its understanding of the sphere of virtue of primary Divine concern: action or belief.

## NOTES

1. John Hospers, *An Introduction to Philosophical Analysis* (Englewood, N. J.: Prentice-Hall, Inc., 1953), p. 146.
2. René Descartes, *Discourse on Method*, Part III.
3. William James, *The Will to Believe and Other Essays* (New York: Dover Publications, Inc., 1956), p. 29.
4. Rene Descartes, *op. cit.*, Part III.
5. William James, *The Principles of Psychology*, II.
6. John Wisdom, *Philosophy and Psycho-Analysis* (New York: Philosophical Library, Inc., 1953), p. 277 n.

# 23

# FAITH, HOPE, AND CLARITY

*by Marvin Zimmerman,* New York University

Is religious faith like everyday and scientific faith; is faith in the existence of God like faith in the axioms of logic and mathematics, in the existence of an external world, in human beings, in the principle of induction, etc.? Does not the ordinary or scientific man take for granted certain unproved beliefs and therefore accept many things on faith, i.e., go beyond the evidence, just as the religious man does? Are we not all in the same boat, after all? It is sometimes said that, just as scientific belief pre-supposes without proof certain fundamental assumptions such as the "axioms" of logic and mathematics, religious belief assumes on faith the fundamental "axiom" of the existence of God. Thus, all beliefs rely ultimately on faith in certain initial, unproved as-sumptions or axioms, without which further belief would be im-possible.

Interestingly enough, this kind of argument proves too much, and is far from being more reassuring about the fundamental assumptions presupposed by religious faith. It would be more cor-rect to say that, in light of recent developments in geometry, mathematics, logic, and physics, their fundamental "axioms" have been seriously challenged to the extent that they were taken to have "empirical" content. Thus, for example, the well-known axioms that two parallel lines can never meet and that a straight line is the shortest distance between two points are no longer taken to be correct descriptions of the physical structure of the universe. The whole point here is that, whatever may have been true in the past, these axioms are no longer accepted on faith or without their being subjected to scientific verification.

# Religious Experience and Truth

We must, of course, distinguish the use of these axioms in "empirical" discourse from their use in the "pure" or "uninterpreted" sense where no application and, thus, no unproved assumptions about the "universe" is intended. Failure to make this distinction clear may very well account for the misconception that scientific belief presupposes certain initial assumptions about the "universe" on faith.

It will be argued that scientific and everyday belief presuppose much more faith than is usually realized; that, for example, they presuppose faith in the existence of an external world, other minds, etc. which like religious faith also goes beyond the evidence.

Now hardly anyone with any philosophical sophistication would wish to deny that all scientific and everyday beliefs are fallible, particularly in light of the difficulties surrounding such notions as certainty, conclusive evidence, possibility of error, and so on. But, from the fact that all beliefs are fallible, it does not follow that all beliefs are *equally* credible, since not all beliefs are supported by the *same* amount of evidence. If it is a fact that both faith in the existence of an external world and religious faith go beyond the evidence, it follows that neither faith is infallible, i.e., can be held with absolute (100 per cent) certainty. But it does not follow that we cannot hold one with greater assurance than the other, depending upon the amount of evidence (if any) we have for each.

The crucial question here is, can we offer the *same* amount of evidence (if any) in support of religious faith that we can in support of the belief in an external world or in other minds. The answer to this and its implications seems obvious. The main point here can perhaps be summed up best by saying that, because both kinds of faith are alike in lacking *complete* evidence, it has been erroneously inferred that they are alike in the amount of evidence we have for each, and thus the degree of credibility we can attribute to each.

Further similarities are alleged by comparing religious faith with ordinary or common-variety faith in human beings, one's friends, family, ideals, ideologies, etc. It is true that sometimes we retain our faith in human beings, our friends, etc. even in the face of evidence to the contrary. But it is also true that this can turn out to be unreasonable or irrational. It may not be unreasonable when we have reason to doubt the evidence to the contrary or when we have other evidence which supports our faith and which appears equally, if not more, reliable than the contrary evidence. In some cases our continued faith is not intended to deny the contrary evidence of human failing or weakness, but rather reflects a recognition, *based on experience,* that human beings are sometimes able to overcome their defects, particularly when other human beings express their faith in them.

However, who would wish to deny that this continued faith can become unreasonable, when there is *continued* evidence to the contrary, when expression of faith in them does not eventually do the trick?

Those who have faith in God already presuppose faith in induction, but not vice versa. Those with religious faith not only assume that God has existed but that he will continue to exist. They assume, therefore, that what has been true in the past will continue to be true in the future, i.e., the principle of induction. But if both religious and scientific faith are unwarranted in the sense that they go beyond the evidence, then those with religious faith make two unwarranted assumptions rather than one. In this respect, is not religious faith more unwarranted than scientific faith?

If it is said that two unwarranted assumptions are no worse than one, then why not permit an *indefinite* number of unwarranted assumptions? The implications of this are obvious.

Even if it is argued that justification of religious and scientific faith is based ultimately on the *need* to have faith, not on whether it is warranted, surely the need in each case is not the same, nor is it of equal importance. Although it is likely to be difficult, if not impossible, to get along or even survive without scientific faith, can the same be said for religious faith? Without belief in the principle of induction, no one would have any more reason to choose the slice of bread rather than the cup of arsenic, to choose the front door rather than the window, but surely, without religious belief many have been able to survive for long periods of time.

189

## Religious Experience and Truth

Religious faith sometimes reflects belief merely in the existence of a higher intelligence who created the universe, but traditionally it is taken to mean in addition belief that this higher intelligence is omnipotent, benevolent, etc. In the traditional sense, is the man of religious faith going "beyond the evidence" in the same sense as one who has faith in the principle of induction? In light of the long history of attempts to reconcile the existence of evil with traditional religious faith, it would seem that going "beyond the evidence" here has meant going "against the evidence." But this is hardly the case with faith in the principle of induction. In the latter case, going "beyond the evidence" would seem to mean believing, in the absence of "all" theoretically possible evidence, because at any given time some of the theoretically possible evidence is unavailable. But it does *not* mean going "against the evidence." We would hardly consider faith in the principle of induction reasonable or rational if it did.

It is misleading, therefore, to argue that, since both religious and scientific faith go "beyond the evidence," the former is no less reasonable than the latter, for the former goes "beyond the evidence" in the sense of going "against the evidence" and the latter does not.

Of course, many have given up the traditional religious faith and shifted over to some other kind. Thus, some will express belief merely in the existence of a higher intelligence who created the universe, without specifying the traditional attributes of omnipotence, benevolence, etc. and which, therefore, presumably avoids going "against the evidence."

Here it is sometimes argued that, since the scientist can never obtain complete certainty, he always selects the best among alternative hypotheses and takes that for the truth. Likewise, the man of religious faith merely selects the "God" hypothesis as the best among alternative possibilities and takes that for the truth. But it would be a mistake to assume that the scientist always selects the best and takes that for the truth. The "best" is sometimes not good enough, particularly where, though the hypothesis does not go "against the evidence," the evidence is very sparse or conflicting. In such cases what is called for is suspension of judgment, not accepting the belief that the "best" is true. And if it is argued that we cannot suspend judgment in the case of the "God" hypothesis because our reason or emotions "require" us to have religious faith, what would we think of a scientist (and there have been some) who likewise felt compelled to have faith rather than suspend judgment in his scientific speculations, where evidence is insufficient?

Furthermore, if one is willing to commit the fallacy *ad ignorantium* of justifying religious faith on the grounds that religious belief has not been shown to be false (this is in itself debatable), one should be no less willing to argue that religious faith is not justified since religious belief has not been shown to be true either.

There is one position a man of religious faith may fall back on in the face of objections and difficulties raised, and that is that his religious faith does reflect the "hope" that what he believes is true in spite of the absence of evidence or even contrary evidence. This attitude is reflected in the frequent use of the assertion, "Well, maybe there is nothing left but hope, but, at least, I can hope, can't I?"

But even here, hope can be unreasonable as well as reasonable, not only when it goes against the evidence, but even where there is mere absence of evidence extending over a long period of time. Here, though hope coupled with suspension of judgment may not appear to be unreasonable *at first,* a time may be reached where even hope becomes unreasonable. And in the case of religious faith, man has been waiting a long time for affirmative evidence to make its appearance.

At this point, if it is said that religious faith reflects a mere "wish" that what is believed is true, we can perhaps all plead guilty to wishing for things we have no reason to believe true or even have good reason to believe false.

191

# PART III

## Meaning and Truth in Theology

## 24

## ABOUT 'GOD'
*by Paul Ziff, University of Pennsylvania*

My text is a text: the utterance 'God exists.' The question is:
does he?

1. The English utterance 'God exists' occurs in religious discourses in English (not in "religious language"—there is no such
thing). The expression 'God' in that utterance is evidently a noun;
furthermore, it is not a count noun (like 'bean') since it does not
require an article. This is not to deny that there is also a count noun
'god' in English. Thus one can say 'If God exists then a god exists'
or even 'God is a god.' This indicates that 'God' is not a noun
like 'man' in 'Man is a rope stretched over an abyss' for one cannot
say 'Man is a man.'

That 'God' is neither a pronoun nor a mass noun in the utterance
'God exists' is indicated by the fact that it is neither a pronoun
nor a mass noun in English religious discourses; that it is neither
a pronoun nor a mass noun in these discourses is indicated by
various facts; e.g., that it does not occur in such environments as
'How much . . . exists?' 'A quantity of . . . exists'; that it takes
'he' as an anaphoric substitute as in, 'That God exists may be
doubted but that some men think he exists, that cannot be doubted';
that the "wh—" form employed in connection with 'God' is
generally 'who'; and so forth.

Hence it is reasonably clear that 'God' in 'God exists' is a proper
noun, i.e., a proper name, or for short, a name.

2. A name may be introduced into a particular discourse either
by both extralinguistic and intralinguistic means or simply by intralinguistic means. Since I take it that no one claims to have learned
to use the name 'God' by extralinguistic means, i.e., no one (that

I am concerned with) claims to have had the referent of the name 'God' indicated to him by ostension, we may take it that the name 'God' has been introduced into those religious discourses in which it occurs solely by intralinguistic means.

'God' then is a name like 'Caesar' or 'Pegasus' but not like your name.

3. To introduce a name into a discourse by intralinguistic means alone it is necessary to associate certain expressions of the discourse with the name. Since these expressions will have certain conditions associated with them, this means that derivatively the name will have certain conditions associated with it.

(To state the matter more clearly but less precisely, what I am saying is probably that which is intended by those who claim that certain names are introduced into a discourse by means of descriptions.)

4. Consider the name 'Dietrich of Leipzig': I tell you that Dietrich wrote theological tracts entitled "On the Divine Pseudonyms" and "Celestial Conundrums." I tell you that he lived in Leipzig about 1400.

I have now introduced the name 'Dietrich of Leipzig' into the present discourse. I have done so by associating with it certain expressions and, thus, derivatively a certain set of conditions. Thus the referent of the name 'Dietrich of Leipzig,' if it has one, is that which satisfied a certain set of conditions, viz., a set having as its members the conditions of being a man, a resident of Leipzig about 1400, the author of certain theological tracts, and so forth.

5. I shall say that, speaking in what I take to be a familiar and relatively unproblematic way, the set of conditions we take to be associated with a name determines our conception of the referent of the name. Thus, given that the name 'Dietrich of Leipzig' has been introduced into the present discourse, you now have a certain conception of Dietrich.

6. Though a name may at one time have associated with it a certain set of conditions, at another time it may have associated with it a slightly different or even radically different set of condi-

tions. If so, one's conception of the referent of the name will most likely have altered.

Thus your present conception of Dietrich may tarnish and alter in time. You may discover that he did not write the tract on pseudonyms; if so, you will then have a slightly different conception of Dietrich. Or you may discover that he did not write the tract on celestial conundrums, but rather a tract on infernal paradoxes, and indeed that he did not live in Leipzig about 1400. If so, you will then have a radically different conception of Dietrich.

A name is a fixed point in a turning world. But as the world turns, our conception of that which is named by a name may change.

7. The questions whether the name 'Dietrich of Leipzig' has a referent, whether Dietrich ever existed, whether any such person as Dietrich ever existed, or whether anything answering to our conception of Dietrich ever existed can all be answered in much the same way.

It is necessary to specify the relevant set of conditions associated with the name and then determine whether anything or anyone ever satisfied the conditions of the set.

8. Questions whether the name 'God' has a referent, whether God exists, whether any such being as God exists, or whether anything answering to our conception of God exists can all be answered in much the same way and in much the same way as the analogous questions about Dietrich.

It is necessary to specify the relevant set of conditions associated with the name and then determine whether anything or anyone satisfies the conditions of the set.

9. But whether God exists is, in fact, a genuine question depends on (at least) two distinct factors: first, on the intelligibility of the conditions associated with the name, and secondly, on the consistency of that set of conditions.

To determine whether the conditions are intelligible and, if so, both self-committing and mutually consistent, it is necessary to determine precisely what they are.

10. The first problem then is to specify the conditions as-

197

sociated with the name 'God.' And it is here that the confusion endemic in religious discourse takes its locus. We need not confuse the excubant theologian's febrile concept with that of a plain or even plainer man.

Different theistic groups are likely to have somewhat different and even competing conceptions of God. Presumably the God of the Christians is identical with the God of the Jews: yet Christians apparently suppose that the referent of the name 'God' satisfies the condition of either having been crucified or having had a crucified son; while Jews apparently suppose that the referent of the name 'God' satisfies the condition of neither having been crucified nor having had a crucified son. (It follows that either Jews or Christians are laboring under a misconception.)

Within a particular theistic group, the members of the group are likely to have different conceptions of God. And even a particular member of a theistic group is likely to have different conceptions of God at different periods of his life. To simplify matters I shall suppose that for the moment we are largely concerned with some particular conception of God.

11. All sorts of conditions have been associated with the name 'God.' For the purposes of the present discussion it is useful to sort some of these conditions into two groups, viz., unproblematic conditions and problematic conditions.

12. Some unproblematic conditions are the conditions of being a being, a force, a person, a father, a son, a creator, spatiotemporal, crucified, just, good, merciful, powerful, wise, and so forth.

I class these conditions as unproblematic because its seems clear to me that each condition is, in fact, satisfied or readily satisfiable by something or someone; furthermore, that each condition is satisfied or readily satisfiable is a fairly obvious matter.

13. Some problematic conditions are the conditions of being omnipotent, omniscient, eternal, creator of the world, a nonspatiotemporal being, a spirit, the cause of itself, and so forth.

I class these conditions as problematic simply for this reason: if someone were to maintain that a traditional conception of God is unintelligible, I should think he would base his claim on the prior claim that such conditions as these are fundamentally unintelligible.

So the question is: are such conditions as these somehow unintelligible?

14. To suppose that the conditions in question are unintelligible is to suppose that one cannot understand them. But understanding admits of degrees—I think there can be no doubt but that some of us at any rate have some understanding of these conditions.

I know that if something satisfies the condition of being an omnipotent being then there is nothing that it cannot do owing to a lack of power, e.g., such a being could transport a stone from the earth to the sun in less than one second. I know that if something is the cause of itself then we cannot succeed in finding another cause. I know that if something is the creator of the world then prior to its act of creation the world did not exist. And so forth. That I can make such inferences indicates that I have some understanding of the conditions involved.

15. The only general sort of reason I can think of to suppose that the conditions in question are somehow unintelligible is that it is evidently difficult to establish whether or not any of them are, in fact, satisfied. But although this is something of a reason to suppose that the conditions in question are somehow unintelligible, I do not think it is a good reason.

Understanding a condition is one thing; knowing how to establish that it is satisfied is another. For example, suppose I agree to do something on the condition that my friend George approves of it. There is no difficulty in understanding this condition though there may be some difficulty in establishing that it is satisfied. Suppose that I agree to do it on the condition that Caesar would have approved of it—there is still no difficulty in understanding the condition though there could be considerable difficulty in establishing that it is satisfied. And now suppose that I agree to do it on the condition that the last man ever to live, were he alive now, would approve of it: There is still no difficulty in understanding the condition and yet I have no idea how to actually establish that such a condition is satisfied.

16. I do not wish to deny that what I have called "problematic" conditions associated with the name 'God' pose all sorts of conceptual problems, including problems of verification and confirmation. Thus, is there a difference between the condition of being a spirit and that of being spirits? If so, how do we count spirits? What principle of individuation is employed? (This is, of course, an old question, but all these questions are old questions.) Again, what is one to understand by creation *ex nihilo*? Of course, as Collingwood pointed out, one doesn't create something out of anything; thus we speak of creating a disturbance, a design. Even so, creation takes place in a certain environment, under certain environing conditions. The conception of first nothing and then something is a difficult one.

But despite such problems as these I do not think that there can be any serious question about the intelligibility of the conditions in question. That they pose problems merely shows, if it shows anything, that the conception of God is a difficult one.

17. Similarly, I am inclined to suppose that there can be no great problems about the self-consistency and mutual consistency of the conditions in question. Again, there are problems of a sort. I would not deny it; how can something satisfy both the condition of being a being and that of being nonspatiotemporal? I suppose numbers might be said to be nonspatiotemporal, but then numbers are not beings. Such problems, however, are readily dealt with in obvious ways: contradiction can always be avoided by an appropriate and judicious feat of logistic legerdemain; conditions can always be weakened, modified, and so made compatible. This game has been played for over a thousand years.

18. Consequently it seems reasonable to suppose that whether God exists is an intelligible question. To answer it we need do nothing more than determine whether the conditions associated with the name 'God' are satisfied. Since that is evidently difficult to do, the interesting question then is: why is it difficult and can it be done, now or ever?

19. The difficulty in establishing whether or not God exists is obviously partially attributable to the character of what I called the "problematic" conditions associated with the name 'God.' All such

conditions seem to involve some extreme form of either generalization or abstraction.

Thus the condition of being omniscient is an obvious generalization over the condition of being informed or learned. The condition of being the creator of the world can be thought of as a generalization over the condition of being a creator. On the other hand, the condition of being a non-spatiotemporal being can be viewed as the result of an abstraction from the condition of being a spatiotemporal being. The ease of such abstraction is testified to by the fact that plain people sometimes say they find it difficult to keep body and soul together.

20. The question we are concerned with is whether a certain set of conditions, conditions involving simultaneous generalization and abstraction, are satisfied. Questions of such a character are, I believe, not unreasonably classed as theoretic questions. Simultaneous generalization and abstraction is frequently a striking characteristic of scientific laws and hypotheses; thus a scientist may speak of all rigid bodies, of all bodies free of impressed forces, and so forth.

That a certain question is reasonably classed as a theoretic question is of interest only in that it indicates that one can reasonably expect to answer such a question only within the framework provided by a theory of some sort.

21. It is or should be evident that the question whether God exists can be answered only within the framework provided by some theory if it can be answered at all. For it is or should be obvious that no simple set of observations unsupplemented by powerful theoretic considerations can serve to determine whether or not anything satisfies the conditions in question, e.g., that of being an omnipotent being. That a certain being did not perform a certain task could not in itself establish that the being was not omnipotent, no matter what the task was. Again, that the being performed the task would not establish its omnipotence, and again that no matter what the task was. Projection or extrapolation of some sort is required but that is possible only within a theoretical framework.

22. But the difficulty in providing a final answer to the question

whether God exists is only partially owing to problems posed by what I have called "problematic" conditions. It is primarily owing to the fact that, in fact, there is not one but indefinitely many questions to answer. That each question is asked by the utterance 'Does God exist?' only shows that we put old names to new uses. The sense of the question 'Does God exist?' depends on the conditions associated with the name 'God': these may vary from case to case and they change in time.

23. Consider a plain man's conception of God: the name 'God' has associated with it the conditions of being an omnipotent being, creator of the world, and so forth. Then in answer to the question 'Does God exist?' one can say this: There is no reason to suppose so; there is excellent reason to suppose that no such being exists.

It is a tenet of present physical theory that no physical object can attain a velocity greater than the speed of light. Consequently, according to present physical theory, no being has it in its power to transport a stone from the earth to the sun in one second. But this is to say that no omnipotent being exists. Hence, according to present physical theory, nothing answering to the plain man's conception of God exists.

Present physical theory may be mistaken; that is always possible. But that possibility is irrelevant here. For no matter what form physical theory may take in the future, it seems reasonable to suppose that it will impose certain limits on experience: the existence of limits is incompatible with the existence of an omnipotent being.

24. Present physical theory, however, does not suffice to establish the nonexistence of God; at best, it suffices to establish the nonexistence of God as now conceived of by a plain man.

Man's conception of the world he lives in changes; that his conception of a creator of the world also changes is only to be expected. In consequence the question 'Does God exist?' may be freshly conceived, and so conceived may call for a fresh answer. That the answers to the old questions have always been no proves nothing. The answer to tomorrow's question is something that one can only be blank about.

# 25

# MEANING AND TRUTH
# IN THEOLOGY

*by John Hick, Princeton Theological Seminary*

I find myself in agreement with the positive conclusions of Professor Ziff's lucid and pregnant paper. I agree that is to say, that the word "God" functions in religious, or at least in monotheistic, discourse as a proper name, and that the question whether God exists is an intelligible and legitimate question. However I do not think that I should be able to accept this latter contention on the basis of Ziff's arguments alone, mainly because what he calls the unproblematic conditions associated with the name "God" seem to me to be far from unproblematic. "God is a force," "God is a person," "God is a father," "God is (or has) a son," "God is a creator," "God is spatiotemporal," "God was crucified," "God is just, good, merciful, wise, etc." None of these affirmations occurs within religious discourse in an ordinary unproblematic sense, and to take them unproblematically is to have taken them out of their proper context and to have destroyed the meaning which they had within their theological setting.

I should therefore like first to discuss further these conditions associated with the name "God," or elements in the concept of God, seeking to supplement from a different point of view Ziff's argument for their intelligibility.

There are, as Ziff reminds us, an indefinite number of different concepts of God, so that the question "Does God exist?" is really a multitude of questions. However we are not obliged to ask all of these questions; we can quite properly restrict ourselves, as Ziff in effect does, to the monotheistic conception of God. In doing so it seems to me desirable to pay close attention to the actual features of the specific God-belief that we are discussing, as these features show themselves in the associated religious ideas and practices which have grown out of, or in interaction with, that particular concept of God. For belief in God is, characteristically, integral to a 'form of life,' a living organism of beliefs, practices, and dispositions through which it finds expression beyond the mere repetition of the somewhat bleak proposition "God exists"—a proposition which is, incidentally, so far from typical of first-order religious utterances that it does not occur at all in the Jewish and Christian scriptures. I shall, therefore, confine my remarks for the sake of concreteness to one specific concept of God, namely the Christian concept. There are of course within Christianity a plurality of overlapping notions of God; but this fact need not concern us here, since I shall choose for discussion ideas which are common to this whole family of concepts of deity.

Ziff divides "the conditions associated with the name 'God' " into the unproblematic and the problematic. Perhaps it is possible to formulate a more precise distinction, which indicates why some of the terms applied to God seem to be more intelligible than others. The apparently more intelligible terms are those whose meanings have already been established in ordinary everyday contexts. Their primary or defining use is secular, but they have been adopted by religion and given a secondary use. Examples are "good," "loving," and "just." One is tempted to find these readily intelligible when applied to God because their primary nonreligious use is already well understood. Others, such as "Spirit," "omnipotent," "omniscient," have no familiar, established use in the language of everyday life. They were (I assume) originally formed for theological purposes; and outside of theological contexts they occur infrequently and generally in poetic or rhetorical roles. These terms, when used by the theologian, are thus "problematic" in that they lack a clear prior use in ordinary secular discourse.

This twofold division has only preliminary validity. However I shall not pursue here the logical classification of the God-predicates, but concentrate instead upon one term from each provisional grouping, which will raise what appear to be the central problems involved in talk about God. Two terms which will serve this purpose are "loving" and "unlimited," giving rise to the two related questions: (i) as to the sense in which such nonreligious terms as "loving" are being used when they are applied to God, and (ii) as to the origin and justification of the notion of unlimited or infinite being, by which love, goodness, power, knowledge, and so on are (so to speak) multiplied in the theological concept of God.

Such a primarily nonreligious predicate as "loving" is not as free from problems in its theological contexts as Ziff seems inclined to give it credit for being. Certainly we know what we mean when we say of a fellow human being that he has a loving disposition. But what does "loving" mean when it is transferred to a Being who is defined, *inter alia*, as having no body, so that he cannot be thought of as performing any actions? What is disembodied love, and how can we ever ascertain that it exists?

The traditional answer is that such terms as "loving," which we have learned how to employ in everyday contexts, are used with reference to God in a way which is not precisely the same as, nor yet totally different from, but which is analogous to their ordinary use. This would seem, however, to be a negative and formal rather than a positive and substantive answer, for "analogous" means essentially "neither univocal nor equivocal." At this point then it seems appropriate to supplement this formal answer by taking account of a further concrete feature of discourse about God by which, within Christianity, the theological meaning of such terms as "loving" is fixed.

The Christian doctrine of the Incarnation is many-sided and has implications in more than one direction. As relevant to our present problem, it points to the historical individual, Jesus of Nazareth, and, regarding him from the special point of view of those who have received him as a divine Savior, it claims that the various attitudes which Jesus displayed toward the men and women whom he met in Palestine were also God's attitudes toward those particular individuals. Jesus' attitudes thus exhibit and reveal certain aspects of God's nature. This is part of the meaning of the statement that God the Son was incarnate in Jesus of Nazareth. In the life of Jesus, then, the love, compassion, and other aspects of God's attitude toward mankind are seen expressed in concrete human actions: "The Logos was made flesh and dwelt among us. . . ." And, accordingly, the first part of the answer to the question, In what sense of "loving" is God said to be loving is: In the sense in which Jesus can be seen to have exhibited this characteristic.

This is however only the first part of the answer. It is further involved in the Incarnation doctrine that whilst Christ was 'wholly God,' he was not 'the whole of God.' His life is believed to have been an authentic, but at the same time a finite and limited, embodiment of the divine attitude toward mankind. Accordingly, when we speak of God discarnate, or God in his transcendent being, we have to put together the incarnated moral characteristics and the 'metaphysical' conception of unlimited being.

This latter idea raises a further and different problem. Whilst the nature or quality of the divine attitudes toward mankind can intelligibly be said to have been exhibited in a human life, their unlimitedness cannot have been similarly disclosed. Jesus, as a human being, was not unlimited in power or knowledge or any other attribute. Infinite characteristics cannot, as such, be incarnated. Nor can they be objects of religious experience. Men of faith have always claimed to be conscious at times of being in the presence of God; there are mystics who speak of moments of overwhelmingly vivid awareness of, or even union with, the Godhead; and some contemporary theologians speak of an 'I-Thou' encounter with God. But whilst all these believe the God who is thus experienced or encountered to be eternal, omnipotent, etc. they do not (or should not) claim to have *experienced* these unlimited qualities. One might observe that a Being whom one in some way meets is, for example, very powerful, more powerful perhaps than any other known force, but one could never observe that he is *omni*potent—and so with the other qualities which God is said to possess without limit.

How then can unlimitedness have become part of the Christian (as also of the Jewish) concept of God?

In his article "Anselm's Ontological Arguments," [1] Norman Malcolm has suggested that, for instance, the idea of an infinite divine mercy forms itself out of man's sense of a guilt which requires such a mercy for its healing, and that the concept of God has other similar connections with the various aspects of human nature and experience. I think there can be no doubt that in principle this is so. The thought of God as unlimited goodness, mercy, and the like fits and meets certain deep needs of the human psyche. Although not proposed by Malcolm from this point of view, these connections form the basis for the Freudian and other theories of God as an unreal creation of man's own inner needs and desires. The same facts are, however, capable of a religious as well as a naturalistic interpretation. Perhaps man needs God because God has made him in this way: in St. Augustine's words, "Thou has made us for Thyself, and our hearts are restless until they find their rest in Thee." It need not, then, be a conclusion damaging to religious belief that the unlimitedness of the concept of God is, as regards its genesis in the human mind, a product of emotion.

However, without doubting that there are a variety of links and correspondences between the believer's emotional needs and his concept of God, I think that another factor of a different, and perhaps even more important, kind can also be identified. This is a rational factor. There is what one may call a logical nisus within the general concept of deity or object of worship toward the *ne plus ultra* of 'that Being than which no more perfect can be conceived.' There is a rational progression from the thought of a number of finite and perhaps competing deities to that of a single all-powerful creator; from the thought of an impersonal cosmic force to that of a personal or suprapersonal Being; from the thought of a nonmoral to that of a moral God, who is 'holy, righteous, wise, and loving'; and these movements of thought point toward and terminate in the concept of God as unlimited perfection. In other words, the search, which is implicit in the activity of worship, for its most adequate possible object, leads to the concept of God which has developed in ethical monotheism. The only serious alternative is that of the religions (notably primitive Buddhism) in which there is no worship.

In all this I am agreeing, although from a different point of view, with Ziff's contention that the things that are said about God are intelligible, and that the question whether there is a being so characterized is, accordingly, a proper question.

Let me now turn, very briefly, to the problem which Ziff considers at the end of his paper, namely how the question of the existence or nonexistence of God might be settled.

I have only time to make one methodological suggestion. To speak of settling this question, as though it were classifiable with questions concerning the existence of physical objects, would be to have mistaken the subject matter. For this is not an issue with regard to which we can properly assert in advance either that it can or ought to be settled publicly, by universal agreement. Religious men speak of an awareness of God which (at any given time) some men have and others lack. Faith is often described as a function of the whole personality in its response to God's actions as these are mediated in and through, and yet at the same time concealed under, the events of the world. We hear of the operation of that mysterious factor, the Holy Spirit. And it seems quite possible, from the religious standpoint, that the question of God's existence might never, at least in this life, be publicly settled. It therefore seems more in accordance with the nature of the subject matter to begin by noting that there is what (adapting Professor Tillich's famous phrase 'the theological circle') we may call the circle of faith. (There are indeed many such circles; but we are concerned here with Christian [and, so far as the following formulation is concerned, Jewish] faith.) This does not refer to a group of people but to the state of implicit and unreserved faith in which God is not thought of as an inferred entity—inferred with however high degree of probability,—but is, the believer would say, directly known as the ultimate personal reality, the holy presence and sovereign will with whom at all times he has to do.

Now within the circle of faith the question Does God exist?

208

does not arise. To ask that question, as a real question, is *ipso facto* to stand outside the circle of faith. For to be within that circle is to be convinced, with a conviction which affects one's whole life, that one is, sometimes at least, aware of God as a reality as indubitable as one's material environment or one's fellow human beings. To many of the Biblical writers, for example, God was apprehended as a will interacting with their own wills; a sheer given reality, as inescapably to be reckoned with as destructive storm and lifegiving sunshine, or the fixed contours of the land. The Biblical writers were (sometimes, though doubtless not at all times) as vividly conscious of being in God's presence as they were of living in a material world. Their pages resound and vibrate with the sense of God's presence as a building might resound and vibrate from the tread of some great being walking through it. And to such people the question "Does God exist?" would be no less absurd than the questions: "Does the perceived world exist?" and "Do the members of my family exist?"

In thus reminding you of the fact of the religious 'form of life' and mode of experience, I am not, needless to say, proposing any kind of backstairs proof that God exists. I am not arguing that what the believer regards as his experience of God should be treated by the nonbeliever as proving God's existence. Clearly it should not. There is no proof of God's existence. I am, however, pointing out that there is a state of faith in which it seems so evident that God exists that the *question* as to whether he exists does not even arise.

Outside the circle of faith, on the other hand, the question does arise, and it is important to consider what form it most properly takes. I suggest that the right question to ask is not: Do I have grounds for believing that God exists? (for it is a tautology that, outside the circle of faith, one does not) but, Do I have grounds for claiming to know that the men of faith are deluded and that what they believe is false; have I warrant for being sure that they are mistaken, or is this for me an open question? It is hard to see how one could claim to know that the religious believer is deluded. (Except, as Professor Ziff has pointed out, on the basis of another and incompatible religious belief. Thus the monotheist and the polytheist will each claim to know that the other is mistaken.) If one does not make that claim, one will say, "I do not know whether God exists; but if he does, possibly one day I may come to be conscious of him."

## NOTES

1. Norman Malcolm, "Anselm's Ontological Arguments," *The Philosophical Review*, LXIX (1960), 41–62.

# 26

## GOD'S EXISTENCE:
## A CONCEPTUAL PROBLEM
*by Charles Hartshorne, Emory University*

Many points in Professor Ziff's interesting paper are well
taken. I shall consider chiefly those matters about which I have
misgivings. Learning to apply the name "God," our speaker
suggests, is like the ordinary process of learning to use names, in
cases where the one named has not been personally encountered.
Let us consider this analogy.

First, is it correct to say that God is an individual whom we have
not personally encountered? Many would contend that in religion
we encounter God, as we never, in any context, encounter Jane
Austen's Mr. Knightley. In a certain sense I agree with this contention. From a definition which I find appropriate of what it means
to "experience" something, or to have it as "datum" of direct
intuition, and from a definition of God which I also accept, it
follows deductively that all experience must have God as datum,
or that everyone experiences God at all times. But I do not urge
this as an objection to our speaker's analysis because the presupposed definition of "datum of experience" does not imply ready
accessibility to consciousness, and an unconscious experience of
God would not teach us how to apply the word. True, some persons claim a conscious encounter with God, but this, at most,
solves the problem for them, not for others. So let us waive this
point.

I still think that there is a difference in principle between the
naming of God and ordinary naming. Kierkegaard puts it strongly:
" 'God' is a concept, not a name." His explanation is clear enough:
the sorts of thing God is conceived to do no one else could possibly

do. Hence the character of God is self-individuating as no other character is. If we say, "Richard is very kind," we say nothing about him which might not be said about many another. And no mere multiplication of adjectives can designate an individual of the ordinary or nondivine sort. But there are adjectives which are suitable only in application to God. Some of these are well-known, such as omniscient, infallible, eternal (in the sense at least of being ungenerated and indestructible). Make me aware of an individual with any of these characters, and I will acknowledge that individual as God.

We have then two apparent classes of individuals: those whose identification must transcend mere concepts and include empirical facts and those who are specifiable by concepts alone. However, since we can conceive of no conceptually specifiable individual other than God, there are not really two classes of individuals in this regard, there is only the one class of empirically specified individuals and the unique, conceptually specified individual who, as the old saying had it, is not in a class of possible similars, but is necessarily *sui generis*.

This distinction among individuals, please note, is a logical or formal, not a material, one. I propose as an axiom that every logical difference in subject matter implies a methodological difference. Thus, because mathematical validity is a logically distinct sort of rightness from factual truth, the evidences to which a mathematician appeals are not those appealed to in physics or psychology. And so the evidences pertinent to the existence of the conceptually specifiable individual cannot be of the usual kind employed for that of empirically specifiable individuals.

Since I know that Dr. Ziff is more learned than some of our philosophers in the history of religious ideas, and unusually thoughtful and objective in judging them, I am rather surprised that he takes little or no account of the point I am making. He does say (secs. 20–21) that the existence of God cannot be handled by simple direct appeal to facts but must be dealt with by the aid of powerful theoretic considerations. I go further: The theoretic considerations are here the whole story. The mere facts are neutral.

God is worshiped, not merely as creator of the actual world, but as the One who would have had to create any other world for it to exist. He is regarded as the actual God of the actual world and and potentially the God of any possible world. Hence factual peculiarities of our world are irrelevant to the question of his existence.

The much misunderstood ontological argument (of which I am publishing elsewhere an extended analysis, as part of a book) is the partial emergence into philosophy of the uniquely conceptual meaning of the term "God." It would be both out of place and impossible to give my complete analysis of this here. But I might say this: The necessity of empirical elements for identification in ordinary naming is logically one with the need for empirical evidence to establish existence. By the other side of the same reason, the purely conceptual identification possible for God alone is logically one with the nonempirical status of his existence. The problem is conceptual, not factual. Ziff's brief reference to the ontological argument does not, I think, do justice to this point. He says (in sec. 8) that one may still ask, does the term "God" have a referent? The reply is that if it does not, then there is a logical flaw in the conception. For this name, unlike all others, by its barest connotation, requires a denotation, so that he who denies the latter implies a logical defect in the former. If, however, there be such defect, then God cannot exist; if there be none, then he cannot fail to exist. Norman Malcolm has recently brought out this point well.[1]

Ziff has astutely said that there is not a single question of divine existence but a different question for each of the innumerable possible ideas of God or, as he neatly puts it, sets of conditions for the applicability of the name. To this I feel constrained to proffer several qualifications. First, there may be descriptions of deity which at first sight seem quite different from one another but which, when more carefully regarded, turn out to be mutually implicative and to represent mere differences of rhetoric or emphasis. Whether the divine nature is said to be supreme will, or supreme knowledge, experience, love, or power, these need not

213

mean different things. Will, knowledge, experience, love, and power belong together, at least in the supreme or perfect form of each. So they may—I should say, must—describe the same nature and the same individual.

Second, certain descriptions seem incompatible, not only with others, but with themselves. Thus if we say that, although God is the absolute, meaning whatever is wholly without relativity, yet he knows and loves the world ( and so is by implication intrinsically related to it) we talk in sheer paradox or outright contradiction. If contradiction goes, anything goes, including as many contrasting contradictions as you please.

It is my belief, and here again I expected to find myself somewhat closer to Ziff than it seems I am, that the standard descriptions of deity in most of the older writings either lack any definite meaning or contain contradictions. God so described, I conclude, could not exist. Our speaker admits apparent logical difficulties in the old descriptions, but he suggests that writers like Philo and Dionysius have shown that these are not insuperable. I am not convinced. So for me there is no proper question of existence, so far as these descriptions of God are concerned, for they fail to define any coherent nature or entity.

Apart from rhetorical differences, there are three ways of conceiving God which differ logically. The three are: (1) God is in all respects infinite (or absolute, eternal, necessary, and self-sufficient, these terms as here used being equivalent); (2) God is in all respects finite; (3) God is in some respect finite and in some respect infinite. I agree, and expect Ziff would agree, with most theologians in regarding a merely finite God as a misuse of the term. Also, as I think William James unwittingly showed, there is no evidence for the reality of such a being. It would have to be identified empirically, and the ontological argument would have no relevance to it. Putting the finitistic view aside, we have but the first and the third view: God is either wholly infinite, or he is both finite and infinite, in diverse respects. Of course we need a rule for distinguishing the respects to which finitude applies from those to which it does not. Otherwise the expression "finite-infinite God" (which was proposed by Brightman), is too indefinite to have much value. The rule, or a rule, must also specify how the "finitude" of God differs from that of ordinary individuals. For the word is not unambiguous. I believe that the rule or rules can be supplied and that this is the sole rational way to define God. The alternative, that God is wholly infinite or absolute, has always led to antinomies and absurdities.

However one may view the choice between the wholly infinite and the finite-infinite God, the element of infinity, whether or not limited to certain aspects, suffices to provide conceptual uniqueness. Either of the concepts is self-individuating. The ontological argument is, therefore, relevant in any case. But the argument does not establish existence, it establishes the disjunction: the existence is necessary, or it is impossible. The question is purely conceptual, but a conceptual question may be answered by a conceptually determined yes or a conceptually determined no. Since both the infinite and the finite-infinite concepts must describe but one and the same deity, at least one of these concepts must be impossible. If only one is impossible, then the other is necessary. If both are impossible, then positivism is the correct position; that is, the term "God" is not at once cognitively significant and logically possible. Thus all the issues are conceptual.

Let us now consider Ziff's argument (sec. 23) that "omnipotence," as the plain man understands it, is refuted by physics. This seems to make the existence of God qua omnipotent a question of contingent fact. I wonder. It seems to me that, and Ziff virtually says as much in the last paragraph of that section, any physics in any possible world would hold that not all things are possible in that world. For this is only to say that there are laws of that world. And if not, no physics. But then is not the denial of "omnipotence" by physics analytic, the a priori faith of any science as such? Also, even apart from physics, does the notion of omnipotence, as thus construed, make sense? If God can nullify any and all laws, which are presumably his own orderings of the world, then it seems that he can both order and not order the world in the same respect. Individuality implies consistency of action;

omnipotence as here understood is destructive of such consistency. I incline to agree with Ziff that the plain man is not innocent of the notions which generate this difficulty, at least, if it is a plain man who, when misfortune strikes him, inquires, why has God done this to me, as though God could perfectly well bend the entire order of the world to the chance needs of individuals endowed with power of choice and constantly dependent upon the choice of other individuals. And if it be replied that the choices might be entirely arranged for the best by God's eternal decision, than I point out that we are here equivocating with the words decide or choose: in God, decision is viewed as genuinely free, it could have fallen otherwise; while in the creatures it is wholly determined by the presupposed divine decision. Between these two meanings of choose, the one fully determined by prior conditions, the other wholly undetermined by conditions, there can be nothing in common. So why speak of divine "decision," when we cannot possibly mean anything by the expression? If the plain man is in such confusion, then so much the worse for plainness, and so much the more need for philosophy.

This is not the place to explain how I think the divine power should be conceived. I must, however, explain that, while the existence of God is not a factual question, there are factual questions concerning God. This is because, though there can be at most but one sort of God who even could exist, still this one God could exist in various concrete ways, or in various concrete states of knowledge, experience, volition, or whatever word you prefer. Thus, for instance, God may, or could have, put himself in a special relation to Jesus of Nazareth, but his existence could not depend upon this relation, for the existence of a man is a mere contingent fact, which presupposes God. Or again, God's knowledge that you and I exist must be as contingent as that we exist, for had we not, God could not have known that we did. The total reality of God must then be as rich in contingent details as the universe, at the very least. Thus I can agree with Ziff that there are innumerable factual questions about God. But they are not questions of his existing or not existing, but of *how* he exists, in what actual "state." The term "actuality" is useful to express the concrete reality of God which is more than his bare existence. So long as existence and actuality are confused, we shall never achieve clarity concerning the ontological argument or any of the classical problems of theism. Actuality, even divine, cannot be necessary, but divine existence can only be necessary. The conditions for the applicability of the name "God" do not include reference to any fact rather than any other. It is all possible facts which are in question in the definition of God. Change the facts and you change the divine actuality, how God exists, but not the necessity that he exists.

Professor Ziff tries to show by examples that propositions may be intelligible though there is no apparent way to establish their truth. I have some misgivings about his examples. "Caesar would have approved of it" means, I think, something like this: Caesar's career up to some point or other causally implies such approval on the assumption of the issue having arisen but without other changes in the career. This presents problems not perhaps easily separable from the question: How could such an assertion be tested?

With respect to the divine existence, the problems are very different. The actual creator of the actual world and potential creator of the possible worlds must be entailed by any conception of world that is consistent. For the idea is that without its creator anything else would be nothing at all. One need, therefore, only abstract from the peculiarities which make one creature different from another to have left the common property, created by God, and this property includes God. Hence God must be knowable from the creatures. However, I hold, with Popper, that the crucial question is not how would an assertion be verified, but how would it be falsified? Empirical statements are falsifiable, whether or not they are verifiable. Now what would it mean to falsify the divine existence? It would mean, in Popper's terms, to observe some positive fact incompatible with that existence. But the definition of God excludes this possibility. God is conceived as independent in his existence of all other things; a fact incompatible with his existence would mean that, were he to exist, he would owe this existence to the nonbeing of the supposed fact. This contradicts the independence in question. Suppose for instance that some very evil but possible world would, if it existed, show that God did not exist; then God, if he does exist, owes his existence to the fortunate accident that the allegedly possible evil world does not exist. We should have to say to God, we owe our existence to you, but you owe yours to the lucky accident that no world incompatible with your existence happens to be. Thus the creator would virtually have a creator.

I submit: it is time that we did our homework and, after nearly a thousand years of delay, learned our little lesson from Anselm. But then, in contrast to Ziff's suggestion that these old thinkers said what was worth saying about the intelligibility of the idea of deity, I think we have something to teach most of them about the relations between finitude and infinitude and the danger of trying to locate God merely on one side of this contrast. I am deeply convinced that they erred here, and that God must be on both sides of the contrast. The finite-infinite God is the only God that possibly could exist. Possibility, however, as Leibnitz correctly said, here means necessity. The modal problem, the problem of consistent meaning, is the only question at issue when the divine existence is under consideration.

The question of divinity is so fundamental that even the basic rules of our language must either require or exclude God. Either all conceivable facts properly understood must manifest God's existence, or no conceivable fact or state of affairs could manifest it. This is the choice—all else is talk, not about God, but about some idol or fetish. And since not all descriptions of God agree, some of them must be merely absurd, some idolatrous, and the rest reducible to a single description except so far as they express characters not included in the identifying conditions for the application of the name. Many characters may be true of God without which he still would have existed and have been himself. Abstracting from these inessential characters, what we have left is only the choice between absurdity and various ways of expressing the one right conception, if any concept can be right in this field. This problem is purely conceptual, and that is why it is the central philosophical problem. For here and here alone individual existence (once more, not individual actuality) and universal principles are mutually inseparable. Here and here alone understanding is the same as knowledge of existential truth. To find this coincidence of understanding and existential knowledge is the unique function of metaphysics. Neither empirical science nor pure mathematics can do this. If philosophy fails to do it, its function must remain in doubt.

In judging the issue between the necessity and impossibility of deity, one may resort to theistic arguments other than the ontological. Properly understood, they are all nonfactual arguments, and their conclusion should be the finite-infinite, not the purely infinite, God. Through failure to understand these and other requirements, the classical formulations and classical refutations alike are unacceptable. The supposition pervading current discussion that our ancestors have done this job for us is abdication of intellectual responsibility.

## NOTES

1. Norman Malcolm, "Anselm's Ontological Arguments," *The Philosophical Review, LXIX* (1960), 41–62.

# 27

## ON GOD'S EXISTENCE

*by Markus Barth, The Federated Theological Faculty,*
*University of Chicago*

1. Professor Ziff might have spoken more directly and with greater power to some of the theologians present if he had put less emphasis upon what he called the problematic conditions associated with the name God. In his paper the term omnipotence is especially used and illustrated and led *ad absurdum* in a way which has little to do with the complicated history of this term or of its equivalents in the Hebrew Old Testament, the Septuagint, the Roman Creed and its derivates, in Scholastic philosophy and theology, and in modern thought. If not all, then many present-day theologians show little or no interest in a concept of God or of omnipotence which would imply that a deity can negate itself, can undo yesterday, or can place an infinite number of angels on the head of a pin. They would rather assert with Augustine, "If God can be what He does not will to be, He is not omnipotent" (sermon 214). Or, to put it into positive terms, they understand the words, "I believe in God the father the almighty" to mean that God has the will and the power to affirm and to manifest his fatherhood in the realm of creation, despite those features of heaven and earth that seem to belie and to deny his faithfulness and righteousness. The power of God's love, rather than the will of God to please speculative expostulations, is meant by the attribute omnipotent. The god of speculative omnipotence, of whom Professor Ziff speaks, may be left to those speculative minds which invented or concocted him. Theologians have no interest in his existence; they would rather join Professor Ziff's side in asserting

that his existence is fictitious and that verbal affirmation of his *Vorhandensein* makes little or no logical sense.

2. The question "Does God exist?," to which Professor Ziff addresses himself, appears to be lacking in logical precision. Does he understand it to be identical with the question "Is there a God?," or, "Does God verify himself as existing?" In the latter case the meaning of the verb exist would lie in a qualified manner of *Da-sein,* even in a personal, historical, and phenomenological stepping out of oneself; this meaning would lie strictly opposite an interpretation of the verb exist by reference to a simple *Vorhandensein.* Both terms, god and exist, are so ambiguous that their indiscriminate combination in a question makes little sense and their possible positive or negative relationship to each other can be stated only after extensive preparatory footwork.

(a) *Concerning God.* In the Old and New Testaments, god is but rarely used as a name (so found in Ps. 22:1; Mark 15:34). *Elohim, El,* and *theos* are pagan nomenclatures used for the description of power, might, manifestation beyond man's grasp, i.e., of *mysterium tremendum.* It is accepted by Jewish and Christian writers that many gods exist (Ps. 82:1 ff; I. Cor. 8:5). The Bible's emphasis lies on the question: Who is this god who calls the patriarchs, redeems from Egypt, gives kings and prophets, destroys the holy city, and who finally gives his son to be slain, raises him, and manifests himself by the Spirit's works? In the context of this question the answer is given: The *Lord* is this god; *our* God is the Lord; it is the father of Jesus Christ; his name I am; god of Abraham, Isaac, Jacob. Therefore, Lord, Father, or Jesus Christ—rather than God—are the names that have to be discussed.

(b) *Concerning existence.* The god of Israel and the father of Jesus Christ is by definition verifying himself. He introduces himself as I am who I am, and as creator, revealer, judge, etc. His self-disclosure never simply reveals that he is;

221

what he discloses is who and what he is. God "manifests his righteousness" (Rom. 3:25–26). By making known what a god he is, he reveals *that* he is one, and that he is to be loved. The existence of this god is most likely not *in genere* of any sort or definition of existence. The question, "Does God exist?" may be rephrased and asked the following way: What does the God of Israel and of Jesus Christ reveal of his being and nature by the manner of his self-manifestation in history? It seems that logical analysis might be concerned with this or a similar recuperation of the much misused term "exist."

(c) *Concerning God's existence.* From (a) and (b) the following conclusion may be drawn: It is a serious and open question (which cannot be solved by professional theologians or ordained clergymen alone) whether and in what ways the Lord is a god different from any other god or gods. The traces, if not proof, of this Lord's existence are the Jews, Jesus Christ, the church, and possibly the Bible—i.e., those phenomena in the world of spirit and matter, space and time, that cannot be observed, understood, and explained except by reference to a god different from other deities. Logical analysis and discriminating linguistic studies are indispensable for any one who wants to speak of that God. My protest against Professor Ziff's treatment of his topic is founded upon the disappointment that his analysis did not hit the real issues at the place and in the manner appropriate to the subject under consideration.

3. Professor Ziff may be aware of the fact that present-day theology, especially so-called Biblical theology, finds itself in a seemingly hopeless impasse in regard to the problem labeled "faith and history." Theologians are using in a most confused and confusing manner, terms like fact, event, history, myth, understanding, meaning, interpretation, historiography, proclamation, acceptance, belief, trust—and philosophy. If they don't know what really is to be made of such concepts, who shall understand them? Linguistic logic and logical analysis should be capable of providing the

university of sciences with workable definitions of such terms. If so, theologians would be not only deeply humiliated but also effectively helped. The fact that, for better or worse, Jewish and Christian theologians have to speak of a god, a revelation, a history, a faith that are not *in genere* but unique, need not exclude, but rather should simulate sharp, discriminating, and well-informed discussion of the issues at stake. Compared with the topic taken up by Professor Ziff, and with its correction as suggested above (2c), the clarification of the exact meaning of terms such as those mentioned may look like a small thing and a much reduced program. But the taking of little steps may prove to be of greater importance than the sound of clanging cymbals.

## 28

# ON PROFESSORS ZIFF,
# NIEBUHR, AND TILLICH
*by W. Norris Clarke, S.J., Fordham University*

## I. On Professor Ziff's Paper, "About 'God'"

One of the special merits of Professor Ziff's paper, and even more, of his remarks in the discussion, was his care in not closing off prematurely the possibility of meaningful discourse about God by adducing oversimplified linguistic impasses of all sorts, as has so frequently been done by other analytic philosophers. In so doing he has rendered a distinct service to philosophical maturity and refinement of concepts in dealing with this difficult problem.

There are two criticisms, however, which I should still like to make concerning his position as expressed in the paper. The first concerns how the term 'God' functions in religious discourse (I accept his distinction between religious language and religious discourse as exact and well-taken for the English language). For Professor Ziff, it functions as a proper name, and, therefore, presumably not as a description. In the case of other ordinary terms in the language, one must indeed choose between these two uses. But it is just one of the unusual features of this most unusual of terms, 'God' that it combines the two functions indissolubly. I would say that, in view of its actual use down the ages in Western religious discourse (monotheistic for many centuries), it functions primarily as a description; but, since one of the notes of the description is that it can be verified by only one referent ('God' means *the one infinite Creator of all other things*), this particular descriptive term can also be, and traditionally has been, used as a direct form of address or as a proper name. Something of the same thing has happened in the case of terms like 'Love,' 'Truth,' etc. though not in so firmly crystallized a manner as with 'God' (it could happen also with a term like 'Sun'), so that one can or could say in the direct address of prayer: "O Love," "O Truth," (or "O Sun"), like "O God." In the case of 'God,' it seems to me that any adequate analysis of the role played by the term must indissolubly join these two uses: description and proper name.

The second point concerns section 23, on the impossibility of the plain man's conception of God being compatible with the requirements for omnipotence. "It is a tenet of present physical theory that no physical object can attain a velocity greater than the speed of light. Consequently, according to present physical theory, no being has it in its power to transport a stone from the earth to the sun in one second. But this is to say that no omnipotent being exists. Hence, according to present physical theory, nothing answering to the plain man's conception of God exists."

The difficulty here is that the requirements laid down for omnipotence applied to actions in the physical world contain a hidden analytical contradiction, which rules out a priori any possible meaning or verification for the term 'omnipotence.' Such a contradiction does not exist, however, either in the conception of the genuine "plain man," nor in that of the careful theologian or theistic philosopher. In effect, the conditions laid down by Professor Ziff come to this: God could not transport a stone a certain distance both *according to* the laws of an Einsteinian universe (which He himself, according to the supposition, has freely set up and freely maintains) and at the same time *in contradiction to* those same laws. Obviously He could not, since it would involve His simultaneous ratification and violation of the same laws with respect to the same object. But I believe it is quite easy to show that not only the theologian, but even more the plain man, understands omnipotence in such a context as signifying the power of God to *suspend* or *change at will* the physical laws He himself has set up, in order to effectuate some good. In other words, a physical impossibility is always a conditioned one, the condition being the continued free willing of the present system of physical laws by God—a condition revocable by the same will; a logical or metaphysical impossibility would alone be an unconditioned one, whose violation would be impossible even to God and would involve no genuine limitation in the order of real being or real perfection, since it would imply the positing of an internally contradictory nonbeing.

## II. On Professor Niebuhr's Paper, "On the Nature of Faith"

Professor Niebuhr's sole aim in his paper has been to do the preliminary work of analyzing the whole spectrum of phenomena which we call 'faith' in our language. He has done what seems to me, for the most part, quite a successful job. In thus trying to separate clearly all the "pure colors" on this spectrum, however, I believe he has in one case separated what in reality are always or for the most part joined together. His major distinction is between kinds of faith having to do primarily with knowledge and kinds having to do primarily with interpersonal trust, confidence, and the like. All well and good in itself and in most of its applications. But I do not think that species I d), "personal knowledge," under the cognitive genus, can be separated from or found without the interpersonal "trust" kind of faith characteristic of his second main genus. He identifies the first with the kind of knowledge Newman called "personal knowledge," and he describes it as follows: "it may be a kind of totality of the apprehending self that apprehends as a psychosomatic-rational-spiritual whole. . . . For J. H. Newman, religious assent is a function of the whole person confronting a totality."

But it is precisely because such an attitude involves the whole person as an existential totality in action that it must include the basic will attitudes of interpersonal trust, confidence, commitment, etc. I believe this is almost certainly how Newman himself understood this type of attitude or faith. Historically, it is quite true that the Hebrews seemed to have focused more explicitly on the trust kind of faith and the Greeks on the cognitive. But it is precisely part of the genius of Christianity that it fused the two into a single and henceforth indissoluble spiritual attitude in its own new and much richer conception of faith as total commitment, at once intellectual and voluntary, of the whole person to God. Again, within Christianity, the Protestant tradition has tended to stress more the trust element and the Catholic the cognitive (in the latter case because its theology has analyzed the original rich whole of Biblical "faith" into the distinct, but not separated, theological virtues of faith, hope, and charity). But it still remains that, if we are not to denature or impoverish the reality we are trying to analyze in the concrete, any act of what Niebuhr, following Newman, calls "personal knowledge," involving the "totality of the apprehending self," "the whole person confronting a totality," must necessarily include the whole will dimension of trust, commitment, etc. Therefore, I would here unite what Professor Niebuhr has, it seems to me, a little too sharply distinguished.

## III. On Professor Tillich's Paper, "The Meaning and Justification of Religious Symbols"

Since we did not have available the text of the paper actually given by Professor Tillich, I must trust my memory in commenting on the gist of what was said, using as a guide his previously published paper on the subject. (The latter paper, by the way, I found to be an extraordinarily rich, profound, and illuminating one—and one with which I could agree to a very large extent. As he understands symbolic language, I do not think there is as much difference or opposition as he would seem to think between it and analogical language as I understand it. A Catholic theologian, Father Gustave Weigel, who knows the thought of Professor Tillich well, is now using the term "symbolic language" more and more as a synonym for "analogical language," and did so, in fact, throughout his own paper at this same gathering.)

# Religious Experience and Truth

The one point I would like to comment on is Professor Tillich's fear that analogy applied to God is "too static" and his attempts to fix and hold in a finite concept the ineffable and utterly transcendent nature of God. I would like to link this with the constant difficulty voiced by logicians, philosophers of science, linguistic analysts, and others during the symposium: by what right can we take terms from ordinary experience and language—which all the theistic philosophers and theologians agree must be done—and apply them with a significant shift and extension of meaning to something, God, which we cannot directly experience (unless we are mystics—and then we cannot communicate literally what we have experienced)? Must not the new elements introduced into the concepts when applied beyond our own experience be necessarily a blank of positive meaning, a pure shot in the dark?

This is a genuine and profound problem, *the* main problem in the philosophy of religion, one might well say. I have time here to point out only what seems to me the key notion which permits a working out of the solution. The objectors commonly presume that what is going on is this: we take a term which has one definite conceptual content as drawn from and applied to our own experience, then when we apply it to God, we add on to it a new element which is quite extraneous to the latter and whose meaning we cannot possibly understand from this experience. If this were the case, we would indeed have made an illegitimate conceptual and linguistic leap.

But the whole point of the application of analogy to God is that the extra dimension of content introduced into the concepts thus applied is not dragged in arbitrarily from *outside* what we discern in our experience. It is rather a dynamic exigency, a thrust, a direction, already imbedded deep *in* the intelligible texture of the finite world of our own experience. As we confront the world with reflective intelligence, the profound and ineluctable exigencies of our intellect and will for total and unconditioned truth, being, goodness, perfection, etc. help us to discern in the finite, imperfect beings of our experience their radical state of deficiency or imperfection, both in the possession of the perfections they manifest as well as in their incapacity to satisfy the exigencies built into our intellectual nature.

The notion of limited and deficient perfection is here the operative one that acts as springboard to point the mind beyond its present experience. Found *within* the beings of our experience, it yet, by the very dynamism that constitutes its intelligibility, points beyond itself to a mysterious source which is pure, simple, unconditioned, hence infinite, plenitude of what we experience here as "only so much and no more," i.e., as radically deficient, limited, and unsatisfying. We do not properly look *away* from the finite to find the Infinite. We rather find the exigency for the infinite written right *into* the intelligible texture of the finite recognized as such, and we find it by looking more deeply *into* the finite itself.

Note that I am not arguing the point here whether or not one can construct a valid proof of the real existence of the Infinite from the finite, though I believe that with care one can. I am making only this point: the meaningfulness of our *language* and *thought* about the Infinite finds its support in the profound human *experience* of discerning within our world the latter's intrinsic character of radical limitation, deficiency, and inability to satisfy our own deepest exigencies of intellect and will. And the notion of deficient or limited goodness is, by its very inner structure, both psychologically and conceptually, a highly dynamic one which necessarily and importunately points beyond itself to a mysterious plenitude in the same line, affirmable—though not representable—in the dim mirror of need, desire, and hope.

Therefore, analogous language which is combined with the peculiar "pointing-concept" of infinity, what we might analogously call the "infinity-operator"—and only such language can be legitimately applied to God—contains within itself all the dynamism of the negative theology whose need Professor Tillich has so clearly seen, and this precisely because it includes within its very meaning-structure the expression of the mind's own act of transcending all possible finite experience.

It may still be objected that, however, we have no positive idea of what, for example, a beyond-finite, or beyond-human, love might be; it might no longer be love at all but something quite different. The answer here is twofold. First, through the causal argument to the dependence of the finite on an infinite Source, combined with reflection on our own exigencies of intellect and will, we can say this much with certainty about what we call "infinite Love": it cannot fall *below* the core of positive perfection, goodness, being, etc. which we have found in the finite participant within our experience, but must be at least all of that and could be, still better, incalculably more. In other words, when we apply the attribute *love* to God we are using it, not as a "ceiling-concept" limiting its content to what our experience of love is, but as "floor-concept," so to speak, indicating *at least* all this positive value and whatever else is better, as long as it does not negate or evacuate the positive content of the authentic value we have experienced in human love. Secondly, we must be careful before applying any concept to God (intrinsic analogy applies not only to terms but to their conceptual content) to see if it can sustain "purification" from imperfection and finitude, i.e., whether its positive core of value is purely positive in what it affirms or whether it affirms some imperfection or limit as an essential and irreducible part of its meaning. Thus *love* would meet this test, not *sexual love;* so would *intellectual knowledge,* but not *knowledge by inference,* and so forth. I trust this may help somewhat to show how sense can be made out of analogical language applied to God.

## 29

# RELIGIOUS EXPERIENCE, LANGUAGE, AND TRUTH

*by Daya Krishna, Saigur University, India*

The hours devoted to discussion in this symposium seemed characterized by a singular unconcern with religious experience, which is the *raison d'etre* of any inquiry being undertaken in this field at all. It may seem futile and foolish to discuss problems in the philosophy of science without taking into account what the scientists in their scientific behavior do and the way they go about doing it. But it certainly did not seem so to most persons discussing problems in the philosophy of religion. There was, for example, much discussion of language in religious discourse but little, if any, attention was paid to the way in which religious concepts arise from, and find their meaning in, the religious experience itself. The 'operationalism' so obvious in the field of science did not seem quite so necessary in the field of religion to most philosophers assembled there.

The lack of interest in religious experience manifested itself in another direction. It was completely forgotten that the truths of religion are not contained in a set of propositions which can be made a subject of analysis and reasoned argument in themselves. Every religion prescribes a pattern of practices, sometimes varying in great detail for different types of persons with different temperaments, which, if pursued, result for most people in the gradual realization of what was meant by those statements. The philosophers assembled seemed to think that 'knowing God' is an easy matter, while to the religious men of all ages it has been the pursuit of a lifetime or in some cultures even of cycles of lives. The point again is that unless it is seen that, according to most religions, something has to be *done* to realize God (or whatever is the equivalent of God in that religion)—a realization in terms of which the religious statements get their meaning and their verification—the philosophical discussions will hang in the air.

The religious discourse, for example, is replete with contradictions. There seems something in the religious experience which necessitates its articulation in statements which appear contradictory to the rational intellect. Should this lead to the view that what religion talks about cannot be valid? It makes claims to truth which in their very nature cannot be true. How would the scientist feel if the philosopher, using the criterion of strict verification, termed most of his discovered principles literally meaningless? Would he not think there is something wrong with the criterion which necessarily makes the philosopher reach such a conclusion? And why have the philosophers themselves increasingly diluted the verification principle till it has reached such an innocuous form as, "our statements about the external world face the tribunal of sense experience not individually but only as a corporate body? "[1]

The prestige of science is too great today, and if the philosophers had persisted too long in the stringency of their criterion, they would merely have exposed themselves to ridicule. Behind the diplomatic retreat, however, there was also the insight that the philosopher could bring no a priori criteria that would prejudge the matter completely. Rather, one had to go to the practitioners themselves to articulate the criteria which they used within the field of their inquiry. And though a philosophical critique of the concepts employed, the methods used, and the criteria adopted is sound philosophical activity, it is such only if it does not make the activity itself impossible. That this has not been seen in the case of religious experience shows only that philosophers share the prejudices of their age and find it difficult to get away from them.

The other great limitation of the discussion, to my mind, was its confinement, perhaps naturally, to Christianity alone. It was as if one were to reflect on aesthetic experience and confine one's discussion to Greek art or the Renaissance masters only. (Today, no one would think of doing it in a discussion on art, but if one were to do it, one would be challenged immediately.) That no one challenged this implicit limitation shows once again the difficulty of getting beyond the perspective of the culture one happens to be born in.

If these limitations are overcome, then issues will be formulated in a different way. Whether God exists or does not exist will not be in the center of discussion. For, even if one were to come to the conclusion that a theoretic concept of God is required to understand intelligibly certain phenomena and that the totality of phenomena indirectly confirm—to a certain degree—such a hypothesis, the religious man will remain completely unsatisfied with it and will, in fact, consider it absolutely irrelevant to the 'knowing' of God in his sense of the term. Theology, it should be understood, is the exact opposite of what the religious man seeks, and however much the theologist may talk of God, he is not supposed to 'know' him at all.

Religion is essentially a *seeking* for something beyond this world with its limitation of space, time, mass, and causality—something that is to be experienced as, or even more, *directly* as the world we experience through our senses. The seeking invariably takes the form, at least in its first phase, of a turning away from this world. The world is not sought to be known or understood. It is simply disregarded or treated as a hindrance that distracts one from the one-pointed pursuit of that which is felt to be beyond or behind the world that appears to sense perception. What is 'beyond' or 'behind' the world obviously is not something in space which one could seek and find. Nor is it some sort of a conceptual scheme in terms of which the world of sense-experience can be interrelated and understood. The concern is not with the world at all, but rather with something that is to be realized by taking our minds away from it. The way, therefore, has always been the withdrawal from the world, the concentration on the Divine, the aspiration for it, and the prayer to it to reveal itself. The core of all religions is religious experience got through withdrawal, aspiration, and invocation of grace. Ultimately, whatever is being sought is supposed to reveal itself in freedom, and thus the element of grace is paramount and inalienable in all religions except in certain of its magical forms which have long been left behind in man's religious exploration.

This experience, while not completely the same everywhere, has recognizable similarities in its different ranges, and thus forms a distinctly determinable realm having certain characteristics of its own. It tends to formulate itself, for example, into contradictory statements simultaneously asserted as true. The language in which religious experience tends to express itself is not the language of mathematics or even of the empirical sciences but of parable and paradox which still claims to convey truth. The philosophers and most educated people believe that a set of contradictory statements cannot describe truth. Religion, the realm of contradictor par excellence, therefore, becomes to them so obviously false or even meaningless as not to require any further consideration at all.

The preliminary question is, then, if a contradictory statement can ever correctly designate a side of affairs. Could not there be an experience which could correctly be formulated *only* in a conjunctive unity of contradictory statements? I think it is too easily assumed in philosophical discussions that the answer to such a question can only be a definite 'no.' Supposing I were to ask someone "Are you happy?" and he were to reply "I am and I am not," would he necessarily be uttering a false or nonsensical statement? (I am not trying to distinguish between the two at the present state of the argument.) Is it quite so obvious that he could only feel either happy or unhappy but not something which could only be described as feeling both?

The objection obviously will take the familiar form. First, it will be suggested that we are ignoring the difference in contexts and what may be called the difference in time-instants, which *alone* could make the sentence meaningful for any further consideration. The statement is supposed to be a cryptic way of saying that I am alternately feeling happy and unhappy in quick succession with respect to different things in my life which force themselves on my attention. Second, it may be suggested that the person just does not

know what he is talking about, that he is talking lightly and doesn't
expect to be taken literally and seriously, or that we are making
an elementary confusion between language and that to which it
refers. Contradiction is characteristic of linguistic discourse, and if
we are asked to avoid it, it is only because linguistic discourse must
be intelligible to perform its function effectively. It may even be
suggested that the problem arises merely because there is no single
word for the feeling in the language. (There may actually be such
a word, but that does not affect the argument.) If there were such
a word we would not feel it to denote a contradictory state of affairs, just as no one thinks that the word 'courage' refers to something which is both cowardice and foolhardiness at the same time.

I do not wish to consider all these objections here in detail,
since some I have considered elsewhere.[2] But I should very much
like to urge that, if someone feels that the alternative formulation
does not adequately describe what he wants to convey, then his own
formulation should be accepted. After all, isn't the person concerned
the one who should be supposed to know best in the whole affair?
And as for intelligibility, how do we know that law of contradiction is a necessary condition for it or that without it language cannot perform its function adequately? Surely, on any 'operational
definition' of 'intelligibility,' if a large number of people behaved
as if they understood, then it cannot but be considered intelligible
to them. I may not understand a thing myself, but I can certainly
*observe* that others are understanding and successfully communicat-
ing with each other. Whether the language is performing its function or not can only be decided by those who are using it. If it
were not performing the function to the satisfaction of those who
are using it, then obviously they would try to change it in a way
that would make it more effective for their purpose. Of course,
the satisfaction may only be minimal and the persons may just
not know that a more effective instrument exists or is possible.
Equally, they may be too lazy to make the extra effort or too easily
satisfied to want something better.

These considerations, however, do not seem relevant, for it is not
that religious people are, or were not, aware of the law of contradic-

tion. Like everyone else, they themselves accept it in many fields of human discourse. It is only with respect to religious experience that all of them feel constrained to question the relevance of the law. It is almost as if beyond a certain range the properties do not hold—a situation which certainly is not unfamiliar to persons in other fields of knowledge.

Basically, the application of the law of contradiction presupposes a sharp, specific, and identifiable application of 'sameness,' and if this is not possible in a situation, it ceases to be relevant. The religious experience is concerned with that which is supposed to be beyond space, time, mass, and causality. There should be little wonder if it expresses itself in a conjunction of contradictory statements asserted as true.

Contradiction may be a characteristic of linguistic statements, but that it is a necessary condition for any language to be a 'language' or for language to be 'intelligible' is empirically falsified by the existence of language in which contradictions abound and which are treated as intelligible by a large number of persons who use them. It may be objected that the use in all such cases is non-cognitive and thus beyond questions of truth and falsehood. The contradictory assertions of religion are supposed to shock the mind out of its habitual grooves of thought, or to be something like poetry, which conveys truth but not of the cognitive kind. However, what if the persons insist that this is not always what they are doing? Some parts of religious discourse as, say, in Zen Buddhism, are obviously of this type and such is consciously intended by the Master. But, equally obviously, others are not of this type, and if one were to treat them in such a way, one would be corrected immediately. As for 'poetic truth,' it has mostly been considered as the truth of the form of our feelings, while religion has always claimed that the truth it discovers is simultaneously a truth about the self and the world.

The claim to truth is the hardest thing to understand for most persons who are scientifically or philosophically trained. Yet it can hardly be denied that there is some sort of verification in terms of experience. A person has to undergo a certain process in order to encounter a certain experience which he takes as verificatory of that which he had been theoretically told by the tradition and the Master. The verification is never complete, and both theoretic reflection and actual experience can reveal new possibilities and actualities which neither the tradition nor the Master knew. The experience and its usual interpretation, of course, do not cohere with the general trend of interpretation in the sciences. And many persons genuinely feel that if they have to bet on one rather than the other, it will be far, far safer to bet on science than religion, for it is almost certain they would gain the whole world and very, very doubtful if they would lose the whole soul. But is it necessary to choose between them? Can't we have the whole world and our soul too?

First, even on the purely scientific plane, there is no such thing as Science, but only sciences. There is not only the great cleavage between physical and social sciences, but within these broad classes there is no unity either. Even within a single science, the generalized theory from which all the facts within that realm can be derived is an ideal unrealized anywhere—including that paradigm of all sciences, the science of physics.

Second, it does not seem quite clear what exactly is meant by the demand that all the fields of human experience, or even all the theories constructed to account for the phenomena in these different fields, should be "coherent" with each other. What, for example, is the "coherence" between Freud's theory of neuroses, Darwin's theory of evolution, and the electromagnetic theory of matter? Or, for that matter, what is the 'coherence' between 'matter' and 'evolution' and 'neuroses' if they are treated as facts and not as constructs in a theoretic system? [3] The theories, it will be observed, are about too-disparate realms for the question of coherence to be significantly raised about them. And once this is accepted, it becomes completely irrelevant to object to religious experience and its usual interpretation on a ground of 'incoherence' with experience and interpretation in other fields. True, if religion makes claims to knowledge about phenomena in other fields which conflict with the evidenced findings in those areas, then it obviously has to give up its claims or substantiate them by the usual processes of establishing a proposition in those realms. Similarly, if a generalized philosophical structure is built on the basis of religious experience, it will have to stand the usual tests brought to bear on the adequacy of any philosophical system whatsoever. But both these admissions do not impugn in any way the claim to knowledge and truth made by religion in its own sphere.

Third, it should be seriously considered how the cognitive claims of experiences which are of great imminent significance should be regarded. Sensory experiences in terms of which verification is sought in the sciences are usually not significant in themselves. Their significance is merely in the context of the theory which is sought to be verified. And it is never a part of the theory that the experience which verifies it should be felt as outstandingly suffused with significance in itself. In religious experience, on the other hand, the supremely significant character of the experience is an integral part of its being as evidence for the truth of the cognition claim based on it. Crystals may be beautiful to watch or the stars a wonderful sight, but it is not a part of the theory in crytallography or astronomy that they should be so.

The alleged incongruence between religious experience and its articulation on the one hand and so-called 'scientific experience' and its articulation on the other need not then be such a serious thing as it usually is considered to be. After all, everything that seems to matter to us and make life meaningful and worthwhile is, at least apparently, incongruent with scientific explanation. Whether it be love or friendship or enjoyment of art or contemplation of nature or courage to be what one thinks one ought to be— all these seem irrelevant to or even positively incongruent with the world as revealed by science. However, neither the scientist nor anyone else gives up these things, ceases to find meaning in them, or waits till someone will discover the cognitive congruence in all the different realms of human experiencing. Why, then, should it be different with religious experience in particular? Why should the exploration in this realm and the relevant theorizing therein wait on the issue of its accord with the experience and the theories in the different sciences?

There is, of course, a theorizing which is permitted and even welcomed in the prevailing academic atmosphere today, viz., the theorizing that drains the experience of all its significance and reduces it to some sort of an illusion which, when its causes are understood, would cease to be mistaken for knowledge or felt as supremely significant. Unfortunately, everything is supposed to have a cause, including an experience that is veridical, and there are no *specific* causes which establish an experience to be illusory. Also, an experience does not lose its significance if its causes are found to be of dubious character unless the belief in the nondubiousness of its causes is a necessary condition of its being felt as significant. The case is similar with that which is supposed to be illusory. No one ceases to feel the beauty of a Greek column just because he finds that its physical measurements are different from what they seem to the eye.

These considerations, it may be urged, apply to all experiences felt as significant, including those of the drug addict and the murderer. Why should the religious experience be treated on a different level, or as cognitively, in a different category than these experiences? The question of abnormality in relation to values and cognitive validity has seldom been discussed in philosophical literature. But it may be asserted with some confidence that, except in the statistical sense, religious experience cannot be considered as abnormal. The capacity for inner freedom, abiding joy, and relevant response to external situations is so pre-eminent and abundant in spiritual persons that compared to them, ordinary, normal persons appear as deficient human beings. The problem of cognitive validity centers around that about which the cognitive claim is made. If the claim is about empirical things, the tests of validity are the same as in the relevant sciences. However, it should be remembered that statements concerning entities, which may be treated as logical constructs out of experiences which are spiritual in nature, seldom concern the world known through sense-experience or reasoning except at the highest level of generality, and they are almost impossible to verify. This does not mean they are unverifiable, but only that their verification is not quite an easy thing to achieve. This should hardly be surprising when even such a simple thing as the geometrical nature of the space we are living in is not quite easily determinable by all the methods of present-day physical science. The situation is even more complicated in the case of religious statements, as they are cognitive and evaluative at the same time. The logic of verification of evaluative statements is hardly developed, and if purely cognitive statements about the whole of the space-time universe (this phrase itself is difficult to give any meaning) are so difficult to verify, how much more difficult it must be in the case of these that are evaluative also.

Therefore, unless the autonomous validity of religious experience is accepted in its own field and the theoretic reflection thereon is carried in the context of this basic acceptance, all that goes on in any discussion about religion will appear completely irrelevant to those who are actually practicing religion.[4]

## NOTES

1. W. V. O. Quine, *From a Logical Point of View* (Cambridge: Harvard University Press, 1953), p. 41.

2. "Law of Contradiction and Empirical Reality," *Mind,* April, 1957. The 'point-instant-context' way of saving the law of contradiction has been discussed and, as far as I am aware, no one has ever attempted to meet the consideration urged there.

3. For a more extended discussion of the problem see "Types of Coherence," *The Philosophical Quarterly,* July, 1960.

4. For some of the issues discussed in this paper see "Mysticism and the Problem of Intelligibility," *The Journal of Religion,* April, 1954.

# 30

# SOME NOTES ON
# ANTHROPOMORPHIC THEOLOGY
*by Paul Edwards, New York University*

1. The kind of God discussed by Ziff and Hick is radically
different from the God, if it can be called a God at all, that Tillich
believes in. When Ziff and Hick address themselves to the question
of the existence of a good, powerful, and wise deity they use the
words "good" and "wise" and "powerful" in a sense or senses in
which they are commonly applied to human beings. We may call
this, without implying anything derogatory, the anthropomorphic
conception of God. Tillich, on the other hand, is quite emphatic
that when "good," "wise," or "powerful," or indeed any other
predicates are applied to God, they are not to be understood in
any of their familiar senses. In contrast to the anthropomorphic
God, one may call this the "metaphysical" conception of God. It
should be noted that a person qualifies as a believer in the
anthropomorphic God whether, like Hick and many figures of the
past, he asserts that God is all-powerful, all-knowing, and perfectly
good or whether, like John Stuart Mill or W. P. Montague, he
claims no more than that God possesses these characteristics to a
high degree. Both the believers in the "infinite" and believers in
the "finite" deity openly acknowledge or tacitly presuppose that the
predicates applied to God are used in one or other of their senses
familiar from the human scene.

Now, I am in the habit of calling myself an "atheist," and I wish
to offer here a few remarks in defense of atheism. But, to avoid
misunderstandings, it is necessary to distinguish two of the senses
in which the word "atheism" is used. First, there is the familiar
sense in which a person is an atheist if he maintains that there is

no God, where this is taken to mean that "God exists" expresses a *false* proposition. Secondly, there is also a broader sense in which a person is an atheist if he *rejects* belief in God, regardless of whether his rejection is based on the view that belief in God is *false*. It is worth pointing out that in this broader sense atheism remains distinct from agnosticism, since rejection and suspense of judgment are two different attitudes. I am an atheist in the first sense regarding certain types of God, but not regarding all. I do think—and here Tillich, for one, agrees with me—that in certain of its familiar uses the sentence "God exists" expresses a false proposition. But I do not think that this is true of all widespread uses of this sentence. Nevertheless I adopt an *attitude of rejection* toward all the kinds of God listed in the preceding paragraph. I reject belief in a metaphysical God because it can, I think, be shown that sentences affirming or denying this kind of God are unintelligible or because, in other words, the metaphysical conception is really a pseudo concept; I reject belief in the infinite anthropomorphic God because it can be shown to be either false or meaningless; I reject belief in the finite anthropomorphic God because it can be shown to be either capricious, uneconomical, and excessively vague or meaningless. An exhaustive defense of atheism in this broader sense is out of the question here. However, in exposing certain confusions in the papers of Ziff and Hick, I hope to indicate some of the considerations favoring this position. I shall also try to show that atheism is not, as Ziff seems to imply, a view which, though reasonable "today," might easily be upset "tomorrow."

2. Both Ziff and Hick hold the view that sentences referring to what I have called the anthropomorphic God are intelligible. It seems to me that this assumption is only true with some important reservations and that, furthermore, some of the arguments offered by Ziff and Hick in support of it are far from coercive.

I have no doubt that when most people think about God and his alleged activities, here or in the hereafter, they vaguely think of him as possessing some kind of rather large body. Now, if we are told that there is a God who is, say, just and good and kind and loving and powerful and wise and if, (a) it is made clear that these words are used in one of their ordinary senses, and (b) God is not asserted to be a disembodied mind, then it seems plain to me that *to that extent* a series of meaningful assertions has been made. And this is so whether we are told that God's justice, mercy, etc. are "limitless" or merely that God is superior to all human beings in these respects. However, it seems to me that all these words lose their meaning if we are told that God does not possess a body. Anyone who thinks otherwise without realizing this, I think, is supplying a body in the background of his images. For what would it be like to be, say, just, without a body? To be just, a person has to *act* justly—he has to behave in certain ways. This is not reductive materialism. It is a simple empirical truth about what we mean by "just." But how is it possible to perform these acts, to behave in the required ways without a body? Similar remarks apply to the other divine attributes.

Ziff does not show himself the least bit aware of the seriousness of this problem. He merely assures us that "the condition of being a non-spatiotemporal being can be viewed as a result of an abstraction from the condition of being a spatiotemporal being." This dark saying he elaborates by pointing to the "ease of such abstraction" which is "testified to by the fact that plain people sometimes say they find it difficult to keep body and soul together." This is merely an irresponsible play on words, since there is not the least reason to suppose that anybody who has occasion to complain that "he cannot keep his body and soul together" is in any way trying to assert the existence of an entity that does not occupy space or is in any sense nontemporal.

Unlike Ziff, Hick makes an attempt to meet the difficulty. "What," he very properly asks, "does 'loving' mean when it is transferred to a Being who is defined, *inter alia,* as having no body, so that he cannot be thought of as performing any actions? What is disembodied love, and how can we ascertain that it exists?" Hick is not satisfied with the "traditional answer" that "loving" is used "analogously" when applied to God, but his own answer, as far as I can follow it, is just as unsatisfactory. He divides it into two parts. I cannot see anything in the second part of the answer which has any bearing whatever on the question of what "loving" can mean when applied to a "being" without a body. In the first part of Hick's answer we are told that the Christian doctrine of the Incarnation is revelant to the problem. The attitudes of Jesus, he says, exhibit and reveal certain aspects of God's nature. He continues, "This is part of the meaning of the statement that God the Son was incarnate in Jesus of Nazareth. In the life of Jesus, then, the love, compassion, and other aspects of God's attitude toward mankind are seen expressed in concrete human actions: 'The Logos was made flesh and dwelt among us. . . .' And, accordingly, the first part of the answer to the question, in what sense of 'loving' is God said to be loving, is: In the sense in which Jesus can be seen to have exhibited this characteristic." I fail to see that this takes us anywhere at all. For the love and compassion displayed by Jesus were love and compassion manifesting themselves in certain actions of a human being *with* a body. Either God has a body or he has not. If he has, then there is no problem. If he has not, the problem is not removed by pointing to a human being, however distinguished or remarkable, who possesses a body.

3. Ziff distinguishes between the "problematic" and the "unproblematic" conditions that have been associated with the name "God." He concedes that while some of the "problematic" conditions may be "difficult," they are nevertheless intelligible. In the case of some of the "problematic" conditions, I am inclined to agree with Ziff, but not for the reason he advances. "I know," he writes, "that if something is the cause of itself then we cannot succeed in finding another cause. I know that if something is the creator of the world then prior to its act of creation the world did exist. . . . That I can make such inferences indicates that I have some understanding of the conditions involved."

Surely this argument is fallacious. There are any number of sentences which in the opinion of practically everybody, atheist or believer, positivist or metaphysician, are meaningless, but which can at the same time be used as premises of valid deductions. From "the Absolute is lazy" it follows that the Absolute is not industrious; from "Box sleeps more rapidly than Cox," it follows that Cox

244

sleeps more slowly than Box; from "everything has increased tenfold in size since yesterday," it follows that my right hand is ten times as large as it was yesterday (which in this context is also meaningless); etc., etc. From "there is a being that created the universe out of nothing," it certainly follows that "there was a time when the universe did not exist." But this would have any tendency to show that the former sentence is intelligible only if it is granted that its consequence is intelligible, which is one of the main points of issue.

Part of the trouble seems to be Ziff's use of the phrase "*some* understanding." There is a sense in which I do have "some understanding" of "the Absolute is lazy"—a sense in which, for example, a Chinese, who does not understand English at all, has no understanding of it and in which I have no understanding of gibberish like "*promax robar dux*." But to say that I have "some understanding" of "the Absolute is lazy" in this sense means no more than that I am familiar with certain rules of substitution governing the relative employment of the words "lazy" and "industrious," etc. In *this* sense we certainly have "some understanding" of "something is the creator of the universe." But this is trivial and irrelevant. Nobody who has seriously discussed the question as to whether we understand "problematic" theological sentences has used "understand" and related terms like "intelligible" or "meaningful" in this sense.

4. Tillich, I gather, agrees with atheists that what I have called the anthropomorphic God does not exist. Hick, on the other hand, maintains that the question cannot be, or at least that it has not yet been settled. "It is hard to see," he writes, "how one could claim to know that the religious believer is deluded." He supports this by drawing a distinction between unbelievers and the "circle of faith." For members of this "circle," or generally for people who are in the state of mind to which Hick alludes, the question of the existence of God does not arise. For those outside the circle, Hick tells us, "the right question to ask is not 'Is there a God?' but 'Do I have grounds for supposing that what the men of faith believe is false?'"

245

Since, however, what the "men of faith" believe (or the only part of their belief relevant to the discussion) is that there is a God, the second question is exactly equivalent to the first. Whichever way the question is asked, it is not at all hard to determine that the believer is mistaken. I think that Hick finds it hard to see this when he asks the question in his way, because he vaguely thinks of "the men of faith" as mystics and takes those who claim that the men of faith are deluded to be denying the existence of their mystical experiences. But whether the men of faith have special mystical experiences or not, their claim, insofar as it is relevant to our discussion, can be put to the test of *ordinary* experience. From the assertion that there is a God who is both all-powerful and all-good (in the ordinary sense or senses), certain consequences follow about the publicly observable world, and these consequences are disconfirmed by what we observe. I need hardly rehash the argument from evil here, and I gather that Hick does not endorse the usual rebuttals in terms of man's free will, the need for contrast, the unreality of evil, and the like.

In reply to Professor Blanshard, Hick conceded that it is impossible to reconcile the existence of God with the fact of evil, unless we assume that there is an afterlife in which presumably everything is somehow put right. There are three very obvious objections to such a reply. In the first place, it depends upon the more than dubious proposition that there is an afterlife. Secondly, Hick, who, I gather, is an empiricist, can hardly argue that because things are pretty bad in this life, they will therefore be wonderful in the next one. It has often been pointed out [1] that, if this life is any clue to the other one, the other life will also presumably be characterized by injustice, suffering, and all sorts of other undesirable features. But, finally, let us grant that there is an afterlife and that everything will be wonderful there. I do not see that this would dispose of the argument from evil. It will still remain true that the animal world was full of pain and suffering, that babies were born blind or with two heads or in other ways deformed, that fine and talented human beings died of leukemia or other dread diseases before they had any real opportunity to enjoy life and make adequate use of their talents, etc. And these facts remain just as incompatible with an all-good and all-powerful God as ever.

When Hick maintains that the question of the existence of God cannot or has not been "publicly settled," he fails to note an ambiguity in the use of the word "settle." Sometimes when we say that a dispute has been "settled" we mean that it has come to an end, that all parties to the dispute (or all surviving parties) have come to hold the same view. At other times we mean that one party has been proven to be in the right and the other or others in the wrong, or something of that sort. Let us call the first sense of settlement "termination" and the second sense "resolution by evidence." It is clear that settlement in one sense does not logically entail settlement in the other.[2] Now, if there are people who are as sure of the existence of God as the people whom Hick describes as members of the circle of faith, they are very unlikely to be shaken in their belief by the presentation of antitheological arguments, no matter how sound these arguments may be. Indeed they are unlikely to be ready to listen to such arguments. Hence, as long as such people survive, the dispute about the existence of God will not have been settled in the sense of "termination." But this in no way implies that the question has not been settled in the other, and philosophically far more important and interesting, sense, namely the sense of "resolution." The existence of a circle of faith in no way shows that there is no strong or even conclusive evidence for atheism. Once the ambiguity in the use of such words as "settle" has been pointed out, the entire strategy of distinguishing between a circle of believers and a circle of unbelievers is seen to be pointless.

5. In addition to the argument from evil, there are other powerful considerations for supposing that there is no such being as the infinite, anthropomorphic God. But Ziff's argument is not one of them. According to present-day physics, no physical object can travel with a velocity exceeding that of light. It follows from this, that, Ziff argues, from the velocity of light and from what is known about the distance between the sun and the earth, a stone cannot be transported from the earth to the sun in one second. Nobody could

achieve this feat. Hence there is no omnipotent being and hence no infinite anthropomorphic God.

This argument is so patently invalid that I find it difficult to believe that Ziff is in earnest about it. Physics does indeed show that nothing can travel faster than light, provided, that is, that *miracles never happen.* The various physical propositions listed in the last paragraph imply that there is no omnipotent being only in conjunction with the proposition that miraculous interruptions of natural uniformities never take place. But this is, of course, precisely what very many believers deny. If it is once granted that miracles do not happen, any other established law would equally prove the nonexistence of an omnipotent being.

6. Is atheism, in the broader sense, liable to be upset "tomorrow"? Ziff answers this question in the affirmative. "The question 'does God exist?' " he writes, "may be freshly conceived, and so conceived may call for a fresh answer. That the answers to the old questions have always been no proves nothing. The answer to tomorrow's question is something that one can only be blank about." Now, if "tomorrow's question" is to be at all relevant to our contemporary discussions of the existence of God, the word "God" will have to be used in a way that is not too dissimilar from its present uses. For example, if anybody were to maintain that the universe, as Hume playfully remarked in one place, was spun out of the belly of an infinite spider, this would hardly count as belief in "God." In fact, I cannot see that any belief would be relevant unless it could be fitted into one or other of the three theological positions which I distinguished earlier—the metaphysical position, the belief in the infinite anthropomorphic God, and the belief in the finite anthropomorphic deity.

How sure can one be that the rejection of these three positions will not be upset in the future? Since I have not discussed the metaphysical belief in this paper, and since Ziff is also not concerned with it, I shall confine myself to the two anthropomorphic positions. Surely nothing could upset our rejection of the belief in the infinite anthropomorphic God. No matter what the future may bring, the evil that has already occurred in the history of the world flatly contradicts the assertion of the existence of such a deity. The situation is different in the case of the rejection of the finite anthropomorphic God. I will grant that new facts might logically weaken rejection of this belief, perhaps to such an extent that any attitude short of complete acceptance would become irrational. The facts I have in mind are extreme versions of the sort of thing that Cleanthes in Hume's *Dialogues* imagined when he described the "heavenly voice." Suppose that, Hume makes Cleanthes say, "an articulate voice were heard in the clouds, much louder and more melodious than any which human art could ever reach: Suppose, that this voice were extended in the same instant over all nations, and spoke to each nation in its own language and dialect: Suppose, that the words delivered not only contain a just sense and meaning, but convey some instruction altogether worthy of a benevolent Being, superior to mankind." Let us make this a little more definite. Let us suppose that the voice made statements about the prevention and cure of cancer and all sorts of unsolved scientific problems, and that, upon examination, every one of these statements turned out to be true. It is clear that if such a voice were heard, Cleanthes would regard this as confirmation of the existence of God in the sense in which he asserts it. I think it is equally clear that most ordinary believers would be jubilant if such events ever occurred, and they too would regard their belief confirmed. Actually, such events would be far from constituting *decisive* evidence even for a finite anthropomorphic deity. They would, however, be powerful evidence for the assertion that one *or* more beings exist who exceed all human beings in intelligence and possibly also in other respects. And one could imagine events considerably more extreme than any here described which would be most plausibly explained by the theory of a single finite anthropomorphic deity. There is, however, not the faintest reason to suppose that any such events will actually occur in the future any more than they have occurred in the past. Hence it seems to me that atheism, insofar as it is an empirical theory or a rejection tied to empirical observations, is not a precarious but a very firmly grounded view. "Tomorrow's questions" cannot upset it. "Tomorrow's facts" could, but there is no reason to suppose that they will; on the contrary, there is all the reason in the world to suppose that they will not.

## NOTES

1. See Bertrand Russell, *Why I Am Not A Christian* (New York: Simon and Schuster, Inc. 1957), p. 13. Cf. "Same thing in the next world," says Jigger in *Carousel*. "For rich folks, the heavenly court and the high judge. For you and me, perlice magistrates, Fer the rich, fine music and chubby little angels—" BILLY: "Won't we get any music?" JIGGER: "Not a note. All we'll get is justice! There'll be plenty of that for you and me. Yes, sir! Nothin' but justice."
2. See my book, *The Logic of Moral Discourse* (Glencoe, Ill.: The Free Press, 1955), pp. 25–28 and 36–41.

# 31

## AMBIGUITIES IN
## THE CONCEPT OF GOD

*by Dorothy Emmet, University of Manchester, England*

The discussions strengthened the impression I had already formed of how highly problematic all concepts become when used with reference to God, and indeed how problematic the theistic concept itself is. I fully agree with Professor Ziff that in talking about God, we must use a recognizable kind of logic and connect the meanings of the terms with something which can be made intelligible in a natural sense. But in distinguishing, as he does, between "problematic and unproblematic conditions," I think he underestimates how problematic even the unproblematic ones become when they are related to the others, as in, e.g., the notion of "infinite Being." When theologians use concepts qualified in this way, they say they must be understood analogically. But they do not succeed in showing what the basic common meaning is which controls the analogy, and therefore the concept seems to suffer what Professor Flew has called the "death by a thousand qualifications." The strength of this analogical way of talking is in showing that God should not be thought of just as "a being" over and above others, only greater and grander (as is no doubt the popular way of thinking). Its weakness is in not showing what meaning can be given to the notion of a kind of being which is not "a being" in this sense.

I believe that these discussions are bound to run into impasses so long as we are in effect trying to think of God as "a transcendent being" over and above others. In a way some of the older thinkers in the classical theistic tradition saw this, for instance when they say that we should talk of Him not as *eus,* but as *esse qua esse,* and when St. Thomas says that God is not a genus, and so not a substance. (Margaret Masterman has recently remarked to me in a personal letter how this abstract side of the older classical theism kept Christianity from becoming a concrete kind of popular thinking, and fed its contemplative tradition. Now, she says, we are losing the abstract side, and the concrete symbolism is accordingly becoming cruder.) The difficulty is to relate these highly abstract notions to something naturally meaningful. The discussions strengthened my belief that there is no future (philosophically speaking, as distinct from popular talk) in the "Supreme Being" type of theism. Tillich is one of the few theologians who seems to see this and say it explicitly. He seems to be trying to explore the notion (also drawn from the tradition) of something which is not "a being," but the "ground" or "power" of being in everything that is. Unfortunately he does not go far enough to meet the difficulties we philosophers have in trying to make these notions (which may well be important notions) intelligible. This is partly because this logical and metaphysical problem gets involved for Tillich with the psychological and personalist problem of people's "ultimate concern." And, since he holds that everyone has some ultimate concern, even, as it emerged, the Teddy Boy for his Ma, we are told that everyone is religious, and the discussion becomes a psychological one, with the meaning of "religious" standing for any serious anxiety or concern. Tillich's corrective to this is, of course, to say that all "ultimate concerns" which stop short of the ground of being are religious, but idolatrously religious. The only non-idolatrous religion would presumably be an ultimate concern for something which we might say was "nothing in particular." I think the next step would have to be to show that it is possible for there to be something which is not anything in particular, and yet at the same time show that the notion is not just vacuous because it makes a difference to us (and the difference must not just be that we are concerned, or anxious, about it, i.e., a subjective fact about us). This would call for exploring some of the older "immanentist" notions, instead of fastening exclusively on the "transcendent" notions, as has happened in recent discussions of philosophical

252

theism. We should need to go further into these notions of "ground" and "power" of being. They are, of course, extremely vague, and it is difficult to see how they can be made less so. But I think the task should be to try, for there might here be a possibility of developing a generalized theistic concept which might eventually be related to empirical concept in a way which might not produce the impasses we find in the notion of a supreme transcendent being, as extended from what Professor Ziff calls "the plain man's conception of God."

*32*

# ON DEFINING THE TERM "GOD"

*by Howard W. Hintz, Brooklyn College*

## *I.*

One of the major shortcomings of this symposium, to my mind, was the failure in each of the sessions to reach any satisfactory clarification of the central term under discussion, the term "God." Some efforts in this direction were made by some of the discussants, but the theologians present never really approached an explicit definition. It must also be said that many of the philosophers present used the term frequently without being any more clear or explicit about its meaning.

The classic principle that any term must be defined before it can be meaningfully used applies with particular force to the term "God" and to any of its synonyms. There are few terms connoting such a wide variety of meanings and conceptions as this one. There are few terms about which so much confusion prevails as to the meaning intended to be conveyed by the user, or the meaning accepted by the reader or listener. It was primarily for this reason that the discussions at all three of the Institute sessions so often floundered in obfuscations, irrelevancies, circular arguments, and question-begging statements. At no time was it precisely clear what the speakers or discussants were actually discussing. Therefore, one wonders whether any significant progress toward a clarification of the problems, much less toward a resolution of them, was really achieved at these sessions.

The central point to be made, it seems to me, is simply this: any serious and extended consideration or discussion of religious belief and experience would do well to begin with a session given over exclusively to *definition* and to clarification of theological terminology. The indispensable prerequisite to any meaningful discussion of theology is the attempt, at least, to ascertain the dimension and limits, the similarities and differences in the theological views entertained by the discussants. This applies primarily and particularly to the various concepts represented by the term "God."

Assuming that there cannot possibly be agreement with respect to the meaning of the term (meaning both in the sense of how they as individuals understand the term and also in the sense of the general understanding of the term) among any group of theologians or philosophers brought together either at random or selectively for the purpose of reflecting various points of view—assuming that any agreement on meaning is impossible to achieve in such a group, then at least the differences and disagreements could be specified, sharpened, and clarified. From such an initial effort toward definition, some progress would be made toward understanding which discussants were talking about God in a traditional Judaeo-Christian, anthropomorphic, theistic sense; which were conceiving of God in a theistic but less anthropomorphic sense; which were using the term in a deistic, nonpersonal sense; which were conceiving of the term in the Buddhist or Zen-Buddhist sense; in the Shavian sense (man creates God in his own image); or which were thinking of God in such broad, vague, general, and completely indefinite senses as "Life-Force," "Creative Principle," "Over-Soul," "Totality of Nature," "Universal Mind," etc. Among any group of philosophers brought together for a discussion of religious issues there very likely would also be some who reject the use of the term altogether because of the alleged impossibility of reducing it to explicit, ostensive meaningfulness, either tautologically or empirically. This position, as well as all others represented, must be clearly and explicitly stated as a preliminary to the consideration of any corollary issues, for *all* other theological issues are corollary to the God-concept itself.

Then, even though the participants might indeed find themselves in wide disagreement with respect to basic concepts, at least each would have a clearer notion of: (1) what he is talking about and (2) what his colleagues are talking about. If it be objected that any such preliminary attempt at definition of the central term would occupy not only the first session of any symposium on religion but all subsequent ones for an indefinite period, one can only suggest that an entire conference devoted wholly to the definition and clarification objective might be far more fruitful than a multiplicity of symposia which talk around the subject endlessly for lack of an understanding of the basic terms and the basic issues.

Finally, if it be asserted that (as at least two of the theologians at the Institute did assert) (1) the concept of God is ineffable and inexpressible, and (2) hence any terms referent to the concept are indefinable, and (3) "we must do the best we can with them without defining them," then I believe it must be further asserted that no meaningful discussion can possibly center around terms which are either undefined or indefinable.

If, indeed, one's concept of God is such that one believes his nature and Being to be ineffable and the terms employed to designate him to be indefinable, then the contention of various types of mystics—that neither the God-concept nor the God-designation are subject to argument, discussion, or verbal clarification—is completely sound. But, on the other hand, it should be pointed out that the philosopher or theologian who consents in the first place to enter into a philosophical examination of the God concept implies by that very act that the terms to be employed are discussable and therefore definable. If he does not imply this he is guilty of a fundamental logical contradiction. What logical or philosophical justification is there for any theologian or philosopher *qua* theologian or philosopher to engage in any discussion of issues, religious or otherwise, of which the basic designative terms are impossible of explicit definition, or at least of meaningful clarification?

The major points raised in the preceding paragraphs may seem obvious. They not only seem obvious, they are obvious. This makes it all the more disturbing that the obvious was so largely disregarded at the Institute sessions.

## II.

These general observations about the inescapable need for clearer definitions of our theological and religious vocabulary leads me to some specific observations about the theological terminology of Professor Paul Tillich. I want to refer not only to points made by Tillich at the Symposium, but to his God-concept as it is stated, restated, developed, and elaborated upon in his major books, in his lectures, and in his discussion comments. The more I read and hear Tillich the more confused I become as to what he means by the term God or what his God-concept really is. (I encounter the same difficulty, but for different reasons, with the theological views of Reinhold Niebuhr.) Nor to my mind does his Appendix, "The Religious Symbol," provide any further clarification of his basic God-concept or of the meaning he attaches to the central theological terms.

In his books, as well as in the comments he makes in informal discussion, Tillich repeatedly defines God as the "Ultimate Concern," or the "Ultimate Reality," or the "Ultimate Meaning." In his numerous explications of the God-concept he elaborates upon these phrases or terms in various ways, often employing illustrative and explanatory devices with impressive effect. On first view, the symbolic interpretation of the God idea which Tillich attempts in his Institute paper seems clear, plausible, and even ingenious. "Devotion to the crucifix," he writes, "is really directed to the crucifixion on Golgotha, and devotion to the latter is in reality intended for the redemptive action of God, which is itself a symbolic expression for an experience of what concerns us ultimately." (See p. 301.) Here we are, back to the oft-recurrent term "ultimate concern." But what is it, exactly, that does concern us ultimately? What concerns us ultimately, we learn from the whole body of Tillich's writings, is life-meaning, life-purpose, life-value. Some sense can certainly be made out of these terms. But what is it that is the symbolic expression of the ultimate concern? It is "the

257

redemptive action of God." Note, it is not God which is the symbolic expression, but "the redemptive act of God." It is the *act* of God, but not God which is the symbol. We must therefore assume that God has some kind of meaning and existence beyond and outside of the symbol which his redemptive act represents. Logically and semantically, this is reassuring, because it is difficult to conceive of how a symbol can perform any *act,* redemptive or otherwise. The term God, therefore, does not stand for a mere symbol. It is obviously more than that.

But in the very next paragraph, Tillich states: "Thus perhaps the concept of 'surplus value' as a symbol of economic exploitation in the consciousness of the proletariat or the idea of the 'Supreme Being' as a symbol of the ultimate concern in the consciousness of the religious community may serve as examples."

Now we are told that the "Supreme Being," which is certainly a synonym for God, is a symbol after all—"a symbol of the ultimate concern." This means that we must translate the statement of the first paragraph to read: ". . . and devotion to the latter [the crucifix] is in reality intended for the redemptive action of the [symbol] God [or Supreme Being], which is itself a symbolic expression for an experience of what concerns us ultimately."

What has happened here is obvious: The action of the Symbol is the symbolic expression of the Ultimate concern which is God which is a Symbol. And we discover that nothing lies behind the first symbol but another symbol—albeit the "ultimate" symbol is a special kind of symbol which can perform *acts*. And at no point, it seems to me, does Tillich, in his further interpretation and explications of the "religious symbol," dispel this fundamental contradiction and confusion. The distinction which Tillich later tries to make between "religious" symbols and all other kinds of symbols is a purely arbitrary one and is to my mind an unsuccessful attempt to extricate himself from the logical contradiction involved in the insistence upon putting God "unconditionally beyond the conceptual sphere." If God is not an object in the empirical world, and if even the symbolic expression which is God is beyond the conceptual sphere, how can we possibly talk about a God-concept or definition? This means not only that we cannot conceive of God as an object or entity in any empirical sense. It means also that we cannot conceive of God even as a symbol, for religious symbols are "unconditionally beyond the conceptual sphere." Why and how does Tillich continue to write and talk about something which cannot be *conceived*—even as a symbol?

The crux of the problem is the ancient philosophical error of refusing to make definite distinctions. If one asks the question of Tillich, "What would it be like not to believe in God?" the only possible answer is, "It is impossible not to believe in God." "Do you believe in anything?" "Yes, I believe in some things." "God is everything, hence some things are included in everything. Hence you believe in God whether you know it or admit it or not." There is an adage which runs to this effect and let us not forget it: 'When all things are called blue, blue loses its meaning.'

The same situation prevails with respect to Tillich's familiar principle of "commitment to the holy." It always turns out that, as it did in the present Symposium, when Tillich is insistently hard pressed by questions as to what such commitment really means, he is forced to admit that commitment to anything, even if it is potently evil (i.e., destructive, hateful, antisocial, etc.) is still commitment to the holy in the sense that it is commitment to what any individual holds sacred or is "committed" to. Thus it is the commitment which is holy and not its object. If you believe in *anything* you believe in God. If you are committed to anything, you are committed to the "holy." Thus not only do the distinctions between *beliefs* vanish, but also the distinctions between *commitments*. No matter what we believe or what we do, we cannot help believing in "God" or being committed to "the holy," even though both our beliefs and our commitments may be temporarily misguided or perverted. (As to how we decide whether a "holy" commitment is true or false except by purely subjective criteria is another question on which Tillich offers no clear answer.)

It is of some importance, I submit, that this major, basic, persistent fallacy in Tillich's theological views not only be recognized (as indeed it has been in certain quarters for some time),

259

but that it be more widely understood and more insistently stated. A more general recognition and statement of the major philosophical weakness in Tillich's whole theological system, centered as this weakness is in the vagueness and circularity of the definition of the original terms, would be of service not only to theologians and philosophers, but also to that relatively large segment of the literate laity (including the hundreds of Harvard undergraduates who listen to him every year) who have been so much impressed and influenced by his books, lectures, and reputation.

Finally and briefly (because of limitations of space), I should like to suggest what I believe lies at the core of Tillich's dilemma. It is the dilemma of both the "liberal" or "modernist" *and* the neo-orthodox theologians of the present time. The problem is anthropomorphism. Naturalism, pragmatism, and scientism have driven some of the more scholarly and philosophically-trained modern theologians to the point where, like Tillich, they feel they must reject anthropomorphism. Is God a Person? Well, not really. He can't be located in space. He does not have a body, a physical brain, nerves, organs in the sense in which human beings possess these things.

And yet the theologians who reject anthropomorphism (God as an empirical object) preach sermons about *HIM,* pray to *HIM,* worship *HIM.*

The fact of the matter is that the beliefs of Billy Graham (whether one agrees with them or not is irrelevant) are more philosophically and logically tenable than those of Tillich. To Graham, God is a person—and a *person* must necessarily be essentially anthropomorphic—whom he worships and to whom he prays. Tillich worships and prays either to a symbol which cannot be conceptualized, or to a fantasy which cannot be objectified in the empirical world.

Professor Ziff is absolutely right. God is a proper name. Either he exists as a person or he does not exist at all. You can't have your cake and eat it too.

260

*33*

# ON PROVING THAT GOD EXISTS
*by William E. Kennick, Amherst College*

Trying to show by argument that God exists is a pastime that has largely gone out of fashion with theologians and philosophers today. There are many reasons for this, but one of these reasons, contrary to the beliefs of many of these theologians and philosophers themselves, is not, I think, that Hume or Kant or anybody else has conclusively shown that there is anything wrong with the standard arguments (ontological, cosmological, teleological) for the existence of God—that is, that Hume or Kant or anyone else has conclusively refuted the arguments. Which is not to suggest, however, that there is something wrong with the critiques of Hume, and Kant, and the rest. There is a third possibility to be explored, namely that there is nothing wrong with the standard arguments for the existence of God or with the standard critiques of these arguments, but that what is wrong perhaps is the standard interpretation of these arguments and of the critiques of them.

The standard interpretation is this: an argument for the existence of God is a piece of evidence for the truth-value of a certain proposition, namely, the proposition that God exists. It is an attempt to show by reasoning rather than by observation or experiment that, in addition to anything the existence of which we know or can know by observation or experiment, or by inductive inference from observation or experiment, there is also something else, namely God. If the premises (p) in the argument for the existence of God are true, then the conclusion that God exists (q) is also true, and q is a deductive consequence of p. (Of course, if p is false, nothing follows about the truth or falsity of q.)

This means that if one wishes to criticize an argument for the existence of God he must either show that the argument is invalid or show that p is false. Now there is nothing formally wrong with the standard arguments for the existence of God, or at least there is nothing formally wrong with them that cannot be repaired with a little dialectical ingenuity—the arguments can always be put in a valid form; one can even exhibit their formal rigor with the techniques of symbolic logic. This means that if one wishes to show that the arguments are unsound, that they do not prove the conclusion in question, he must show that p is false. This is why the standard critiques of the arguments are largely devoted to showing that existence is not a predicate, or that it is false that every event has a cause, or that it is false that the chain of causes of design implies the existence of a designer, and so on.

It appears that we understand all of this and that it is obvious. What I wish to suggest is that it is not as obvious as it appears. Despite the facts that we can: recognize arguments for the existence of God when we see them, form such arguments, accept or reject them, and hence must be able to understand them and to appreciate the work they do—nevertheless when we voice the standard interpretation of them we say things about them, about what they are, and what they do which will not stand the test of a closer scrutiny. I wish, therefore, to exhibit certain features of the traditional arguments for the existence of God, and of the usual critiques of them, which suggest that the standard interpretation is mistaken.

The utterance 'God exists' may be used to express either an empirical proposition or an a priori proposition.[1] (It may, of course, be used in other, nonassertive, ways; but these ways have nothing to do with the standard interpretation of the arguments for the existence of God and may hence be ignored here.) By an empirical proposition I mean merely one whose actual truth-value is not its only possible truth-value; and by an a priori proposition I mean one whose actual truth-value is its only possible truth-value. I say nothing about whether all true a priori propositions are necessarily true because they are analytic or tautologous, nor do I say anything about whether all false a priori propositions are false because they are self-contradictory. There may be what are called synthetic a priori propositions, and 'God exists' may be such a proposition.

"The God of the geometers," said Pascal, that is, the God of the theologians and philosophers, "is not the God of Abraham, Isaac and Jacob." The concept of God employed by an Anselm, an Aquinas, or a Descartes is not the same concept as that employed by the ordinary, or even the extraordinary, religious man. Hence it is not surprising that the utterance 'God exists' should be used differently by each. By 'God,' the theologian and philosopher mean 'a being than which no greater can be conceived' or 'a necessary being,' and as the utterance 'God exists' is used by the theologian and philosopher it is most frequently used to express an a priori proposition. Certainly it appears to be used in this way by those theologians and philosophers who offer arguments for the existence of God, and they are the ones we are interested in here. They do not treat the utterance 'God exists' as expressing a proposition which is merely probably, even highly probably, true.[2]

It is well known that those who accept the ontological argument believe that the proposition that God exists is a priori true. But they are not alone in this. Aquinas, for example, rejected the ontological argument, but in Pt. I, Q. 2, Art. 1 of the *Summa Theologica* he clearly holds that the proposition that God exists is inherently self-evident, by which he means that it is a priori true. He holds that a proposition can be self-evident (*per se notum*) in either of two ways: it can be inherently self-evident (*per se notum secundum se*) though not self-evident to us (*per se notum quoad nos*), or it can be inherently self-evident and also self-evident to us. A proposition is inherently self-evident, he says, when the predicate is included in the essence of the subject, as in the proposition 'Man is an animal.' This proposition is also self-evident to us because we know what is meant both by 'man' and by 'animal.' If, however, we did not know what is meant by 'man' or what by 'animal,' then the proposition 'Man is an animal' would be inherently self-evident though not self-evident to us. Now the proposition 'God exists' is inherently self-evident, "for the predicate is the same as the subject,

263

because God is His own existence," but it may not be self-evident to those who do not know what is meant by 'God.'

Whether Aquinas's account of what makes an a priori proposition true will or will not do—and it may be mistaken—what is of interest here is that he holds that 'God exists' expresses an inherently self-evident proposition, i.e., one that is a priori true, just as it is a priori true that man is an animal. This is what it means to hold that God's existence is necessary.

Again it has been argued [3] that, if 'God exists' is an empirical proposition, then some observable fact must in principle be relevant to its truth or falsity. Thus, to falsify the proposition that God exists, one would have to be able to observe some fact incompatible with the assertion that God exists. But this is impossible. God's existence is independent of, and therefore compatible with, every and any contingent fact. If it were not, God would 'owe' his existence to the fortunate fact that the disconfirming fact in question does not exist. But anyone who understands what 'God' means knows that God cannot 'owe' his existence to anything other than himself. Therefore 'God exists' is not an empirical proposition but an a priori proposition, and if it is true it is necessarily true and if it is false it is necessarily false. Hence, God's existence is either necessary or impossible. [4]

The soundness of this or any other argument for the claim that 'God exists' expresses an a priori proposition is not what is at issue here. What is at issue here is this: Assuming that 'God exists' is an a priori proposition, what are we to make of the arguments for the existence of God?

Now let 'p' represent the conjunction of premises of any argument for the existence of God, and let 'q' represent its conclusions. According to the standard interpretation, p is evidence for the truth of q; if p is true, q is true, and q is a deductive consequence of p. But if q is a priori true, as has been claimed, then this cannot be the case. Certainly it cannot be the case in any nonontological argument for the existence of God. (By an 'ontological argument' I mean merely one that is devised to show that not-q is necessarily false.) For if q is an a priori proposition, its truth-value is totally unaffected by the truth-value of p; p is not a truth-condition of q. Hence p is neither evidence for the truth of q, nor is q a deductive consequence of p.

In a non-ontological argument for the existence of God, p is a conjunction of propositions. At least one of these conjuncts must be an empirical proposition (e.g., some things are in motion); the remaining conjuncts are usually a priori true, or are at least thought to be a priori true (e.g., anything that is in motion is moved by something else). Now it is pointless to attack the a priori conjunct(s), as is usually done, because, although the a priori conjunct(s) alone imply the conclusion, the empirical conjunct alone also implies the conclusion. *Any* empirical proposition alone implies an a priori true proposition, as a truth table will show. So that the following, which is sometimes erroneously cited as the first of Aquinas's 'Five Ways,' will actually do just as well as Aquinas's own argument: 'If some things are in motion, then God exists; some things are in motion; therefore, God exists.'

But if this is so, then p cannot be evidence for the truth of q as the standard interpretation alleges. The existence of motion, causality, degrees of goodness, purpose, design, beauty, and so on is no more evidence for the existence of God than is the existence of rest, chance, evil, purposelessness, chaos, ugliness, or, indeed, nothing at all. For whatever empirical proposition, true or false, is substituted for p or is made a conjunct of p, p implies q if q is a priori true. To put the point in another way: everything and anything is evidence for the existence of God, which means that nothing is evidence for the existence of God.

This perhaps explains why theologians are unwilling to accept the presence of evil or of undeserved suffering in the world as showing or tending to show that there is no God. Of course, they do not show that there is no God, i.e., that 'God exists' is false, for the simple reason that nothing *can* show this.

Furthermore, if q is a priori true, as is claimed, q cannot be a deductive consequence of p in a non-ontological argument for the existence of God. For q is a deductive consequence of p if and only if 'p and not-q' is necessarily false and the necessary falsity of 'p and not-q' can be removed by the removal of p. But not-q alone is held to be necessarily false, hence the conjunction of not-q and any other proposition will be necessarily false.

What then is the function of a non-ontological argument for the existence of God? Clearly the premises of such an argument do serve some purpose, even if that purpose cannot be the one indicated by the standard interpretation. And clearly also it will *not* do to argue 'If some things are ugly, then God exists; some things are ugly; therefore, God exists'—this is no argument for the existence of God at all, despite the fact that logically it is directly analogous to all non-ontological arguments for the existence of God, i.e., despite the fact that 'Some things are ugly' does imply 'God exists' just as much as does 'Some things are in motion.' What purpose, then, *can* the premises of such an argument serve if the conclusion has the character that it is alleged to have?

The standard way of meeting an ontological argument for the existence of God is to say that it makes the mistake of assuming that existence is a predicate, i.e., that 'exists' denotes a quality, attribute, or characteristic of things. But this will not do. No one has shown that existence is not a predicate. What may have been shown is that 'exists' is not used in exactly the same way or ways as 'growls' or 'runs' or 'is red,' but this does not show that existence is not a predicate. It does not show this because, as far as I can see, it cannot be shown either that existence is or that existence is not a predicate, any more than it can be shown, in William James's puzzle, that the man does or does not go around the squirrel. (Which raises an interesting problem as to the nature of such philosophical questions as 'Is existence a predicate?') It is therefore always open to the proponent of the ontological argument to claim that at best all this shows is that existence is just a different kind of predicate from 'growls' or 'is red.'

Whether existence is or is not a predicate is not the important issue. The important issue is whether there can or cannot be a proposition which is at once existential and a priori true. But if that is the issue, then it is quickly settled in favor of the proponent of the ontological argument, for 'There is an infinity of prime numbers' is both existential and a priori true. And if that is both existential and a priori true, there can be no reason why 'God exists' cannot be both existential and a priori true, and no reason why there could not be an argument to show this, just as there is an argument to show that there is an infinity of prime numbers.

Granted, then that there is an acceptable a priori argument, i.e, a valid ontological argument, for the existence of God, whether it be one of those offered by Anselm or some other, does it show that God exists? In some sense, it must. For if it shows, as *ex hypothesi* it must, that 'God exists' is a priori true, or, what is the same, that 'God does not exist' is necessarily false, then it shows that God exists. But does it show this in the way that the standard interpretation supposes?

To tell someone that tigers exist is to give him information about the world; to tell him that purple swans exist is to give him misinformation about the world. This is because neither 'tigers exist' nor 'purple swans exist' is a priori true or a priori false. A proposition can give information or misinformation about the world if and only if it is not an a priori proposition, that is, if and only if it is an empirical proposition. The truth-value of an a priori proposition cannot be determined by what the world is like or by what it is not like. For since the truth-value of an a priori proposition is its only possible truth-value, the world may be as different from what it is as you like, it cannot affect the truth-value of a proposition that has its truth-value necessarily. To put it another way, an a priori proposition is true (or false) of all possible worlds, but a proposition which is true (or false) of all possible worlds is true (or false) of none.[5]

In a non-ontological argument for the existence of God, moreover, no more information about the world is conveyed by the argument as a whole than is conveyed by the empirical premise(s) taken alone. Thus, if 'some things are in motion' is the only empirical premise of the argument, the conjunction of this and the other premises (e.g., everything that is moved must be moved by something else; the chain of movers cannot be infinite) together with the conclusion, yields no more information about the world than does 'Some things are in motion' taken alone.

Now the proposition 'God exists' or 'There is a God' looks like the proposition 'Tigers exist' or 'There are tigers.' For this reason it may lead some theologians and philosophers to suppose that it is, or to forget that it is not, informative of the nature of the world. But if God's existence is indeed necessary, as many of these same theologians and philosophers contend, then the proposition that God exists cannot be informative of the nature of the world. It does not tell us that in addition to tigers and rocks and men and trees and . . . there is also God, except in the bad-joke sense in which one might say that in addition to tigers and rocks and men and trees and . . . there is also an infinity of prime numbers. Perhaps this is why Professor Malcolm thinks that "it would be unreasonable to require that the recognition of Anselm's demonstration as valid must produce a conversion." [6]

If what has been said is correct, or nearly correct, it raises the question about what we are to make of the standard arguments for the existence of God. As long as 'God' is taken to mean a being than which no greater can be thought, that is, a necessary being, they cannot reasonably be construed to be what they appear to be, namely, pieces of evidence for the truth-value of a proposition about what exists or does not exist. The standard interpretation of arguments for the existence of God fails, I have tried to show, on two counts: (a) in its interpretation of the function of the premises of an argument for the existence of God, and (b) in its interpretation of the conclusion of an argument for the existence of God. But if the standard interpretation fails to provide a theory that satisfactorily explains what an argument for the existence of God does—and clearly it does do something—what theory will satisfactorily explain this? I have not offered or suggested such a theory. I have merely tried to show that there is something here that calls for explanation.

# NOTES

1. Professor Ziff, in his paper above, treats the proposition that God exists as an empirical proposition or hypothesis. In the discussion following the reading of his paper, however, he said that he takes the proposition that God exists to be 'something like a necessary truth.' ' "Pegasus does not exist," ' he says, is something like a necessary truth. Because if someone understands what is meant by "Pegasus," he understands that Pegasus is a mythical creature. "God does exist" is in this respect like "Pegasus does not exist." ' In his paper, Professor Ziff is speaking with the plain man and he clearly shows the difficulties that the plain man must face; in his remarks during the discussion he was, momentarily at least, speaking with the theologians, whose difficulties are different.

2. See E. L. Mascall, *Existence and Analogy*, (London: Longmans, Green and Company, Inc., 1949), Preface.

3. By Professor Hartshorne during the discussion following the reading of Professor Ziff's paper.

4. For a similar line of reasoning leading to the same conclusion, see Norman Malcolm, "Anselm's Ontological Arguments," *The Philosophical Review*, LXIX (1960), 45–51.

5. I say nothing here about what it is that does determine the truth-value of an a priori proposition—whether, for example, all a priori propositions are merely verbal. It strikes me that this is an independent issue, the upshot of which cannot affect what has already been said.

6. Norman Malcolm, *op. cit.*, 62.

# 34

# IS GOD SO POWERFUL THAT
# HE DOESN'T EVEN HAVE TO EXIST?

*by Kai Nielsen, New York University*

Ziff has made a reasonable case for (1) the contention that in a very *wide* sense of 'intelligible' 'Does God exist?' is an intelligible question and (2) that, given the conditions traditionally associated with the word 'God,' the correct answer to this question should be 'No.' God's omnipotence is incompatible with the limits imposed on experience by physical theory. There are thus excellent grounds for denying the existence of the God when God is conceptualized as many plain men conceptualize Him.

Theologians are not satisfied with the plain man's concept of God. The theologians present at the Institute did not challenge Ziff's evidence that, *given* this plain man's conception of God, there is excellent reason to believe that God does not exist. They challenged instead that very conception of God. We do not, they argued, understand 'eternal,' 'omnipotent,' etc. in the straightforward way Ziff's plain man does. Scholastics speak of analogical predication, and Tillichians try to make a case for a special sense of 'symbol' in religious talk. Only Hick appears to be an exception to this. Hick claims that the existence of God is an empirical issue. Yet it is an empirical issue only in a very unusual sense, for God's existence can only be confirmed by certain experiences after we have shuffled off these mortal coils. Hick, and others like him, argue that no conceivable experience during *this life* could confirm or disconfirm the existence of God, and no conceivable post-mortem experiences could *falsify* or *disconfirm* the existence of God. They will not use 'God' in such a way that God's existence could possibly be put to a test. On Ziff's plainer use, the existence of God is an experimental issue, but theologians—and modern believers affected by their febrile concepts—will not treat such a question as a question that could be settled by evidence. At best, on the theories of eschatological verification of Hick and Crombie, we might by-and-by in the hereafter find evidence for the existence of God, but 'God exists' is used by them in such a way that it cannot be falsified. It is argued that the plain man's understanding of God is anthropomorphic and demonic. A "subtler" understanding of religion makes it clear why all questions of evidence are beside the point. In fact, Bultmann goes so far as to say that to talk of God in this way is "not only error and foolishness: it is sin." By such moves the believer is protected from the wolves of disbelief.

Ziff realizes that the concept of God has changed and is changing. Negative answers to the old questions will prove nothing vis-à-vis questions that arise about God when 'God' is used in a different way. Yet theologians do not want to use 'God' in such a way that all the old conditions associated with 'God' are lost. Tillich, for example, is not unaware that his theological endeavor involves a restatement of the very meaning of the word 'God,' but he and all the Crisis Theologians wish to capture the real world of the Bible; they wish to restate for modern man what is genuinely crucial in the Judaeo-Christian tradition. They do not simply wish to give essays in redefinition, in which the tokens 'God' and 'religion' are given radically new uses. But at the same time they realize that the old arguments and the old conceptions will not do. Here Hume, Kant, and contemporary analytic philosophers have won a decisive victory. Yet these Crisis Theologians believe that the most crucial things in the strange world of the Bible have not been touched by such sceptical considerations.

Perhaps we can put new wine in old bottles; perhaps new conceptions of God are feasible. Yet Tillich's approach, via a kind of quasi-Platonic metaphysics, a confusing interpretation of religious symbolism, and an analysis of ultimate concern will not do the trick. It is a loquacious obscurantist theology which stands in the way of a genuine understanding of religion. It is set up in such a loose and incoherent manner that it allows us to equivocate on

271

almost all the crucial conceptual questions that arise about religion. This is well demonstrated by Alston for Tillich's contentions about religious symbolism; he also effectively points out the conceptual chaos in Tillich's talk about 'being-itself,' 'the unconditioned transcendent,' and "being grasped by Being." Yet someone trying to defend Tillich might argue that there is another crucial strand to Tillich's thinking that is not touched by Alston's analysis. This strand was much in evidence in the first part of his talk to the Institute and it is much in evidence in his writings. Under pressure, a defender of Tillich might argue that this strand of Tillich's thought is even more fundamental than his conception of the ground of being and religious symbols. I shall argue that this side of Tillich's thought is equally useless for elucidating the nature of religion.

Tillich has argued that religious symbols are representative. They have an inherent power because they somehow participate in the very majesty of that which they represent. They open up dimensions of reality which otherwise would not be open. But it is crucial, Tillich argues, to know the referent of religious symbols. No account of religious language is adequate which does not give an account of the referent of the word 'God.' Tillich contends that a main way of going astray in thinking about religion is to think that religious symbols have objects as their referents. This is an anthropomorphic conception. It consists in making God into a mere thing, a Being—even a supernatural Being—among beings. But God cannot be limited in this way. God is the unconditioned transcendent. Religious symbols point not to objects but to a *dimension* of objects. But Tillich also claims that his use of 'dimension' is metaphoric. In view of this, just what could Tillich intend when he says that religious symbols point to a dimension of objects? We are not told; Tillich's metaphor is not explained; we do not know what must happen or not happen in order for it to be the case that a symbol stands for a dimension of objects. If we are told that Tillich's use of language here involves a metaphor that *can not* be explained, then such a defender of Tillich is abusing 'metaphor,' for 'metaphor' is not used in that way.

There is a way to know God, Tillich argues, that would enable us to undercut the difficulties connected with understanding religious language. We have religious encounters in which these very "dimensions" of depth in the natural are directly apprehended. In religious experience we encounter "the whole of the sacred." We have feelings of holiness. To have those feelings is to have that sense of ultimacy whose adequate object is being-itself, the unconditioned transcendent. If we have these feelings of holiness we can come to intuit the unconditioned transcendent. We can, if we will carry on a scrupulous "qualitative analysis," come to grasp "an ultimate metaphysical structure of existence." Our feelings of holiness enable us to know the referent of 'God.' Thus we have in our very direct experience a concrete check on our abstract claims for religious symbols.

In arguing this way, Tillich ignores an elementary conceptual point; namely, that, from statements about feelings or from sentences expressing feelings, no statements of a nonpsychological sort can be derived, nor do such utterances by themselves constitute a sufficient reason for asserting the truth or the falsity of a nonpsychological statement. At best they teach us something about ourselves and our fellow men, but they tell us nothing of God.

I may feel nauseated by Professor Jackal's table manners, but this does not entail that Professor Jackal's table manners are nauseating. 'Nauseating' has many referents and what it is taken to refer to will depend on the sentence in which it occurs and the context in which it is used. (After all, 'nauseating' has different referents in 'Jackal's table manners are nauseating' and 'Kadar's cant is nauseating.') Red-blooded Americans will say that Professor Jackal's table manners are nauseating if he stirs his tomato juice with his finger, picks his nose at the table, belches at dinner, gobbles his food, and wipes his mouth with the back of his none-too-clean hand. But it is perfectly possible for us to assert that Professor Jackal's table manners are nauseating without feeling nauseated by them, and I might feel nauseated by them without their being nauseating. I might have an intense but secret hatred of Professor

Jackal, and this could make me feel nauseated by his table manners when, in fact, they were unobjectionable.

Similarly I may *feel* guilty without *being* guilty. A couple may go to a party and, during the course of the party, their apartment may, through no fault of their own, catch on fire and their child and baby-sitter may burn to death. As a result, they may *feel* overwhelmed by guilt without being guilty, as someone may feel nauseated by X when X is not nauseating. Again we have independent tests for someone's being guilty. One's feelings of guilt do not establish one's guilt.

Contrast these two cases with what can be said about 'feelings of contingency.' When I reflect that someday I shall cease to be, that the world changes, that religions and whole civilizations alter and eventually come to an end I may come to have feelings of contingency in a very acute way. I may come to *feel* that the universe is contingent, but this does not mean that the universe is contingent or even that there are good grounds for saying that it is. The fact of the matter is that we may well have what is called 'a *sense* of contingency' or '*feelings* of contingency' without even knowing what it would be like for it to be either true or false that the universe is contingent. My feeling that Professor Jackal's table manners are nauseating would normally be taken as *evidence* for the claim that Professor Jackal's table manners are nauseating, even though 'X feels nauseated by Y's table manners' does not entail 'Y's table manners are nauseating.' But for this to be so we need *independent criteria* for what counts as nauseating table manners. We have such criteria. People who belch during dinner or slurp their soup are said to have nauseating table manners. We, on the other hand (as Tillich knows full well), do not know whether it must be the case or must not be the case for it to be either true or false that the universe is contingent or noncontingent. We can intelligibly speak of *feelings* of contingency, but we do not know what must be the case for the sentence, 'The universe is contingent,' to be used to make a true assertion.

Philosophers like Feuerbach and Dewey do not deny the obvious, namely, that the human animal has complex religious feelings or experiences, but they do question whether those feelings or experiences are correctly understood as Divine Encounters or experiences of God. Feuerbach in particular offered an elaborate alternative account of these experiences that did not envoke anything incompatible with a naturalistic account of the world. And here Feuerbach is on safer ground than Tillich, for sentences about feelings or sentences expressive of feelings only entail sentences of the same logical type. Tillich seems to be completely oblivious of this elementary and well-worn claim.

Tillich might claim instead that religious experiences can be said to constitute good reasons for the claim that there is being-itself or the unconditioned transcendent. But if he does, he must show both that such psychological states are inadequately accounted for by the far simpler naturalistic accounts, and that his turgid, quasi-Platonic metaphysical framework can give an intelligible account of those or any other experiences. (Even if the current naturalistic accounts are inadequate, it would not at all follow that Tillich's account is even intelligible, let alone adequate.) Tillich has not done these things; and if he were to try he would again run afoul of the difficulties Alston brings up about what could be meant by 'the ground of being,' 'being-itself,' 'the unconditioned transcendent,' 'being grasped by being' and the like. Such phrases do not *have* a meaning or use; they must be *given* a meaning or a use. Alston shows that Tillich's account of religious symbolism does not enable us to understand what Tillich means by these opaque phrases. How could we possibly know whether our experiences were experiences of the unconditioned transcendent, etc.?

While at times Tillich denies that "beyond all symbols the unconditioned transcendent should be directly intuited," at other times, as we have seen, he argues that we can, if we will attend carefully to our experience, come to grasp the reality embodied in religious symbols. He claims that we can intelligibly request that "reality itself should be looked at immediately and be spoken of in such way that its position in and before the unconditioned transcendent would receive direct expression."

It is intelligible to say that I am directly aware of being tired, guilty, afraid, in pain, lonely, bored, nauseated, and the like, but it could not be said that I am directly aware of being confronted with the unconditioned transcendent, an adequate object of ultimate concern, Being-itself, or the ground of being anymore than I could be said to be directly aware that I am *contra-causally* free, have a soul which is a simple undividable substance, or that I have a superego. Such theoretical concepts are precisely what we can not be directly aware of. They are used to interpret or explain our experience and not as simple designations or descriptions of it. Furthermore, Tillich's phrases are not a part of ordinary discourse; native speakers of English do not know how to use them—they must be given directions for their use. Tillich has not given us these directions. Thus we are at sea as to what he could *mean*. This being so, there is no possible way for us to rectify our perplexity over Tillich's strange claims by careful attention to our feelings of holiness or concern.

There is an allied consideration that further evidences the intellectual bankruptcy of Tillich's position. Tillich talks a lot of being ultimately concerned or unconditionally concerned. He says, "The experience of ultimate is concern." Now in a way these are fine phrases; they have a grand emotive ring; but unfortunately we have no criterion for deciding when a concern is *ulitimate* or *unconditioned*. Just when *is* a man's concern an ultimate concern, as distinct from a proximate one? We are not told. Though we all have ultimate concern, ultimate concern, Tillich tells us, is in the last analysis only concerned ultimately with Being-itself. But how does he know this? And what is meant by 'being concerned with Being-itself'? Again we are asked to affirm or deny something whose meaning has not been sufficiently explicated to be something we could affirm or deny.

Like Kierkegaard and Barth, Tillich is shrewdly aware that agnostics and atheists are often very concerned with religion. They are closer to God than many of the faithful for they think about Him more. God is important enough to deny. But the agnostic or atheist is doing something that is inconsistent in a practical way, for believing in God, Tillich tells us, is simply being ultimately concerned. One cannot really be an atheist, for in denying there is a God one expresses ultimate concern; one expresses a "passionate longing for ultimate reality . . ."; one "rejects religion in the name of religion." As Tillich sums it up, "You cannot reject religion with ultimate seriousness, because ultimate seriousness or the state of being ultimately concerned is itself religion." Then Tillich adds his coup de grace: everyone is religious since everyone has ultimate concern, the atheist most particularly for he has a high degree of ultimate seriousness. Tillich observes, as if it were a psychological generalization, that he has never known a man who did not have ultimate concern.

Now assuming what is not the case, namely that we know what is to count as '*ultimate* concern,' it remains the case that Tillich's argument has at least two major flaws.

First, believing in God or being religious is not simply being in a state of ultimate concern. The concept of ultimate concern brings out quite nicely an important constituent in religion that philosophers are apt to forget. To believe in God involves taking on a certain attitude, having a certain concern, but while this perhaps is a necessary condition for genuine religious belief it is not a sufficient condition. The great agnostics of the nineteenth century were quite aware they were concerned, but their religious trauma was precisely that they could not believe in God. To persuasively define 'believing in God' so that anyone who is deeply concerned about religion *eo ipso* will be said to believe in God is to indulge in an arbitrary form of linguistic imperialism that can only confuse issues. It *may* be the case that one cannot believe in God without being ultimately concerned, but 'believing in God' does not *mean* 'being in a state of ultimate concern.' My ultimate concern may be to avoid an atomic holocaust and to find happiness for myself and others, but to say that if I have such a concern I must be said to believe in God is to play with words. That is not how the religious language-game is played; the forms of life we characterize as Judaism and Christianity are not like this. Tillich can indeed play his own grandiose game, making up his rules as he goes along; by doing this, Tillich can evade the intellectual difficulties connected with faith. Yet what do such maneuvers actually accomplish? Tillich can convert nonbelievers into believers by redefinition. But as they stand, his stipulations are arbitrary; if he were to defend the adequacy of his ventures in redefinition, all the old difficulties about belief and unbelief would re-emerge. Tillich's maneuver has has done little but spread sloppy thinking and evasiveness.

Tillich indeed tells us something true and important when he tells us that to be religious involves much more than the intellectual assent to certain doctrinal propositions; it involves, in addition, adopting a way of life and the taking on of *certain* very pervasive attitudes about our own lives and the lives of others. But it does involve adopting *certain* attitudes and *having certain* concerns, not just any attitude or any concern.

There is a second objection that should be made against Tillich's claims about ultimate concern. It is indeed true that many professional atheists or freethinkers are terribly involved with religion. They have a real need to deny God. Furthermore, there is a sense in which we can speak of being religiously antireligious. Many of the same motivations go into humanism, Marxism, or Freudianism that go into religion. But we must be careful in our claims here. While there are clear similarities between the dedicated Freudian and the Christian believer, there are crucial differences as well. Stressing the similarities does nothing to show that all people are ultimately concerned.

Tillich, however, confidently claims he has never known a person without ultimate concern. Without feeling any need to make psychological or sociological investigations, he asserts confidently that all people are ultimately concerned. Yet it looks as if what starts out as a psychological insight, namely, 'Many people who would deny it are really very concerned with religion,' turns into a pseudofactual hypothesis, namely, 'All men have ultimate concern,' (I say 'pseudofactual' for it is not like 'All men have livers.') We know what it would be like for someone to be a man and not have a liver, but as Tillich uses the phrase we do *not* know what it would be like for a man *not* to have ultimate concern. Arguing with Tillich over this is like arguing with an egoist over egoism.

Whenever cases are brought up which would ordinarily be thought *not* to be cases of ultimate concern, Tillich always argues that in some hidden way they do exhibit ultimate concern. Even the playboy must—at some periods in his life—exhibit ultimate concern, and this ultimate concern remains as part of the total configuration of his personality. Tillich makes no serious effort to give evidence for his claim. What starts out as an empirical generalization is unwittingly converted into a tautology. 'All men have ultimate concern' is not, of course, a tautology in ordinary language; but Tillich, by his odd linguistic behaviour, *makes* it into a tautology by so using 'Being a man' and 'having ultimate concern' that we cannot say that 'So and so is a man but so and so does not have ultimate concern.' Once again Tillich has arbitrarily tinkered with language. (If it is denied that Tillich is really engaging in such linguistic gerrymandering, then it is essential to explain in a straightforward manner under what conditions it would be *unwarranted* for a Tillichian to say that a man is ultimately concerned.)

Perhaps I have been too quick in this last argument? It will be objected that my tone here is too harsh and sceptical—Tillich is not being all that arbitrary. It will be said that even if Tillich's above remark applied only some of the time it would still be a profound observation; although '*ultimate* concern' and '*unconditioned* concern' are indeed vague, we do know what it is to be intensely and passionately concerned with our fellow men and with making sense of our lives. Hindu seers have taught us about the ambiguities and ambivalences in our search for what "we really want." Pleasure, success, and service are not always sufficient. They are indeed important but they are not enough; they are not all we seek. Most of us, at any rate, also aim for things that are less tangible, less definite. And we all live in a world in which we must learn to face death, loss of love, defeat, and the frustration of our deepest longings. Man is concerned with these things. Having been born he must—as a matter of brute fact—suffer and someday die. Similarly men seek—without any very clear idea of what they are seeking—what sometimes is called, not without irony, "true happiness." Men

279

who are not concerned with such things would, in a plain sense, scarcely be human, for being so concerned is what it is to be a person. A man not so concerned would, in a moralistic sense of 'human,' not be human or (at least) not be fully human. (Here we have indeed two more tautologies, but, for all that, they are profound.) When Tillich says 'All men have ultimate concern,' can he not be understood to be saying something like this? So understood, is not this both significant and profound?

There is indeed something in such remarks. So construed, 'being ultimately concerned' does not entail 'believing in God,' but there is *a sense* in which it is entailed by 'being human.' (There is also a sense in which there is no such entailment.) Someone without these concerns does not *deserve* the name "human being." Yet we must not forget that 'human being' in such a use no longer means 'human being' in its most straightforward and direct sense. The words are being used with an evaluative force so that, on such a use, it is quite possible that there are some human beings who are not human. Secondly, we should still beware of taking the high a priori road. Tillich, and most of us I suspect, are talking about God-seekers both among the believers and unbelievers. But what about all the good folks huddled around the T.V. sets in Westchester and elsewhere? Do they all have these anxieties? Do we have any grounds for saying they all have ultimate concern? I would first like to see 'ultimate concern' made a little more precise, and then I would like a little raw empiricism about who is and who isn't afflicted with it. No doubt Tillich has his finger on something important in any characterization of the human animal (it's still a long way to God), but until his Germanic superstructure gets washed in the detergent of plain statement we will remain bespattered with a kind of Hegeloid mud.

I have tried here to finish the job ably begun by Alston. I am sure that it will be said that I have misinterpreted Tillich, but Tillich writes in a fashion which almost begs for misinterpretation. I have discussed central concepts in his system, and these concepts lead to the difficulties I mentioned. If such criticisms are *not* to the point it should be shown clearly why they are not to the point.

Religion is indeed a difficult and complex matter; religion is mysterious and baffling, but, as one need not be fat to drive fat oxen, so one need not be mysterious and obscure in talking about what is mysterious and obscure. And verbose grandeloquence is not a symptom of profundity.

Ziff is right in claiming that there are many different conceptions of God. 'God' is a name and "a name is a fixed point in a turning world. But as the world turns our conception of that which is named by a name may change." At the present this is going on at an accelerated rate with 'God.' Tillich's odd talk and the odd talk of Crisis Theologians generally has had the effect of altering for many people their very first-order uses of religious concepts. There is not the gulf between the "excubant theologian's febrile concept" and the plain man's concept that Ziff thinks there is. Many plain Protestants carry with them Paley's conceptions though they have never heard of Paley, and there is likely to be a little mismanaged Aristotle and Aquinas in all good Catholics, and, the grammar of ultimate concern, like the cocktail party, has become an adornment of many college graduates. Ziff has shown that the existence of God is not rationally warranted on a reasonably definite plain man's conception of God. Tillich and many like him use 'God' in such a way that God is so powerful that He doesn't even have to exist. If we wish to play with words in Tillich's way, we can indeed avoid the impediments to religious belief. But for men who wish to live nonevasively, Tillich's conceptions are not conceptions about which he can simply remain blank. Tillich doesn't put new wine into old bottles, he puts in grape soda and then labels it *Chateau Latour.*

# 35

## DO THE GODS EXIST?
*by Cyril C. Richardson, Union Theological Seminary*

### *I.*

My remarks are in response to Professor Ziff's paper. I have three objections to his analysis of the question, "Does God exist?" First, the 'God' he is describing and talking about is, from a Christian point of view, an idol. He is part of the furniture of the universe and comparable to a Mr. Dietrich throwing stones faster than light. Second, I do not think Professor Ziff gives an adequate logical analysis of 'existence' propositions. Third, he does not see there are several different questions hidden in his initial one.

Limitation of space forbids me to deal with Professor Ziff's argument point by point. There are clearly many language differences between us, which could only be cleared up after hours of dialogue together. Here I must confine myself to four issues:

(a) Rephrasing the initial question
(b) An analysis of 'existence' propositions
(c) The four questions involved in the initial one
(d) The meaninglessness of talking about gods throwing stones faster than light.

### *II.*

I have rephrased the question in the plural ("gods") for three reasons. First, believers and nonbelievers can often be less emotional in their discussions together when polytheistic rather than

282

monotheistic propositions are at issue. Christians do not believe in polytheism, while nonbelievers, in a Christian (or semi-Christian) culture, do not react against polytheism as strongly as against monotheism. Second, we can use the definite article, "*the* gods." Whether 'God' is a proper name or not in an 'existence' proposition appears to me quite irrelevant. It is, as I shall argue later, a 'description word.' The presence or absence of the article is insignificant. "God" happens to serve in English for the proper name of 'god' (cf., Zeus or Yahweh), as well as for the ambiguous *deus* or *ho theos* of Latin and Greek (cf. *le Dieu,* in French).

Third, the reasons generally advanced in Western thought for monotheism or for a single absolute are manifestly false. They derive from a logic of infinity which is intuitive but indefensible. I cannot argue that here. All I wish to point out is that, since Georg Cantor began to formulate a logic of infinity, serious doubts attach to the reasons usually put forward for a single 'god.' This does not mean that talk about a single god is meaningless. It only means that we do not need to restrict ourselves by dubious conventions, as if talking about 'gods' in the plural were illogical.

## III.

'Existence' propositions have as their logical subject a 'description word.' Whether this is a common noun, a proper name, or another kind of expression, the logical subject *serves only as a description.* It is a cypher for one or more predicates upon which we agree. The predicates are 'analytical' in the sense they are all implied and necessarily implied in the word. They, and they alone, are what we have agreed to talk about. They are established by the language rules of dictionaries, and such revisions and limitations of these as we wish to impose for our discussion. "Do griffins exist?" Very well: we shall first define 'griffins,' and agree we are talking about a *description,* of which the predicates are half-lion, half-eagle. "Did Caesar exist?" Very well: we shall agree on a description, the predicates being a military genius, writing about Gaul, and being murdered. We cannot proceed to the problems of "exist" until we are clear that the logical subject is a description and only a description.

In 'description propositions,' on the other hand, it is quite different. The logical subject is not a 'description word' but a 'pointing-at' word. Here 'existence' (whatever that may be) is *necessarily presupposed* or *necessarily denied*. We ask, for instance, "Is that cat a male or a female?" There is no point in the question unless 'that cat' exists. Similarly we ask, "Did Mr. Pickwick win his case?" There is no point in the question unless we have already accepted Mr. Pickwick's existence.

To return to 'existence' propositions. The dictum, 'existence is not a predicate,' is at least true to this extent that with respect to finite objects, attributes, and occasions, 'existence' cannot be part of a description. It cannot be translated into "is a physical object," "is a psi entity." Griffins are certainly physical objects, but I doubt if they exist. The grammatical predicates "is real" and "is actual" are not *logical* predicates. What, then do they mean?

I suggest they affirm that *at least some physical observations* have been, or can be, made. I say "at least," for more than such observations, universally verifiable in principle, are generally involved. Some 'theory' enters too. But at basis the physical observations are indispensable. "Do griffins exist?" means, "Have at least physical observations been made which would verify the description 'griffin'?" The same applies to attributes. When the painter says, after hours of argument with my wife about the new color for the living room, "There ain't no such color, lady!" he means, "No physical observations have been, or could be made, to satisfy your description of that color."

What, then, is the difference between 'imaginary' griffins and 'real' ones (if there are such)? I should say that the 'real' griffin is the cause, external to myself, of certain physical experiences which I might have. These, further, almost always involve the unexpected. That is what is meant by making physical observations. By "external to myself" I mean external to my body and its functioning (sensation, will, mind). By 'cause' I mean whatever you want to mean by 'cause.' 'Imaginary' griffins, on the other hand, are rearrangements of my past experiences, images of which *I* am the immediate cause. They are not external to me. No physical observations of them have been made. (Painted griffins are another question, involving a different description of 'griffin'.)

When we ask, "Do the gods exist?" we have to decide what description 'the gods' entails. Of what predicates are these words a cypher? It may be well to state only a single predicate, which I shall call "the Infinites." Others are of course involved, such as positive being, personality in some sense, and some kind of 'distance' from the universe. But 'the Infinites' is the heart of the matter. Whatever is said about 'the gods' is always 'qualified' (or better, 'expanded') by the word 'infinite.' Are they good? Infinitely so. Are they happy? Infinitely so. Are they enduring? Infinitely so. Are they powerful? Infinitely so.

"The Infinites" removes all boundaries. Hence all physical observations become impossible. The gods are not part of the furniture of the universe. They dwell 'above'; they do not have 'bodies'; every attribute which they do have is 'infinite.' Yet, despite the fact no physical experience can verify them, that does not preclude experiencing them in a way appropriate to their infinity. The way, to be sure, is indirect. They are experienced *through* things, persons, occasions (e.g., theophanies, incarnations). But they can be experienced. At least that is the claim we must now examine.

## *IV.*

The fundamental issue, the first question hidden in the question 'Do the gods exist?' is this: Are there experiences of the Infinites? If this is allowed in any sense whatever, we may pass to the second question. If it is disallowed, we must enquire about the character of those experiences which other people have claimed to be experiences of the 'Infinites.' Further, we must enquire whether there are techniques for inducing such experiences in those who claim never to have had them.

The second question is: Are you the sole cause of such experiences, or do they come to you from 'outside'? If they are accompanied by the feeling of the unexpected, the feeling of being overwhelmed, the sense of the anxiety and the sheer mystery of being 'you,' and the amazement that there is anything at all, it would seem as if they came from 'outside,' as if you were aware of being plunged into an immensity which could only be characterized by 'the Infinites.' Their existence is guaranteed by this awareness which can be universally experienced.

The third question is to discover the fitting way to talk about the causes of these experiences. Confronted by the enigmas of birth and death, by the crises of joy and suffering which every human being encounters, by the dissatisfaction of 'explaining' oneself in terms of one's parents and ancestry or in terms of one's immediate environment, one leaps into a strange world. How shall we talk about 'them' who are knocking, as it were, on the doors of the self? If we talk at all it is in images, analogies which point only to the Mysteries which confront us and which we cannot grasp. There are many analogies and ways of talking about them. But three are basic. We can call the Infinites 'the gods,' attributing to them positive being, and some characteristics of personality. Here the images evoked provide the ultimate security and cleansing of the self. We can call the Infinites 'the Universe.' Here the images evoked offer the embrace of the womb, the warmth of being united again with the 'isness' of life. We dissolve ourselves in the sea of being. Finally we can call the Infinites 'the Nothingness.' Here the images call us to final resignation and to acceptance of the meaninglessness of existence. Here the death wish conquers.

It would be my contention that these are the three possible answers to the religious question which the classical arguments for 'God' have raised. It is needful, however, to appreciate the context within which these arguments proceed, and the fact that there is no single answer to the questions posed. Further, the unity of the Infinites is by no means established by these arguments.

The cosmological argument asks about the cause (or causes) of the world. We may say the world has *no* cause, since 'cause' refers only to relations between objects, persons, and occasions within the world. 'Cause' can have no other meaning. In this case and by virtue of this decision, the Infinites are the Universe itself, and the religious attitude is one of nature, mysticism, pantheism, and absorption into the living being of the All.

Again, we may decide that 'Nothingness' is the ground or cause of the universe, that things, persons, and occasions 'spring' into being out of the void of Nothingness and then disappear into Nothingness. They 'pop' in and out of being. It is well to note here the analogous use of language. 'Spring,' 'pop,' or any such expression is an analogy. The way of analogy is not confined to talk about the gods. It is endemic to all religious and antireligious discourse.

Finally we may say the gods are the cause of the universe. Here a distinction is made between the relative sense of 'cause,' for relations *within* the universe, and a use of cause by way of analogy to speak of the relation of the Infinites to the world. This relation can be either that of creation or of begetting and generation.

The ontological argument similarly has three answers. We can say *"aliquid quo maius nihil cogitari possit"* is Nothingness, since every concrete image can be imagined to be yet greater, and there is nothing than which nothing greater can be conceived. Again, we can say the Universe is that than which nothing greater can be conceived. This argument rests on the principle (which I believe to be sound but cannot argue here) that only descriptions of the actual are logical, viz., that any description if *prolonged far enough* either contains a self-contradiction or else describes something which has been, is, or will be actualized. Finally, *"aliquid qua maius nihil cogitari possit"* may be a description of the gods, and in this one instance alone 'existence' is a predicate. The basis for this is not logical, however, but psychological: the experience of the Infinites and the decision to view them as external both to the self and to the world.

The fourth and final question implied in "Do the gods exist?"

is this: how shall we choose between the images of the Infinites as the gods, the Universe, and Nothingness?

If the 'Infinites' exist and we have experienced them, how shall we name them? (To name them is necessary, for without naming them we do not know how to handle ourselves before them.) I do not think there are any ways of verification or any other terms of choice other than those of earnestly seeking and of finally being grasped by one or other of the sets of images which are given in our culture or rediscovered from our heritage. Only religious genius creates new religions, or new antireligions, and even here the past heritage is to some degree determinative. We are encountered and embraced. We experience the Infinites passively. We feel we give ourselves to the decision, being irresistibly driven thereto in a total context of the community in which *they* have found *us*. We are decided for, though we have striven to decide. We have found fulfillment, but we have also taken a risk. That is why we should listen to every voice of the Infinites as they speak through the structures of reason and mystery, lest we have decided for idols and cast ourselves down before demons.

## V.

My final observation is that it is meaningless to treat omnipotence (as Professor Ziff does) in such terms as throwing stones faster than light. Omnipotence refers to infinite power. Any statement, then, about 'the gods' must qualify or expand its terms infinitely. We should have to say, "The gods infinitely throw infinite stones infinitely faster than light." Such a concatenation of words appears to me to be senseless. However, side by side with infinite statements about the gods, it is possible to make relative or finite statements. The conditions of these do not qualify the infinite statements, since these latter cannot be qualified in principle. This is one of the curious features of any adequate logic of infinity. In consequence, if we speak about the gods throwing stones, we do so in the only context in which this is intelligible to us. For that is what we mean by 'throwing stones.' Implicit in the very words are certain structures of space-time which we take for granted. That these structures will always be this way, or have always been this way, is something we assume by induction and for the support of which we have only statistical probability. Consequently, to speak of throwing stones faster than light is to deny the structure within which "throwing stones" is intelligible. It is similar to speaking of an object being both on the earth and on the moon at the same time. We cannot see what this would mean, other than that a different space-time structure than ours would be implied. But we cannot give it any concrete sense. In such a different structure words would have new and odd meanings. If, then, we have some reason to speak of the gods throwing stones, and we are claiming to speak intelligibly, we simply mean that they do it within the structure familiar to us. Otherwise we should not speak of their 'throwing stones' at all.

But is there any reason to speak of the gods throwing stones? The only reason would be one in which the movement of some stones was "theophanic"—an occasion in which the Infinites were experienced by someone or by a community. Such an occasion would be similar to Moses' encounter with Yahweh (the Infinites) on first beholding some type of flaming azalea in the desert, or the Israelites' encounter with Yahweh in their first acquaintance with the drops of carbohydrates extended by insects in the desert ('manna'). In such a theophanic movement of stones, a religious community could intelligibly speak of the gods throwing stones. There would be a movement of stones within a space-time structure familiar to us, and whatever may have been the scientific causes of the movement (the falling of meteors, for example), the point of the assertion would be that this occasion evoked the experience of the Infinites and was pregnant with that sense of awe and over-whelming power which makes one aware of the gods. I cannot see any other reason which would lead to speaking of the gods throwing stones. Without such a theophanic experience, the words would have no context and be completely meaningless.

## 36

# FRUSTRATING STRATEGIES IN
# RELIGIOUS DISCUSSION
*by Paul F. Schmidt, Oberlin College*

Everyone has observed how discussions in religion often seem to end without even approaching a resolution of points of disagreement. I think that this is due to certain logical strategies built into the very fabric of religious claims. The discussion of the main papers in this conference by Ziff, Niebuhr, and Tillich, as well as some commentators contains examples of these logical strategies. I want to present the logical moves that allow these strategies to completely frustrate continued philosophical discussion. This presentation will show why religious discussions are interminable, and what has to be done to enable them to overcome this defect.

For our first case, let us look at the discussion of faith as stated by Niebuhr in his contribution. He begins, at a level none of us have any difficulty with, by describing a number of ways in which the term "faith" is used in reference to our human, natural, and ordinary language and experience. We understand what it is to trust another person; to have faith in him (Niebuhr calls this the Hebrew meaning). Likewise, we understand what is involved in the belief that the sun will rise tomorrow; we have faith that this is the case. " 'Faith' is used in contexts in which such other words as knowledge, opinion, conviction, apprehension, sight, etc. frequently occur." Niebuhr calls this the Greek meaning. He gives an admirable account of these uses. Now, what is religious faith? Well, it is not just any one of those. It is like some of them in some ways, but different (*Meaning of Revelation*, p. 23 ff., 77 ff.). Faith in God is something like faith in my friend, but not entirely; faith is a way of knowing, but not just a feeling of conviction that such and such is the case. The signals to observe in these preceding statements are the qualifiers at the end 'but not . . .' and 'but not just. . . .' With these the strategy begins. We enter upon a peculiar chain of stretching and shifting the use and reference of the term faith. This is shown by the fact that if I ask: Is faith in God like faith in my friend, or is faith in the Commandments like faith in the accuracy of scientific reports? In each case the answer is yes and no. The answer cannot be a straightforward yes because there would remain nothing distinctive about religious faith. The stretching and shifting has begun. The next point to inquire into is: How much is it like or in what respects is it like it? But one meets the same strategies; namely, no precise quantitative measure is provided, nor a sharp list of respects. The shifting and stretching of use and reference continues further and further until I no longer have an understanding of the terms. In religious discussion, extreme and moderate forms of stretching and shifting will occur, leaving philosophic discussion in more or less frustration.

This sequence of moves brings us finally to the following situation: if I understand faith as just any of Niebuhr's human, natural, ordinary senses, then I miss something essential to the character of religious faith; and, on the other hand, if I claim to grasp the character of religious faith, then I must modify and go beyond these human, natural, ordinary senses of faith. The evidence that this is the situation comes out if a person tries to equate religious faith with either the human-interpersonal or natural-knowledge senses. The believer will deny such an equation. Faith that the sun will rise tomorrow will be rejected in the light of specifiable items, while faith that God is merciful never specifies what items would lead to its rejection. Faith (trust) in my friend can turn out to be a sad illusion, but faith in God for the believer cannot turn out to be an illusion. If it did he would not be said to possess religious faith.

How does the stretching and shifting take place? Consider the following statements "I have reasonable assurance that the water I drink is not contaminated. I have faith that proper chemical precautions are taken. No one has any reason to doubt that the water is safe. No one in his right mind would question this water. If you want to understand these (religious) beliefs you must have faith in them. Nothing whatsoever could alter my faith. I must believe that this is so. These are the articles of my creed, my faith." Look back over these statements. Notice these stretches and shifts. They begin with a reasonable assurance in a definite context; move to definite belief carefully related to a chemical warrant; on to a general reference to any reasons; next, even the vague reference to any reasons drops out, and a shift to a quality of mind is made; then, a shift to inclusion of a commitment for understanding the belief-that; on to a complete rejection of evidential considerations or need of commitment; and finally the stretch and shift yields a sense of faith as pure categorical axiom far different from the human natural level we began with. In some cases the shifting and stretching goes so far as to frustrate understanding. It frustrates understanding because we do understand what is meant by faith on the human natural side but have little or no understanding on the other side after the stretching and shifting. Yet religion tries to combine the two sides together.

The mechanism which allows the stretching and shifting is the lack of a definite specification of a criterion for the recognition of religious faith. What happens is that a criterion is implicit in an example used to illustrate faith. A counter case is then offered which meets the implicit criterion but would not be acceptable as an example of faith. The religious person then shifts the implicit criterion by use of another example. A counter case is offered; another stretch or shift is made through use of yet another example. This strategy continues making it impossible to pin the discussion down.

What the theologian wants is a bridge from the ordinary, understood sense of faith to religious faith. But such a bridge can be built only if a construction of definite criteria is laid down, a caisson that will stay in place. Such a caisson is not provided. Philosophic discussion cannot proceed.

Let us consider another example. In connection with Professor

Hick's paper, there ensued some discussion of 'loving': God's love for man; one person's love for another. Of course, we understand what it is for one person to love another; that is, at least, what sort of behavior would generally take place. We can even understand some rather unusual sorts of loving relations between human beings. Sometimes we can grasp what is involved in some psychoanalytic cases of loving, although in these the shifting and stretching has sometimes gone so far that definite criteria of recognition are not clear. Now we are supposed to move across a bridge to understand God's love. But unfortunately God's love is compatible with the occurrence of events in the world that would never be allowed as loving behavior among men. What this indicates is that we no longer have a clear criterion of loving. The religious concept of loving has been stretched and shifted so much that any occurrence in the world is compatible with God's love of man. This is brought out by asking a believer to specify an event that would be incompatible. No answer is given. Philosophic discussion is dead in its tracks. Various protective shifts may be employed at this point. Professor Hick used an ancient one: the circle of faith. Those within the circle would understand; those without would not. But no criterion is offered to show who is within and who is without. In saying this I do not mean to question Professor Hick's deep sincerity, for which I have great respect. But I do think this is the logical situation underlying this sort of position.

Professor Tillich employs the same logical strategy at a crucial point in his position with respect to the concept of ultimate concern or ultimate commitment. " 'God' is the answer to the question implied in man's finitude; he is the name for that which concerns man ultimately"; and "whatever concerns a man ultimately becomes God for him" (*Systematic Theology,* p. 211). A man's religion is the object of his ultimate concern. What is the criterion for recognizing one's ultimate concern? What a man is deeply and passionately interested in. Suppose a cynic or playboy claims to have no deep, passionate interest. Is he without religion? Oh no, everybody has such an ultimate concern even though he may not be aware of it. Professor Tillich took this line when someone asked him about the playboy. Already the shift has gone too far when it allows 'ultimate concerns' we are not aware of. It is clear that one could say nothing to dislodge this claim once the 'unaware' shift is made. This is brought out by asking Professor Tillich to specify a case which would not be one of ultimate concern. There are none. But if there are none, philosophic discussion cannot proceed.

There is another twist of strategy in this example that is worth notice. When asked about the cynic who claims to have no ultimate concern, the reply tactic is to argue that the cynic's ultimate concern is to have no ultimate concern. This is vicious. The criterion for an ultimate concern is now so stretched that whatever he claims, positive or negative, passive or active, is said to be his ultimate concern. Notice the stretch and shift from a particular deep and passionate interest we began with, that is, a meaning of ultimate concern we could understand in human behavior, to a meaning so wide in scope as to be vacuous of *specific* differences. In addition one should mention that there are very serious logical problems in such self-referring claims in which a denial of any ultimate concern is taken as a member of the class of ultimate concerns. Logical paradoxes ensue if such class memberships are allowed. Finally, what goes on in this case can be brought out by asking whether any person could be without an ultimate concern. Efforts may be made to avoid an answer, but if pressed the answer is usually no. This begins to look dangerously like an analytic claim disguised as an empirical claim about human nature.

In the discussion of the Institute on this point, we recognized that the meaning of "religious" was being stretched when Professor Tillich called Professor Hook religious, stretched even more when Marxism, then Hitler and Nazism are included as religious, and stretched to the breaking point when it embraces the cynic.

What goes on here is precisely the same as with religious faith and God's love. At first, no definite criterion of ultimate concern is laid down, so we shift along from case to case in the discussion trying to pin down a criterion. The cases carry us further and further from our normal and understood use of the term. Finally, an implicit criterion comes into view framed in such a way that no case offered in discussion would dislodge the thesis. Discussion is frustrated. Only the specification of a definite criterion such that examples for and against are possible can make discussion plausible.

In Professor Ziff's paper "About 'God' " the use of this strategy is more subtle and employed in a different way. It comes in with his discussion of whether or not problematic predicates (omniscience, omnipotence) are intelligible. Their intelligibility is linked to understanding, of which he admits degrees, and understanding means that one can make some inferences from the concept. For example, "I know that if something is the creator of the world then prior to its act of creation the world did not exist." Consider the concept of omniscience. What inferences shall we draw from it? One is likely to say: If there is an omniscient being, then he possesses complete knowledge. What kind of complete knowledge? Does God know every property and relation for all objects and events, past, present, and future? Or if God desired (willed) to have knowledge of any property or relation he could have it? Or does God know every property and relation of what has come to be but not of what has not yet come to be? Or is God's knowledge limited but sufficient to all his possible needs? Or is God's knowledge limited but far superior to any other being?

I want to make two points about omniscience. First, from the concept of completely perfect knowledge, there are a variety of inferences about its possible character, some of which are incompatible with others. Our preceding list makes this clear. Second, does not the list indicate how much the concept of knowledge has been stretched and shifted from its use for human knowledge to divine knowledge? Can we say we understand this concept in its divine sense when it yields incompatible inferences about what it might be? Of course, a theologian can select just one of these. But, by what criterion? Doesn't this criterion for selection tend to shift, depending on what theological problems he is dealing with? For example: evil or predestination. Professor Ziff links the intelligibility of a concept to making inferences involving it. My doubts about such intelligibility arise from the question of how such inferences

295

are made. Consider the following cases. First, the concept of "poisonous." If this plant is poisonous, then eating it will kill me or make me very sick. The logic of the concept of poisonous is clear because we use it according to definite rules or criteria. We know what we 'suppose' when we suppose this plant is poisonous. Second, consider the concepts of completely perfect knowledge. Do we know what we 'suppose' when we say: if God has complete knowledge then. . . ? I am suggesting that these are strange sorts of 'ifs' and 'supposes.' They are like saying: if a man had no sensory experience than. . . ; or if a person felt no pain then. . . ; or if a child is reared without any human contacts then. . . . Philosophy, unfortunately, has made frequent use of such strange suppositions. The point is that we do not know what would follow from these strange suppositions because we do not have a standard use or criterion for the logic of such conceptions. I suggest that examination shows that suppositions about God are strange suppositions in which the logic of the concept has no standard. Because of this lack of a definite standard, discussions about God are bound to end in frustration.

Consider the concept of creation *ex nihilo*. We understand the logic of the concept of creation with respect to objects in our natural human experience. There are standards, rules, or criteria for its intelligent use. For the divine use, I am asked to imagine a creation out of nothing. But this violates one of the standards for the logic of the ordinary concept of creation, namely, the supposition of antecedent factors from which the thing is created. By what do I replace this violation? What new logical tracks are allowed under this strange supposition? No standards or rules are specified. We leave firm ground for quicksand. Any inferences might be made. Discussion has a free field, the opposition team has been eliminated, the game of philosophic discussion cannot be played. Worst of all, in the case of creation *ex nihilo,* we are asked to combine in our understanding of this divine trait the very features which are incompatible in the logic of the ordinary use of the concept of creation. The logic of this ordinary concept does not allow the feature of coming to be in combination with the feature of no antecedent factors out of which it is created. The divine use is so stretched and shifted that I find it unintelligible. I submit that Professor Ziff's problematic predicates have built into their logic the same strategy of shifting and stretching that we found in Tillich, Hick, and Niebuhr.

# APPENDIX:

## The Religious Symbol

# THE RELIGIOUS SYMBOL
*by Paul Tillich*

## 1. The Symbol

The religious symbol combines the general characteristics of the symbol with the peculiar characteristics it possesses as a religious symbol.

The first and basic characteristic of the symbol is its figurative quality. This implies that the inner attitude which is oriented to the symbol does not have the symbol itself in view but rather that which is symbolized in it. Moreover, that which is symbolized can itself in turn be a symbol for something of a higher rank. Hence, the written character can be called a symbol for the word and the word a symbol for its meaning. Devotion to the crucifix is really directed to the crucifixon on Golgotha, and devotion to the latter is in reality intended for the redemptive action of God, which is itself a symbolic expression for an experience of what concerns us ultimately.

The second characteristic of the symbol is its perceptibility. This implies that something which is intrinsically invisible, ideal, or transcendent is made perceptible in the symbol and is in this way given objectivity. The perceptibility of the symbol need not be sensuous. It can just as well be something imaginatively conceived, as in the example already given of the crucifixion or as in poetic figures. Even abstract concepts can become symbols if their use involves a perceptible element. Thus perhaps the concept of "surplus values" as a symbol of economic exploitation in the consciousness of the proletariat or the idea of the "Supreme Being" as a symbol

301

of the ultimate concern in the consciousness of the religious community may serve as examples.

The third characteristic of the symbol is its innate power. This implies that the symbol has a power inherent within it that distinguishes it from the mere sign which is impotent in itself. This characteristic is the most important one. It gives to the symbol the reality which it has almost lost in ordinary usage, as the phrase "only a symbol" shows. This characteristic is decisive for the distinction between a sign and a symbol. The sign is interchangeable at will. It does not arise from necessity, for it has no inner power. The symbol, however, does possess a necessary character. It cannot be exchanged. It can only disappear when, through dissolution, it loses its inner power. Nor can it be merely constructed; it can only be created. Words and signs originally had a symbolic character. They conveyed the meaning which they expressed with an inherent power of their own. In the course of evolution and as a result of the transition from the mystical to the technical view of the world, they have lost their symbolic character, though not entirely. Once having lost their innate power they became signs. The pictorial symbols of religious art were originally charged with a magical power, with the loss of which they became a conventional sign language and almost forfeited their genuine symbolic character.

The fourth characteristic of the symbol is its acceptability as such. This implies that the symbol is socially rooted and socially supported. Hence it is not correct to say that a thing is first a symbol and then gains acceptance; the process of becoming a symbol and the acceptance of it as a symbol belong together. The act by which a symbol is created is a social act, even though it first springs forth in an individual. The individual can devise signs for his own private needs; he cannot make symbols. If something becomes a symbol for him, it is always so in relation to the community which in turn can recognize itself in it. This fact is clearly evident in creedal symbols which at first are merely the signs by means of which the members of the group recognize each other. "Symbolics" is the science of the distinctive marks of the different churches, that is, the science of creedal distinctions. But all other symbols could

302

also be considered in this light. Thus universal "symbolics" is conceivable as a general science of the self-expressions of all groups, tendencies, and communities.

These general characteristics of the symbol hold for the religious symbol also, as the various examples show. Religious symbols are distinguished from others by the fact that they are a representation of that which is unconditionally beyond the conceptual sphere; they point to the ultimate reality implied in the religious act, to what concerns us ultimately. All other symbols either stand for something that has also an unsymbolic objective existence aside from its ideal significance, as, for example, a flag can represent a king, and the king in turn represents the state; or they are the forms giving expression to an invisible thing that has no existence except in its symbols, as for example, cultural creations like works of art, scientific concepts, and legal forms. It is only in symbolic fashion that such intangible things as these can be given expression at all.

The situation is essentially different with religious symbols. They must express an object that by its very nature transcends everything in the world that is split into subjectivity and objectivity. A real symbol points to an object which never can become an object. Religious symbols represent the transcendent but do not make the transcendent immanent. They do not make God a part of the empirical world.

## 2. Theories of the Religious Symbol

The theories of the religious symbol are valid also in many respects for the symbol in general. In the consideration of these theories, however, we shall always come to a point where the independent and specific problems of the religious symbol will arise and require a solution. The theories of the symbol can be classified into negative and positive theories. The negative theories are those that interpret the symbol as reflecting an aspect of reality that is not consciously intended in the symbol. They deny that the symbol has an objective reference and attribute to it merely a subjective character. A definite subjective state and not the actual facts referred to in the symbol is expressed in the symbol. These theories are especially dangerous for religious symbols, since the latter do not refer to a world of objects, yet they intend to express a reality and not merely the subjective character of a religious individual.

On scientific and systematic grounds these theories are ultimately reducible to two types: the psychological and the sociological theory of the symbol. Both types have acquired historical significance because they have effectively, though one-sidedly, recognized one aspect of the development of symbols: they have shown that the psychological and social situation is decisive for the selection of symbols in all spheres. Going beyond this, they attempt also to show that symbols have no other reality than to serve as an expression of the psychological and social situation; that is, these negative theories set forth a genetic theory of the symbol itself. The two prophetic personalities of the nineteenth century, Nietzsche and Marx, gave the decisive impulse to this tendency. This fact indicates that these theories are devised for combat and that they aim to do away with something, to destroy a symbol-complex. The object of their attack is the symbolism of bourgeois society including that of the churches supported by bourgeois society. The means employed in their attack is the argument that these symbols are an expression of a definite will to power and have no other reality than that which is conferred upon them by this will to power.

Marx used the expression "ideology" to describe this function of symbols, and he made it into an unprecedentedly powerful political symbol. Symbols are ideologies. The intellectual content, that is, the objective reference of symbols, or that which is expressed in them, is a political subterfuge that is consciously or unconsciously created for the sake of dominance. This thesis has not, to be sure, been followed up by a tested application in the various fields of symbolism. Wherever this has been attempted (and it was not done in the writings of Marx), the result has been a complete failure.

Wherever there has been a discussion of the inherent character of symbols and of their effect upon the social situation, the more rigid theory has been relinquished and the objective reference of symbols has been recognized. This retreat is unavoidable, for a consistent carrying-through of the theory would brand the theory, along with its political symbolical power, as itself an ideology that could only make the claim to be an expression of the proletarian social situation, but by no means an expression of real relationships. Thus the symbol "ideology" would itself be an ideology. It would also remain inconceivable how the will to power could make use of different kinds of symbols, if a cogent relevance to the facts were not inherent in the symbols.

The theory of symbols deriving from Nietzsche has in our day received substantial support from the psychology of the unconscious (depth psychology). The Freudian analysis of the unconscious in a similar way interprets cultural and religious symbols as arising out of unconscious processes. The obscure and mysterious realm of dreams is held to be a symbol area of the first order. When we examine the unconscious, we see the no less mysterious symbols of mythology in a clearer light. All symbols are interpreted as sublimations of vital and instinctive impulses which have been repressed. This interpretation has been employed with greatest success in connection with those symbols that are lacking in any objective foundations, like the dream and the myth. In this way they are deprived of their objective reference.

But this theory has not been carried out consistently either. In the concept of sublimation the problem is concealed rather than solved, for this conception implies not only a pointing-up or refining of the instinctive impulses but also a turning of the impulses towards areas of reality that, so far as their content is concerned, have nothing to do with impulses. Therefore an earnest attempt at carrying out the theory has never been made so far as it concerns the symbols that have objective reference. This holds especially for the science of psychoanalysis whose own inherent character is all too clearly the basis that supports the whole theory. Before it one always comes to a halt—and for just the same reason as obtains for the theory of ideology. All the more insistently, however, the question is raised

305

by the psychology of the unconscious concerning those symbols that have no objective empirical basis.

When psychoanalysis, for example, interprets the use of the father symbol in reference to God as an expression of the analytical father-complex (just as sociology on its part interprets it as an indication of the dominance of the male), we must raise the question as to how far the significance of this explanation extends. Obviously no further than its next assertion: that the *selection* of this symbol is to be explained by the father-complex. But the interpretation that in general the setting-up of religious symbols is determined by complexes is not valid. In other words, a theory of the religious symbol is not given but rather a theory as to how religious symbols are selected. Nor is anything more than this possible, for the positing of an unconditioned transcendent can by no means be explained on the basis of the conditioned and immanent impulses of the unconscious. But the final thing has not yet been said on the question of the selection of religious symbols; the possibility has not been taken into account that the vital impulses which induce the selection of the father symbol are themselves the operation of a primordial shaping of life, and therefore the intuition of the Unconditioned in this symbol expresses a truth which, though limited, is yet an ultimate, and therefore a religious, truth. The same thing would hold also for the sociological theory of the selection of symbols. Psychological and social impulses control the selection; but they can themselves be viewed as symbols for an ultimate metaphysical structure of existence. This consideration deprives these theories of their negative implications even when they are correct, namely, in their explanation of the *selection* of symbols.

With the consideration of the cultural-morphological interpretation of symbols we make a transition from the negative to the positive theories. In common with the negative theories, they make the selection of symbols dependent upon a subjective factor, the soul of the culture. But this factor is not, as it is asserted to be by the negative theories, unrelated to the objective reference of the symbols, but rather has an essential relation to it. Indeed, it is by means of this relationship that the subjective factor is defined as "the soul of the culture." The vital and the cultural are not separate from each other, but rather they constitute a unity within the creative, formative principle of a culture. All cultural creations are symbols for a definite, psychic, formative principle. This symbolic character does not, however, negate its objectivity.

The central phenomenon of the cultural-morphological theory is "style." In the style of works of art, concepts, legal forms, and the like, the soul of the culture from which they derive finds expression. By means of this conception of style all aspects or forms of cultural life become symbols. The morphologist of culture is concerned with style and not with the precise details of the development of a culture. Thus he will incur the strictures we have associated with the negative theory. Indeed, he must do so, if he looks upon morphology as an absolute principle, that is, if he denies all objective connection between the creations of the different cultural epochs. In this theory he exposes himself to the danger that his theory will itself be interpreted only as a symbol for a psychological-cultural situation. At least when dealing with his own science he too must come to a halt.

The symbols that are most of all threatened by this theory are those symbols that possess no objective references and can be interpreted as immediate forms of expression of the soul of the culture and as such can be interpreted as detached from every realm of fact. Against this threat we must assert: the fact that the soul must express itself religiously when it expresses itself immediately cannot be explained in any other way than by the fact that the soul is religious, that the relation to the unconditioned transcendent is essential or constitutive for it. The fact that religious symbols are distiguished from all others in power of expression and immediacy, can be explained only by the fact that that which pertains to the soul, and this holds also for the soul of a culture, must be defined precisely by the relation to the unconditioned transcendent. When this "soul"—apart from all objective, empirical relations—expresses itself, it does so religiously. It is in this context that the connection between the vital and the cultural elements in the "soul" can be understood, namely, from the fact that each element, in transcending itself, meets the other at the point of transcendence: the vital element, by breaking through its own immediacy (for which perhaps the instinct of death, as maintained by Freud, is an expression, although it is absolutely incomprehensible on the basis of the vital); the cultural element, insofar as none of its forms can be exempt from the crisis that they encounter as a result of the demands of the objective world as well as of the meaning of life itself. This fact explains how a "style" of culture possesses a symbolic power that has religious significance. Insofar as the psychic element or the "soul" is expressed in the style, the relation to the unconditioned transcendent is expressed in it. The sphere of religion insofar as it is expressed in symbols embraces the whole autonomous culture. Thus a science of the symbolics of culture worked out from the religious point of view, becomes a necessary task. Naturally this consideration has to do with only one side of culture. The various independent spheres of things remain intact; the symbolic character of cultural creation is "broken" by its objective, empirical character. The symbolism of style is a "broken," indirectly religious symbolism. But it is for this very reason that it has a fundamental significance for the understanding of the religious symbol in general.

We have presupposed the difference between the symbolic and the objective character of cultural creations. This conception, however, is opposed by the critical-idealistic theory of the symbol. The latter identifies the symbolic and the objective character and thereby gives to the concept of the symbol a new form and a tremendous extension. As a result of the work of Cassirer, this conception today stands in the foreground of symbol theory. We shall combine the exposition and criticism of this theory with an exposition and criticism of Cassirer's theory of mythical symbols.

The myth is viewed as a definite form of the cultural interpretation of existence and thus, in accordance with idealistic presuppositions, it is viewed as an objective creation. A symbolic reality is attributed to the laws according to which myths are formed. The myth is classified along with the other cultural spheres that are also manifested in symbols, such as language, philosophy, art, etc. The subject matter of myth is therefore not to be considered as in any special way symbolic. It has a symbolic element in common with all cultural creations, for a cultural life exists only in symbols. To be sure, a precultural and presymbolic world of intuition does exist, but not a reality transcendent to symbols. Cultural reality is in its essence symbolic reality; not because in itself it reflects a reality but rather because, being free from the relation to any thing-in-itself beyond the empirical, it creates a world of cultural objects. At this point we shall turn aside from the epistemological problem and raise the question as to how mythical and religious symbolism are related to each other. The answer given by critical idealism is that originally mythical and religious symbolism are interfused. But gradually religious symbolism rises above mythical symbolism, struggles against it, and overcomes it. This answer grasps the problem and formulates it. But it does not contain the solution: if mythology is in its essence a cultural creation like science, art, law, it is difficult to understand why it should be destroyed; indeed it is impossible that it should decline, for it has its own proper and necessary place in the meaningful structure of cultural life. If religion, on the other hand, is an autonomous area of meaning, we must ask how it is possible that it was originally embedded in myth. In short, the evolutionary and the transcendental conceptions of the myth contradict each other.

This tension is resolved as soon as it is pointed out that the myth, far from having disappeared, has only altered its form. Thus the conflict between religion and myth would not be a conflict with myth as such but rather of one particular myth with another. And this is what appears to me to be the case. The struggle of the Jewish prophets against pagan mythology was a struggle of the ethical henotheism of the old religion of the desert against the ecstatic polytheism of agrarian religion, a struggle of Yahwism against Baalism. But the mythical element is just as active in the religion of Yahweh as in the religion of Baal. To be sure, something has happened to bring in question the myth in its immediacy: the Yahweh myth is an historical myth, that is, it is related to the empirical realities of history. It has the realism of the historical. Yet transcendence has in a radical fashion insinuated itself into the mythical figure of Yahweh. Yahweh acquires the unconditionedness which is intended in the religious act. But the myth is not thereby removed. Empirical history remains always related to a superempirical, a transcendent history, which extends from the primitive period of innocence on beyond Yahweh's choice of his people to the end of history. Unconditioned transcendence as such is not perceptible, If it is to be perceived—and it must be so in religion—it can be done only in mythical conceptions. Of course these mythical ideas thereby lose their immediate meaning, they point beyond themselves, just as, conversely, history, when interpreted mythically, always remains real history demanding actual decisions. Nor does mysticism eliminate the myth, though it has broken the immediately mythical consciousness, for example, in India. The highest concept of even an abstractly transcendent mysticism has necessarily a mythical element still within it. The lower forms of the myth are not negated but are rather deprived of their ultimate reality just as all real facts are deprived of their actuality. The mythical consciousness can therefore be either broken or unbroken; in any case, it does not disappear. If one decides to characterize only the unbroken mythical mentality as mythical, then of course the myth is overcome in religion and it is shown to be nonessential. If, on the other hand, one calls every intuition of transcendence mythical, then there is no such thing as an unmythical attitude and the myth is shown to be essential. The usage is unsettled, presumably not because of the lack of scientific clarification but because of the inner dialectic that characterizes the concept of myth.

The objects of mythical intuition are at the same time the objects of scientific and philosophical investigation. With the appearance of science they enter as such into a new dialectic. There begins a transformation of the objects of mythical intuition into objects of mere empirical experience. A separate objective world arises and confronts the rational, perceiving subject. As a result, the subjective factor which is adapted to all immediately mythical data, the inner living connection of the consciousness with everything existing and with the inwardness of everything real, disappears or is repressed. Insofar as science thus builds up its own world of objects, it repels the myth. But, for the purpose of constructing this world of "things," science needs concepts that are transcendent to reality. In this way science comes into a new mythical situation and itself becomes myth-creative; thus, concepts like evolution, will to power, life, etc. have a mythical character. They no longer serve only for the construction of the empirical order, but rather indicate the transcendent presuppositions of this order. But since the element of the Unconditioned is firmly implanted in each of these presuppositions, and since the presupposition of all thinking (which is below the "abyss of being") signifies both the limits and the abyss of objectification, there comes into science an element of the religious, mythical mentality. Hence, it is possible for the ultimate presuppositions of science to be classed with the highest concepts of abstract mysticism or of abstract monotheism. In this way there arises an abstract myth that is no less a myth than a concrete one, even if it is broken in its immediacy. Indeed, the living meaning of creative metaphysics is that it involves just such an abstract myth. And from this fact it derives both its doubtful character as a science and its religious power.

Under these circumstances one must reject the classification of mythology as an independent type of symbol-creation different from science and religion. In both science and religion mythology is an element that cannot be eliminated, even though it may be broken. Plato recognizes this when on the one hand he puts science in opposition to myth and on the other must acknowledge the indispensability of myth to science. All metaphysics reaches a point where its concepts are myths not only in fact but even in the sound of its words. The myth is, therefore, an essential element of everything in the intellectual and cultural sphere. Nevertheless, it is necessary to distinguish between the unbroken and the broken form of the myth. In the unbroken myth three elements are linked together: the religious, the scientific, and the truly mythical elements: the religious element as relatedness to the unconditioned transcendent, the scientific as relatedness to objective reality, the truly mythical as an objectification of the trans-cendent through the medium of intuitions and conceptions of reality. This unity was possible only so long as the unconditioned-ness of the religious transcendent and the rationality of the world of things were hidden from consciousness. Thus the creations of the mythical consciousness could appear as satisfying both the religious and the scientific claim (of course, the contrast between religion and science as such was not evident at that time). This situation could not continue indefinitely. The breaking-down of this unity signifies a transition into an autonomous religion and into an autonomous science, and thus it signifies the breaking-down of the original mythical mentality. At the same time, however, the mythical stands forth in its purity and in its true character, as a necessary element in the construction of a meaningful reality. Thus it becomes clear that the myth is the central concept of those symbols in which the unconditioned transcendent is envisaged either mediately or immediately.

On this basis not only the original connection of the myth with religion and with a general awareness and understanding of the world becomes intelligible, but also the fact that the myth by its very nature must always strive to achieve again this original unity. Wherever the objective world is recognized in its relatedness to the unconditioned transcendent, and wherever the unconditioned transcendent is interpreted from the point of view of the objective world, the unity of religion with the desire to understand the world is restored in the mythical symbol. Thus science becomes a myth despite its rational autonomy, and religion absorbs certain aspects of the understanding and knowledge of the world, despite its own transcendent autonomy, in order in these ways to sense the tran-scendent. In our time, however, this development is more a tendency than a reality. Its success would involve a thoroughgoing transformation of both the scientific and the religious mentality.

It must not be supposed that mythical symbols constitute one sphere of symbols beside other spheres. For, in contrast to the others, they are "unfounded" symbols, that is, they are determined essentially by their symbolic character. If it is presupposed in accordance with critical idealism that cultural creations do not give expression to a thing-in-itself, but rather that reality is the cultural and objective sphere constituted by these creations, then it is quite clear that the world of mythical objects has an imaginary and figurative character entirely different from that of the world of artistic objects. The work of art expresses wholly intrinsically the reality that it aims to express. The work of art as a figurative thing does not point beyond itself to a reality of a different order. When it tries to do so, as in symbolic art, a special intention is present, the peculiarity of which shows that art as such does not create symbols but rather a meaningful reality of its own. Insofar as it has a symbolic character, it acquires a mythical character also. It surrenders its own character as pure art in order to express a transcendent meaning. The same thing is true for science. The attempt to present a historical figure as a symbol raises this figure to the mythical level and gives to the empirically historical a certain figurative character in favor of its transcendent meaning. The fact that the view here alluded to is advocated only by a small group of historians (the school of the poet Stefan George) again indicates that science, although it does create its own peculiar structures of meaning, does not create symbols. (The secondary level of linguistic and written sign-symbols does not come into consideration for our question.) If, nevertheless, the meaning structures of art and science are called symbols, no other objection can be made to this usage than that one must search for a new word for symbol in the narrower sense. The category of the mythical, therefore, includes essentially that of the symbolic, and that in distinction from the other areas of meaning which include the symbolic exactly to the degree that they are subservient to the mythical. That this connection is never completely absent has been shown by the discussion of the symbolic character of "style."

The fact that mythical symbols are from the objective, empirical point of view without a basis—even when cultural creations are involved—and the fact that they are for this reason symbols in the genuine sense, indicates the inadequacy of critical idealism. In its place we propose a transcendent realism. The thing referred to in the mythical symbol is the unconditioned transcendent, the source of both existence and meaning, which transcends being-in-itself as well as being-for-us. On the basis of this presupposition, which cannot be further dealt with here, the ensuing discussion of the religious symbol will proceed.

## 3. Types of Religious Symbols

We distinguish two levels of religious symbols, a supporting level in which religious objectivity is established and which is based in itself; and a level supported by it and pointing to objects of the other level. Accordingly we call the symbols of the first level the "objective religious symbols" and those of the second level, the "self-transcending religious symbols." The objective religious symbols will occupy the central place in our discussion. Indeed, all the previous discussion has been concerned with them. They are themselves to be subdivided into several groups.

The first and basic level of objective religious symbolism is the world of divine beings which, after the "breaking" of the myth, is "the Supreme Being," God. The divine beings and the Supreme Being, God, are representations of that which is ultimately referred to in the religious act. They are representations, for the unconditioned transcendent surpasses every possible conception of a being, including even the conception of a Supreme Being. Insofar as any such being is assumed as existent, it is again annihilated in the religious act. In this annihilation, in this atheism immanent in the religious act, the profoundest aspect of the religious act is manifest. Wherever this aspect is lost sight of, there results an objectification of the Unconditioned (which is in essence opposed to objectification), a result which is destructive of the religious as well as of the cultural life. Thus God is made into a "thing" that is not a real thing but a contradiction in terms and an absurdity; demanding belief in such a thing is demanding a religious "work," a sacrifice, an act of asceticism, and the self-destruction of the

314

human mind. It is the religious function of atheism ever to remind us that the religious act has to do with the unconditioned transcendent, and that the representations of the Unconditioned are not objects concerning whose existence or nonexistence a discussion would be possible.

This oscillation between the setting-up and the destruction of the religious object expresses itself immediately in the living idea of God. It is indeed true that the religious act really signifies what it refers to: it signifies God. But the word "God" involves a double meaning: it connotes the unconditioned transcendent, the ultimate, and also an object somehow endowed with qualities and actions. The first is not figurative or symbolic, but is rather in the strictest sense what it is said to be. The second, however, is really symbolic, figurative. It is the second that is the object envisaged by the religious consciousness. The idea of a Supreme Being possessing certain definite qualities is present in the consciousness. But the religious consciousness is also aware of the fact that when the word "God" is heard, this idea is figurative, that it does not signify an object, that is, it must be transcendent. The word "God" produces a contradiction in the consciousness, it involves something figurative that is present in the consciousness and something not figurative that we really have in mind and that is represented by this idea. In the word "God" is contained at the same time that which actually functions as a representation and also the idea that it is *only* a representation. It has the peculiarity of transcending its own conceptual content—upon this depends the numinous character that the word has in science and in life in spite of every misuse through false objectification. God as an object is a representation of the reality ultimately referred to in the religious act, but in the word "God" this objectivity is negated and at the same time its representative character is asserted.

The second group of objective religious symbols has to do with characterizations of the nature and actions of God. Here God is presupposed as an object. And yet these characterizations have an element in them that indicates the figurative character of that presupposition. Religiously and theologically, this fact is expressed in

# Religious Experience and Truth

the awareness that all knowledge of God has a symbolic character.

The question concerning the reality and the real differentiation of the attributes of God likewise indicates that we are concerned with symbols here. But this by no means signifies that these statements are lacking in truth or that these symbols are interchangeable at will. Genuine symbols are not interchangeable at all, and real symbols provide no objective knowledge, but yet a true awareness. Therefore, the religious consciousness does not doubt the possibility of a true awareness of God. The criterion of the truth of a symbol naturally cannot be the comparison of it with the reality to which it refers, just because this reality is absolutely beyond human comprehension. The truth of a symbol depends on its inner necessity for the symbol-creating consciousness. Doubts concerning its truth show a change of mentality, a new attitude toward the unconditioned transcendent. The only criterion that is at all relevant is this: that the Unconditioned is clearly grasped in its unconditionedness. A symbol that does not meet this requirement and that elevates a conditioned thing to the dignity of the Unconditioned, even if it should not be false, is demonic.

The third group of objective symbols are the natural and historical objects that are drawn as holy objects into the sphere of religious objects and thus become religious symbols. In the foreground stand the historical personalities that have become the object of a religious act. It would of course be entirely contradictory to the religious consciousness if one characterized these personalities, or what they did and what happened to them, as symbols. For the peculiarity of this kind of object of the religious consciousness depends precisely upon their historical reality, their reality in the objective sense. The use of symbolism with regard to this world in which the holy is supposed to be really present would involve a denial of its presence and hence the destruction of its existence. And yet this denial is inevitable as soon as these holy realities are looked upon as being rationally objective. For in the context of the rational world of concrete objects they have no place. And if it were possible to give them such a place, for instance, with the help of occultism, the thing aimed at in the religious act, that is, the intuition of the unconditioned transcendent, would not be grasped. These historical personalities, insofar as they are considered as symbols, therefore, have no place in the objective world. More than this, they cannot have such a place even though it be to their advantage as historical figures. This signifies, however, that these objects that possess a holy character are not empirical, even if they can only be conceived of as existing in the empirical order. This means that they are symbols, they represent the presence of the unconditioned transcendent in the empirical order. That this presence is viewed as an empirical event (for example, the resurrection), indicates the figurative character that attaches to every objectification of the transcendent. It is therefore correct to say that Christ or the Buddha, for example, insofar as the unconditioned transcendent is envisaged in them, are symbols. But they are symbols that have at the same time an empirical, historical aspect and in whose symbolic meaning the empirical is involved. Therefore both aspects, the empirical and the transcendent, are manifest in this kind of symbols and their symbolic power depends upon this fact. The same thing holds for them as for the name of God: all of these are symbolic, and in such a way that in both cases the unsymbolic reality is expressed—in the one case, the empirical, in the other, the transcendent. It is the task of historical criticism, which runs along parallel to atheistic criticism, to prevent these groups of symbols from degenerating into false objectifications. Religion is greatly indebted to modern research on the life of Jesus, in that it has accomplished this task by recognizing the problematic character of the empirical element and by emphasizing the importance of the symbolic element. It is never possible, however, to alter or to recreate a symbol by means of historical criticism. This group of symbols can also be measured by the standard of how effectively the unconditioned transcendent is expressed in them. The rise and decline of symbols is a matter of the religious and not of the scientific mentality.

The fourth group of objective religious symbols involves the level of symbols that we have characterized as "pointing" symbols. It is the immensely large class of signs and actions of a special significance that contain a reference to religious objects of the first level. This whole class of symbols can be divided into actions on the one hand and objects on the other that symbolize the religious attitude. In the first category belong, for example, all cultic gestures, to the second, all illustrative symbols, such as the cross, arrows, and the like. An elaboration of this class of symbols would be tantamount to working out a theory of the phenomena of religion in general. This is not at the moment feasible. Only one point significant for the principle in question may be mentioned here. All these symbols can be conceived as objective symbols of the third group reduced to a lower power. They all had originally more than "pointing" significance. They were holy objects or actions laden with magical sacramental power. To the degree in which their magical-sacramental power was reduced in favor of the unconditioned transcendent on the one side, and in the direction of the objectification of their reality on the other, they were brought down to the level of the "pointing" symbol. This process is never wholly completed. Even in radically critical religions like Judaism and Protestantism the conservatism of the religious mentality has preserved the magical-sacramental attitude toward reality. Concerning the other great forms of religion it is much better to be silent. Even in the mere "pointing" symbols, so long as they are living, there remains a residue of their original sacral power. If this is wholly lost, it is no longer justifiable to speak of symbols; the symbol is now replaced by conventional idioms which may then be raised by means of religious art into the purely esthetic sphere. And this can happen not only to divine signs and attributes but also to the divine beings themselves, as history has demonstrated. This observation leads to the conclusion that the second level of religious symbols, the "pointing" symbols, are transitional in character. And this is based on the nature of things. So long as symbols are imbued with sacral power the religious act is oriented toward them. When the religious act is no longer oriented toward them, that is, when they lose their sacral power, they degenerate into mere signs. This transition, however, involves so large an area of the religious life that one is justified in assigning to it a

318

special place. At all events, this one conclusion is evident, that the real religious symbol is the objective symbol, which in its four groups represents the unconditioned transcendent.

## 4. The Rise and Decline of Religious Symbols

Religious symbols are created in the course of the historical process of religion. The inner impulse of this historical process has been made clear through the consideration of the myth. It is a tendency that is twofold, toward religious transcendence and toward cultural objectification. Religious criticism manifests itself in the opposition of the divine and the demonic. As a result of this criticism religious symbols are forced inevitably into the status of the demonic. At first their reality is not destroyed, but it is weakened; the real symbolic power lives on in the sphere of the divine. The thus weakened demonic symbols can still have a long life; eventually, however, they tend to withdraw and become mere signs, or wholly to disappear. Scientific criticism does not in itself have the power to make religious symbols disappear. Wherever it seems to have this power, a deflection in the religious consciousness has already taken place. Wherever scientific criticism is effective, it leads not to a demonization, but rather to a profanization of the symbols. The decisive means for bringing about the profanization of symbols is the exposing of their symbolic character. For this reason the religious consciousness always protests against the characterization of its objects as symbols. In this respect nothing is changed by proving that reality can, indeed must, be embraced in the symbol. The shimmering quality that attaches to all objects to which the concept of the symbol is applied can, by the peculiarly religious sense for reality, be recognized only as a negation of its reality. Thus the question arises as to what can be or become a religious symbol in the cultural situation of our day.

On the whole the situation is such that the contents of categories arising out of the scientific and philosophic mode of creating concepts have the immediate persuasive power that fits them to become symbols. The fact that in the most highly educated circles the attitude of certainty towards scientific concepts is shattered and that the mythical character of these concepts is recognized, does not even in these circles greatly affect the self-evident symbolic power of these concepts. The idea of God illustrates the kind of change to which religious symbols have been subjected. The idea of God has, by misuse through objectification, lost its symbolic power in such measure that it serves largely as a concealment of the unconditioned transcendent rather than as a symbol for it. The recognition of this, its unobjective, symbolic character, has a chance of influence only insofar as the "ring" of the unconditioned transcendent can still be heard in the word "God." Where this is not the case, the proof that the intellectual content of the idea of God is symbolic can only hasten its loss of power.

This situation with regard to religious symbols, a situation which is fraught with great danger, may give rise to the desire to treat that which is referred to in the symbol without using symbols. Of course this cannot mean that beyond all symbols the unconditioned transcendent should be directly intuited. Rather it signifies that reality should no longer be used as material for symbols. It signifies that reality itself should be looked at immediately and be spoken of in such a way that its position in and before the unconditioned transcendent would receive direct expression. Undoubtedly, it might well be the highest aim of theology to find the point where reality speaks simultaneously of itself and of the Unconditioned in an unsymbolic fashion, to find the point where the unsymbolic reality itself becomes a symbol, where the contrast between reality and symbol is suspended. If this were really possible, the deepest demand of the religious consciousness would be fulfilled; religion would no longer be a separate thing. This in no way signifies, however, that religion should be reduced to an artistic or scientific approach to reality. It signifies rather an immediate concern with things insofar as they confront us unconditionally, that is, insofar as they stand in the transcendent.

But against this idea, which would involve especially in our day a great unburdening of the religious consciousness, an emancipation from the burden of a symbolism that has lost its self-evident character, there arises a serious objection: the idea rests on the presupposition that an unmythical treatment of the unconditioned transcendent provides the religious possibility of fully penetrating reality. This possibility, however, presupposes that reality stands in God, that is, that reality is eschatological and not present. In our time the idea prevails that certain realities with symbolic power must be placed above other realities without symbolic power; this very fact indicates that reality as a whole is separated from what it ought to be, and is not transparent of its ultimate meaning. Only insofar as this were the case, would reality itself acquire symbolic power and thus the realm of special symbols would become unnecessary: reality and symbol would become identical.

# INDEX

Abélard, 122
Abraham, 53, 221, 263
Absolute, the, 30, 52, 53, 54, 84, 85, 214, 244, 245
Actions: and belief, 68, 182, 185; commitment to, 125; conviction and, 68; discussed, 182; divine, 9; faith and, 68; holy, 5
"Actuality": divine, 217; the term, 217
Aesthetic, 66; experience, 5; ideals, 83; motivations, 154; values, 40
Affirmation, verbal, 221
Agnosticism, 242, 276
*Alice's Adventures in Wonderland,* 39
Allegory, 72
Alston, W. P., 80, 272, 281
Ambivalence, 279
Analogue, 93
Analogy, 15, 17; definition of, 72; doctrine of, 42; false, 112; intrinsic, 230; language of, 227, 230; principle of, 72
Analysis: linguistic, xii; philosophical, xi
Animist, 134, 136
Anselm, St., 116, 207, 218, 263, 268, 276
"Anthropocentric" doctrine, 71; circle, 74; tendency, 71
Anthropology and theology, 71, 72
Anthropomorphism, 157, 241–42, 248, 249, 255, 260
Anxiety, 5, 7, 20, 74
Apologetics of faith, 106, 166
Apprehension, 94; and faith, 114
Aquinas, St. Thomas, 128, 263, 281; doctrine of analogy, 42; truths of faith and reason, 117
Arguments: cosmological, 87; for existence of God, 262; nonfactual, 219; nonontological, 264 ff.; ontological, 264 ff.; teleological, 87

Aristotle, Aristotelianism, 85, 105, 281
Ark of the covenant, 35
Art, 232 f., 306; enjoyment of, 238; pure, 113; religious, 76; pictorial symbols of, 302; representational, 141; spectator of, 76; and symbol, 51, 313; works of, 303, 313
Asceticism, 314
Assent, 167; religious, 226
Assumptions, 168 ff.; and Christian beliefs, 169; epistemological, 156
Assurance, 95, 96 f., 112, 292; feeling of, 181; need for, xi; and prior success, 114; verification of, 111
Atheism: and belief, 62; criticism of, 317; defense of, 241; as an empirical theory, 249; in religious act, 314; in Western tradition, 62
Atheist, 241, 276–77, 278; and Really Ultimate, 68; and risk, 128; Tillich, agreement with, 245; two senses of, 241, 242
Augustine, St., xi, 94, 105, 116 f., 128, 207, 220
Austin, J. L., 118, 119, 129
Autonomy, 312
Averroes, 148 f.
Awe, 62, 289; definition of, 157; feeling of cosmic, 162; religious, 158

Baal, 309
Bain, A., 120
Barth, Karl, 117; on Feuerbach, 74, 75
Barth, Markus, 276
Behavior, 293; and belief, 120; human, 295; scientific, 231
Being, 8, 61, 66, 243; benevolent, 249; described, 205; ineffable, 256; non-spatiotemporal, 200, 201; and perfection, 207; personal, 207; powerful, 206; spatiotemporal, 200, 201; suprapersonal, 207;

322

328

Symbols (*Cont.*):
meaning structures of art and science, 313; mythical, 313; object outside, 36; objective, 315 ff.; objective reference of, 305; given objectivity, 301; origins of, 48 f.; participation in reality, 4; perceptibility of, 76, 301 f.; "pointing," 318; pointing of, 4, 29, 33; political, 5; presentational, 36; in present-day culture, 319 f.; and reality, 4; of reality, 86; referent, point to, 8; relation to what they symbolize, 49; religious, *see* Symbols, religious; representative, 3, 271; and resemblance, 49; rise and decline of, 317; shepherd as, 12, 14, 17; as sublimation, 305; supernatural, 16; and symbolized, 48; as symptom, 51; term misapplied, 3; theories regarding, 303, 306, 308; "ultimate," 258; utterances as, 41; for word, 301. *See also* Referents; Signs; Symbolism.

Symbols, religious, 22 f., 35, 61 f., 74, 227 f.; acceptability of, 302 f.; abstract claims for, 273; and being-itself, 19 ff.; criteria, negative, 10; positive, 11; defined, 12; demonic, 319; distinguished from other symbols, 303; and dynamics, 25; figurative quality of, 301; in form of historic recollection, 74; and idolatry, 11, 23 f.; innate power of, 302; interpretation of, 3; justification of, 3; measure of, 11; and object, 303; objective, 314; origination of, 9; participation of, 19; perceptibility of, 301 f.; plurisignification of, 12; as pointer, 6, 23 f.; primary, three levels of, 8 f.; psychological theories of, 303; referent for, 6, 7, 21; in religious history, 7; secondary, 8, 9; listed, 9; sociological theories of, 303; and supernatural beings, 14; traditional, 12; and ultimate concern, 19, 21; and ultimate reality, 5; unattained goals as, 16; and unconscious processes, 305; understanding of, 3, 8; validity of, 10, 303

*Systematic Theology,* 56, 293

Taubes, J., 70, 75

Tautology, 263, 279
Taylor, A. E., 94 f.
Telepathy, 178
Terms: nonreligious, 205; theological, 170. *See also* "Actuality"; "Exist"; "Faith"; "God," the term; Knowledge; Loving; Pain.
Tertullian, 117, 143
Thankfulness, 158 ff.
Theism, 228; arguments of, 219; classic, 217, 251 f.; problematic, 251
Theologians: Cappadocian, 57; Catholic, on faith, 116; Crisis, 271, 281; and philosophers, xi ff., 3 ff., 228, 268; Protestant, 122 f., on faith, 117
Theology: aim of, 320; canons of, 151; critique of, xi; dialectical, 74; discourse in general, 73 f.; Jewish and Christian, 223; modern, 127, 222; obscurantist, 271; problems, 295; shift from Catholic to Protestant, 71–73; systematic, 74; theory of error in, 46
Theophany, 285, 289
Thought, act of, 182
Tillich, P., xiii, 41, 50 ff., 67, 149, 208, 227 f., 250, 270 ff., 297; on God, 241; religious symbols, evaluation of, 22–24
Time, 9, 233, 234
Tolstoy, L., 152
Tradition: Catholic, 227; Christian, on faith, 103 ff.; Protestant, 227; religious, 67, 150
Transcendence, 59
Transfiguration, 37 f.; as meaning of of Crucifixion, 38. *See also* Crucifixion.
Trinity, Holy, 57
Trust, 101, 129, 146, 222, 226, 227
"Trust," the term, 170, 173 ff., 177, 180, 181
Truth, 42, 190, 225, 231; action relevant to, 121; a priori, 266; of art, 151; claim, 119, 122–23; claim to, 236; conditions, 43 f., 162; contradiction and, 234; defense of, 156; demonstrability of, 151; desire to know, 84; disinterested, 154; dynamic, 120; empirical, 243; factual, 212; of faith and reason, 117; and "faith that," 124; false and true, 136; and heart, 113;